OPERA, SEX, AND OTHER VITAL MATTERS

BOOKS BY PAUL ROBINSON

The Freudian Left

The Modernization of Sex

Opera and Ideas: From Mozart to Strauss

Freud and His Critics

Ludwig van Beethoven: "Fidelio"

*Gay Lives: Homosexual Autobiography
from John Addington Symonds to Paul Monette*

Opera, Sex,

AND OTHER

VITAL MATTERS

Paul Robinson

THE UNIVERSITY OF CHICAGO PRESS

CHICAGO & LONDON

PAUL ROBINSON is the Richard W. Lyman Professor in the Humanities at Stanford University. He is the author of a number of books, including *Opera and Ideas: From Mozart to Strauss* and *Gay Lives: Homosexual Autobiography from John Addington Symonds to Paul Monette,* the latter published by the University of Chicago Press.

The University of Chicago Press, Chicago 60637
The University of Chicago Press, Ltd., London
© 2002 by The University of Chicago
All rights reserved. Published 2002
Printed in the United States of America
11 10 09 08 07 06 05 04 03 02   5 4 3 2 1

ISBN (cloth): 0-226-72182-5
ISBN (paper); 0-226-72183-3

Library of Congress Cataloging-in-Publication Data

Robinson, Paul A., 1940–
    Opera, sex, and other vital matters / Paul Robinson.
        p.   cm.
    Includes bibliographical references and index.
    ISBN 0-226-72182-5 (cloth : alk. paper) — ISBN 0-226-72183-3 (pbk. :
alk. paper)
    I. Title.
    AC8 .R546   2002
    081—dc21

                                                        2001004444

⊗ The paper used in this publication meets the minimum
requirements of the American National Standard for Information
Sciences—Permanence of Paper for Printed Library Materials,
ANSI Z39.48-1992.

For Peter Stansky

CONTENTS

Opera, sex, Freud. These three have been, somewhat mysteriously, the central preoccupations of my scholarly life—and of my personal life as well. On first blush the three might not seem to have much to do with one another. But I am convinced that they are in fact intimately related. In introducing this collection of essays, I would like to reflect on my improbable triad, while also exploring certain tensions in my work that may baffle the reader as they have baffled me.

Over the years I have published six books, two on opera, two on sex, and two on Freud. All of them, I would maintain, are ultimately about modern intellectual history, the subject in which I was trained and that I was hired to teach at Stanford more than three decades ago. I'm not surprised, however, that nobody seems to recognize the principle of unity that links them. My academic career, I like to boast, has been dictated by my passions: I have written only about subjects that excite me, indeed that I love. But at a price: I have not established the sort of clear and stable intellectual profile that most scholars hope to cultivate. I am not readily identified as an intellectual historian. Indeed, I am not readily identified as a historian at all. Some think that I'm a musicologist, others that I'm a sexologist, and still others that I'm a psychoanalyst. Nor does anyone know where to look for my books in the bookstore. My colleagues can find their collected writings sitting proudly alongside one another in the history section, while mine are scattered hither and yon. Only reluctantly do they add up to a "career."

Perhaps I should acknowledge, in full candor, that sex has always been the master figure in this trinity—God the Father, so to speak. After I published my last book, *Gay Lives,* the *Stanford Report* ran an article about me in which a friend offered the following testimony: "Ask any student what Paul is known for and you'll get a one-word answer: sex. He's fascinated by sex and is a constant, funny critic of various forms of puritanism." I plead guilty to the charge and am even flattered by the characterization. I have no doubt that this obsession reflects the experience of growing up gay in the 1950s, when the possibility of fulfilling my desires seemed unimaginable. Ten years of repression, when I thought about sex all the time but did virtually nothing, focused my mind indelibly on the subject, just as it trained me in the arts of sublimation and thus set the stage for my career as an intellectual. Once the homophobic barriers began to crumble in the late 1960s, I naturally wanted to write about this all-important experience of my young life—both to excoriate the cultural and religious forces that had caused me such unhappiness and to celebrate figures like Herbert Marcuse and Norman O. Brown who had challenged them.

My interest in opera is no less deeply rooted in the experiences of my youth. I took piano lessons at an early age and later turned to the trumpet and then the bass violin. A pivotal experience of my childhood was discovering my grandmother's collection of 78-rpm recordings. I remember in particular listening to the Appassionata Sonata performed by Rubinstein and the Emperor Concerto performed by Schnabel. During high school my life revolved around the band, in which I played trumpet, and the youth orchestra, in which I played bass. My discovery of opera, in college, thus grew out of a well-established love of instrumental music. Once again two particular recordings made an unforgettable impression: Cesare Siepi's 1955 *Don Giovanni* and Callas's 1959 *Lucia.* I can still hear them, virtually note for note, in my inner ear.

In one respect music took me away from the body and its mundane concerns. It opened up a realm of beauty untouched by the gross and ephemeral urges of the flesh, a realm of pure spirit whose charms, though originating in physical sounds, seemed ethereal and eternal, like the world of ideas. So from early on I experienced a kind of tug-of-war between my sexual and my musical passions, and doubtless music, like my burgeoning intellectual life, often served as a vehicle of sublimation.

But not entirely, because from the first, music was also an intensely sensuous experience. It set up vibrations in the ear, and in the soul, that echoed rather than contradicted those in the body. The singing voice in particular had (and still has) for me an uncanny physical appeal: I want to hear, over and over, the delicious and utterly individual sounds produced by certain voices, sounds I desire irrespective of the words the singer happens to be uttering or any thoughts those words might inspire. Opera, like all music, remains for me an event in the mind, but it is also an event in the body. In my essay "The Opera Queen" I offer some more pointed speculations about the connection between opera and homosexuality, but opera queenery, I'm persuaded, is merely one instance of a deeper connection between music and sexuality. In my case the connection was reinforced by my first sexual experiences, which occurred in the high school band. Music and sex, I found, had an elective affinity. Much of my writing—as represented in this collection—might be thought of as an elaboration of that affinity.

My relationship with Freud has been more complex but reflects the same tension between the physical and the mental. Freud first came to my rescue as a senior in college, when, having exhausted Roman Catholicism as a way to deal with my recalcitrant urges, I found in him a splendidly dispassionate analyst of human sexuality as well as an incisive critic of the familiar repressions and prejudices of our culture. He appeared to me, in other words, as a sexual liberator. To be sure, he did not give me permission to become a homosexual—although later I would argue, in my essay "Freud and Homosexuality," that he is more the gay man's friend than his enemy. But Freud taught me conclusively that our desires are to be taken seriously and should not be sacrificed to the vapid fulminations of religion and philosophy. It was the first step toward exiting the closet.

Although Freud has remained for me a friend of the body, I also came to see him—as I read more of his writings in graduate school and beyond—as one of the most powerful thinkers of the modern age. I grew to admire him, along with Marx and Darwin, as the inventor of a system of thought whose originality, comprehensiveness, and intricacy command respect purely as an intellectual achievement. The liberator of the body, in other words, had also become for me an exemplar of mind.

You might say that my almost schizophrenic desire to celebrate both the spirit and the flesh found perfect fulfillment in Freud. His work became the centerpiece of my emerging professional identity as an intellectual historian, just as his resolute materialism and erotic candor underwrote my emerging sexual identity. I have remained loyal to him—as the essays gathered in chapter 14 testify—even in the face of the severe criticism to which he has been subjected in recent years. One does not willingly give up the heroes of one's youth, especially not when they have provided sustenance to both body and soul.

This collection has been organized to reflect my three obsessions. Part I gathers the essays I've written on opera since the publication of *Opera and Ideas* in 1985. In all of them I am concerned, as I was in my book, with the connections between opera and intellectual history. Chapter 1 reproduces the critiques of *Opera and Ideas* written by two eminent philosophers, Peter Kivy and Bernard Williams, and in my response I examine some of the book's underlying assumptions—especially about the nature of intellectual history—assumptions that were left largely implicit in the book. Chapter 2, "Reading Libretti and Misreading Opera," defends my conviction that ideas in opera are of interest only when they find expression in music. Put negatively, it mounts a systematic critique of the effort to interpret operas from their librettos. The two following essays extend to Mozart's *Magic Flute* (chapter 3) and Beethoven's *Fidelio* (chapter 4) the sort of intellectual analysis I brought to *The Marriage of Figaro, The Barber of Seville, The Trojans, Don Carlo, Die Meistersinger,* and *Der Rosenkavalier* in *Opera and Ideas*. I show how both operas can be usefully (though not exhaustively) interpreted in terms of the intellectual concerns of their time, those of the Enlightenment and the French Revolution. Again, while the connection I seek to establish is conceptual, I insist that it becomes interesting only when it finds musical articulation. The ideas I pursue must be sensuously embodied.

In the remaining four essays of Part I the link between opera and ideas is more muted or indirect. "Verdi's Fathers and Daughters" (chapter 5) examines three operas of Verdi's middle years—*Luisa Miller, Rigoletto,* and *Simon Boccanegra*—with a view to explaining their shared focus on paternal love; it too argues its case from the music, to wit, from the father-daughter duets that figure so prominently in all three works. The following two essays invert my usual formula: instead of looking for ideas in opera, I take issue with what I consider overintellectualized approaches to the genre. In "Is *Aida* an Orientalist Opera?" (chapter 6) I chastise Edward Said for detecting his favorite intellectual prejudice—the tendentious opposition of East to West—in Verdi's most famous opera, when the evidence, especially the musical evidence, won't support him. In a similar vein, "The Wagner Problem" (chapter 7) argues that Wagner has been taken too seriously as a thinker. Where the intellectual gravitas of most other opera composers is underestimated, Wagner's operas, I complain, are approached like philosophical treatises, usually to the neglect of their dramatic and musical virtues. Finally, "Richard Strauss, Ambivalent Modernist" (chapter 8) considers the troubled relationship between the twentieth century's most important opera composer and the dominant aesthetic tradition of the era, modernism. In this essay, too, I argue against my usual inclinations, for I am eager to defend Strauss the musician against his cultured despisers. Ideas matter in opera, but only up to a point.

The essays in Part II can be considered emanations of the two books I've written on sexual topics, *The Modernization of Sex* (1976), a sympathetic analysis of the thought of Havelock Ellis, Alfred Kinsey, and William Masters and Virginia Johnson, and *Gay Lives* (1999), a study of autobiographies written by gay intellectuals and novelists. My approach to sex is similar to my approach to opera. Like opera, sex is generally thought of as subintellectual—a phenomenon of the senses. But I maintain that it, too, belongs to intellectual history, because the way we think about sex is profoundly influenced by prevailing ideas and values. At the same time I am convinced that sex, like everything else, benefits enormously from the application of intelligence: both our sexual opinions and our sexual behavior are improved by scrutiny. The essays in this section, one might say, bring mind to bear on this most incomprehensible and disruptive human experience.

The first piece, "The Opera Queen: A Voice from the Closet," forms an obvious link with the essays in the previous section. It asks why gay men have been so transfixed by opera, and it looks for an answer in the ideological contingencies of the closet. Opera, I propose, gives voice to an otherwise unutterable self-affirmation; it speaks the gay man's identity when he can't speak for himself. In "Homosexuality: Choice or Destiny?" (chapter 10) I take stock of the recent argument over how we should think about homosexuality, whether as a naturally occurring phenomenon or a historically specific creation. The argument, which pits "essentialists" against "social constructionists," is best understood, I suggest, as a fight between two generations of gay men and, to a lesser extent, between gay men and lesbians.

"Sex Studies and Sex Books: Four Reviews" (chapter 11) is devoted to exposing the nonsense that passes for sexual wisdom in middlebrow culture. It pillories the shabby but hugely successful books, like those of Shere Hite, that pretend to reveal our sexual mores, while the empirically serious studies of sexual behavior by professional sociologists go largely neglected. Chapter 12, "For the Love of Big Brother: The Sexual Politics of *Nineteen Eighty-Four*," is a close reading of the sexual argument, express and implicit, of one of the twentieth-century's most influential novels. I show that sexual repression is an integral feature of Orwell's totalitarian society and that the cult of Big Brother depends on the sublimation of homosexual desire—a revelation not deemed to please Orwell's conservative apologists.

The section concludes with the most intimate piece in the collection, "'Dear Paul': An Exchange between Student and Teacher," my correspondence with a gay undergraduate in the summer of 1979. In that far away and strangely blessed time before the shadow of AIDS, we thrash out the trials and tribulations of a homosexual existence. The exchange reveals interesting generational differences, just as it confirms certain abiding predicaments, and it ends with my reflections about the teacher's responsibilities toward students in sexual distress—as well as the pitfalls of involving oneself in students' private lives.

The last part of the book, "Other Vital Matters," begins with Freud, but it contains a more heterogeneous gathering of essays, united mainly by their devotion to the life of the mind. All of them might be considered products of the rationalist component of my mental makeup, the side of me that values rigor and lucidity and believes devoutly in the importance of ideas. The three essays on Freud (chapter 14) constitute a defense of his intellectual achievement and, one might say, his political correctness.

In the first I sort out the different strands in the recent criticism of Freud and pass judgment on their relative merits and potential to do permanent damage to his reputation. The picture, I suggest, is less bleak than some imagine. The other two essays argue that Freud was neither hopelessly misogynist nor a homophobe, and that in their essentials his ideas serve the cause of both women and gays.

In "H. Stuart Hughes and Intellectual History" (chapter 15) I pay tribute to my mentor in intellectual history, who was among the first to advance the case for Freud's preeminence among twentieth-century thinkers. I use the tribute as an occasion to identify with Hughes's practice as an intellectual historian and to distance myself from recent tendencies in the discipline. With Hughes I argue that intellectual history should attend to the ideas of important innovators (like Freud and Weber) and to the way such ideas both shape and reflect the conceptual landscape of their age. Here I part company with those scholars who would turn away from the great thinkers to track the diffusion of ideas, or those for whom the primary task of the intellectual historian is to deconstruct ideas and thinkers, revealing their contradictions and lacunae.

Another feature of Stuart Hughes's practice with which I strongly identify is his commitment to the plain style—to prose distinguished by clarity and economy and thus accessible to the broad literate public. That commitment is the inspiration for the three essays on writing gathered in chapter 16. "Why Write?" contemplates the absurdities of the writerly life and ultimately comes to its defense. "Lost Causes" and "The Philosophy of Punctuation" make the case—with appropriate delicacy, I hope—for correct usage and punctuation. At stake in the battle for good writing is the possibility of reaching beyond the claustrophobic limits of our individual disciplines—of speaking to an audience outside the ever more hermetically sealed world of the academy. The academy is my home, but I have never felt comfortable with its penchant for crabbed and opaque language.

Every collection of essays ought to have at least one extravagance, and mine is the little reverie on cats in chapter 17. Some readers—I received many angry letters when the piece first appeared—seemed to think my remarks were inspired by aversion to the little critters. But nothing could be further from the truth. Rather, I seized on the domestic cat as an occasion to reflect on certain features of the human condition, above all on the burdens that civilization, or what Freud called "Kultur," imposes on us. Cats, I suggest, remind us of our lost innocence and freedom.

The reader will have noted a strong autobiographical impulse in this Preface. Autobiography is, I suppose, an indulgence of old age. In any event, as the years have passed I've become ever more interested in autobiography, both my own and others'. In 1999 that interest culminated in the publication of *Gay Lives: Homosexual Autobiography from John Addington Symonds to Paul Monette*. But the impulse was already present much earlier in my life, and evidence of it is unmistakable throughout this collection, especially in pieces like "The Opera Queen," "Dear Paul," and the tribute to Stuart Hughes. Thus I feel it is appropriate to end with an Epilogue of unmitigated autobiography, the account of my liver transplant. Yet even here, where I am most personal, I try to draw some implications for intellectual life. In terms of the antithesis between body and soul with which I began, the essay aims at a kind of synthesis in which the blunt realities of physical life get their just due but their spiritual consequences are not ignored.

WE HAVE TRAVELED a long way from *The Magic Flute* to liver transplantation (by way of the opera queen). The collection aptly represents the range of my interests as well as their perhaps extravagant heterogeneity. It also exposes the contradictory intellectual pressures that have driven my career as a scholar and writer. In this Preface I've focused on the contradiction between body and soul, flesh and spirit, the sexual and the aesthetic. But I could as easily have stressed the tension between the academic and the demotic—between my identity as a scholar and my desire to reach a larger intellectual public—a tension that is reflected in the different publications for which I have written, from the *Cambridge Opera Journal* to the *New Republic*. But I entertain the hope—perhaps the delusion—that one need not choose between aesthetic contemplation and physical pleasure, any more than one must choose between scholarly seriousness and intelligibility. We can love both sex and opera, just as we love both analytical complexity and plain speaking.

ACKNOWLEDGMENTS

Earlier versions of the essays reproduced
in this volume appeared as follows.

Chapter 1: Peter Kivy's review of *Opera and Ideas* appeared in *Cambridge Opera Journal* 1, no. 1 (March 1989): 87–93, and is reprinted with the permission of Cambridge University Press.

Chapter 2, originally titled "A Deconstructive Postscript: Reading Libretti and Misreading Opera," is reprinted with the permission of the publisher from Arthur Groos and Roger Parker, eds., *Reading Opera,* © 1988 by Princeton University Press.

Chapter 4, "*Fidelio* and the French Revolution," in *Cambridge Opera Journal* 3, no. 1 (March 1991): 23–48, is reprinted with the permission of Cambridge University Press.

A shorter version of chapter 5, "Verdi's Fathers and Daughters," was written for a Royal Opera House, Covent Garden, program.

Chapter 6, "Is *Aida* an Orientalist Opera," in *Cambridge Opera Journal* 5, no. 2 (July 1993): 133–40, is reprinted with the permission of Cambridge University Press.

Chapter 7, a review of Jean Jacques Nattiez, *Wagner Androgyne: A Study in Interpretation,* appeared in *Cambridge Opera Journal* 7, no. 1 (March 1995): 81–85, and is reprinted with the permission of Cambridge University Press.

Chapter 9, "The Opera Queen: A Voice from the Closet," in *Cambridge Opera Journal* 6, no. 3 (November 1994): 283–91, is reprinted with the permission of Cambridge University Press.

Sections 1 and 3 of chapter 11, reviews of Shere Hite, *The Hite Report on Male Sexuality* and of Alan P. Bell, Martin S. Weinberg, and Sue Kiefer Hammersmith, *Sexual Preference* appeared in *Psychology Today* 15, nos. 7 (July): 81–84 and 12 (December): 105–8, and are reprinted with permission from *Psychology Today,* copyright © 1981 (Sussex Publishers, Inc.). Section 2, a review of Linda Wolfe, *The Cosmo Report,* appeared in *The New Republic,* 2 December 1981, pp. 36–37, and is reprinted by permission. Section 4, a review of Edward O. Laumann, John H. Gagnon, Robert T. Michael, and Stuart Michaels, *The Social Organization of Sexuality,* is reprinted by permission from the *New York Times Book Review,* 30 October 1994, Copyright © 2000 by the New York Times Co.

Chapter 12 appeared in a publication of the Stanford Alumni Association, Stanford University, and is reprinted by permission.

Chapter 13, "Dear Paul: An Exchange between Student and Teacher," in *Salmagundi* 58–59 (Fall–Winter 1982), is reprinted with the permission of the publisher.

Section 1 of chapter 14, "Freud under Siege," originally appeared in *Halcyon 1985,* published by the Nevada Humanities Committee, and is reprinted by permission; section 2, "Freud and the Feminists," is reprinted by permission from *Raritan: A Quarterly Review* 6, no. 4 (Spring 1987); section 3, "Freud and Homosexuality," is reprinted with permission from *Constellations: An International Journal of Critical and Democratic Theory* (March 1999).

Chapter 15 was published in two installments in *The Intellectual History Newsletter* 9 (April 1987): 229–35 and 22 (2000): 88–91, and is reprinted with the permission of the publisher.

Chapter 16 appeared in three installments in the *New Republic* (31 March 1979, pp. 21–23; 26 January 1980, pp. 25–26; and 26 April 1980), and is reprinted by permission.

Chapter 17, "Cats," first appeared in the Spring–Summer 1979 issue of *Stanford* magazine, published by Stanford Alumni Association, Stanford University, and is reprinted by permission.

The Epilogue, "My Afterlife," is reprinted by permission from *The Stanford Historian* 19 (Summer 1995).

OPERA

CHAPTER ONE

A Symposium on *Opera and Ideas*
with Bernard Williams and Peter Kivy

I published my study of opera and intellectual history, Opera and Ideas, *in 1985. Three years later it was made the subject of a symposium at the annual meeting of the American Society for Aesthetics. Two eminent philosophers, Peter Kivy of Rutgers and Bernard Williams of U.C. Berkeley, offered more-or-less friendly critiques of my argument, to which I then responded. Peter Kivy faults me for failing to distinguish consistently between a composer's express intellectual intentions and his unconscious adherence to prevailing notions. Bernard Williams takes issue with my interpretation of Wagner, suggesting that by focusing on* Die Meistersinger, *rather than* Tristan und Isolde *or the* Ring, *I give a skewed account of Wagner's ideas. While addressing their specific complaints, I try to show how both philosophers raise fundamental questions about the practice of intellectual history, particularly how one characterizes the intellectual style of an era— the vexed issue of the Zeitgeist.*

Peter Kivy, "Paul Robinson's *Opera and Ideas:*
From Mozart to Strauss"

I

A sensible man quickly flees from anyone who presumes to tell him how music "expresses ideas." Even when the music is operatic, he knows better. For chances are it is the libretto that will turn out to be what expresses the ideas, not the music. And since the librettist's ideas are usually banal anyway, either the ideas expressed by the opera will not be worth the trouble, or the ideas will be those of the critic, whose imagination will be substituted for the lack of that faculty in the librettist, as in the cases of Kierkegaard's and E. T. A. Hoffmann's fantasies over *Don Giovanni*, in which case we are at a third remove from the musical expression of ideas.

It was with these presuppositions in mind that I warily approached Paul Robinson's book *Opera and Ideas: From Mozart to Strauss*, only to find, happily, that he is not only a sensible man, acutely aware of the pitfalls of his enterprise, but that he has skillfully contrived to avoid them all, at least most of the time. He has, indeed, written a very convincing book on how opera "expresses ideas" (at least in a qualified, and somewhat liberal, sense of "express," as I shall point out later on). And he has managed to write a book not on how libretti express ideas but on how operatic *music* does. "Opera is first and foremost a musical phenomenon," Robinson quite correctly observes, "and throughout the following chapters I have at all times forced myself to talk about music." By and large Robinson has been steady to this text.

Professor Robinson is a historian. His specialty is intellectual history, and his views on opera are clearly intended to be understood as a part of that discipline. The argument of his book is "that operas reflect the intellectual climate of their age and that we experience them differently—indeed more interestingly—when this intellectual factor is taken into account." He has three clearly discernible yet related goals, a historical and a critical one, both dependent upon a third: interpretation. That is to say, Robinson tells us what the operas he is concerned with are about (interpretation) and how their subject matter reflects the intellectual movements of their times (history of ideas), and he presents this operatic expression of ideas as an object for musical appreciation (criticism).

Now, there is a danger here of conflating these very distinct yet related goals. And that danger emanates from the word "reflect," which Robinson frequently uses to describe the relation of music to ideas. For the rather pallid, and somewhat vague, connotations of that word contrast, in a crucial way, with another word, also used by Robinson to describe the music-idea relation, namely, the word "express." Where the former suggests unconscious causation (the mirror reflects), the latter demands conscious intent (speakers express). And where music reflects rather than expresses, it is a nice question whether we can go with Robinson the rest of the way to the conclusion that music is "about" what it "reflects" (as opposed to "expresses"), or whether what it "reflects" is a proper object of aesthetic appreciation.

Here is an example to clarify what I am getting at. Robinson says, in the synopsis of his first chapter: "Mozart, I suggest, was the operatic spokesman of the philosophes, Rossini the unwitting mouthpiece of their conservative opponents; where *The Marriage of Figaro* argues the operatic case for Reason and Humanity, *The Barber of Seville* mocks those very ideals." Now it is clear that Robinson is making a stronger claim with regard to Mozart than with regard to Rossini. Mozart is a "spokesman" for the Enlightenment, Rossini the opposition's "unwitting mouthpiece." But an unwitting mouthpiece does not express ideas with his utterances, for they are merely the symptoms, not the expressions, of those ideas. And being merely the symptoms, they do not, it can be argued, have any "content": they are not "about" those ideas, any more than spots are "about" measles. If, then, Rossini unwittingly reflected the ideas of European conservatism, rather than intentionally expressed them in his music, his operas, qua music, cannot be about those ideas, and the "content" (which is not really content at all) cannot be the proper object of aesthetic contemplation.

We may now observe that as critic Robinson must make out a stronger case than merely as intellectual historian. Read purely as intellectual history—which is one possible and rewarding way of reading Robinson's book—it has accomplished its task successfully either when it has established that a given opera "expresses" the ideas of its time or when it has established that it merely "reflects" them. But read as criticism as well—read, that is, as an argument that a given opera presents the ideas of its time as part of an aesthetic object—it has accomplished its task only when it has made the stronger claim: not merely that the composer has unwittingly reflected the ideas of his time but that he has in some sense or other consciously, willfully expressed them; in other words, that he has been the workman, not the tool.

Thus, in evaluating the arguments of Robinson's book, one must at all times, I suggest, bear in mind the distinction between expressing ideas and merely reflecting them, as well as that between doing intellectual his-

tory and doing opera criticism. For the criteria of success will be different
if the goal is intellectual history, and the relation of reflection sufficient;
or if the goal is appreciation through intellectual history, in which case
the relation must be expression, with its more stringent evidential requirements. With these distinctions and caveats in mind, then, let us look
now at some of the specific claims Robinson makes about specific works.

II

In contrasting Mozart's *Marriage of Figaro* with Rossini's *Barber of Seville*, Robinson remarks upon the phenomenon, familiar to us all, of the
emotional disparity between the two operas, in spite of their common
characters and similar intrigues: "One leaves a performance of *The Barber of Seville* having laughed a great deal and delighted by its many
musical felicities. But while the operagoer has also laughed—though
probably not so uproariously—during *The Marriage of Figaro*, and
while its tunes also return to haunt him, it is not uncommon to leave
Mozart's opera profoundly moved, and this Rossini's can never achieve."
Part of the purpose of Robinson's first chapter is to try to explain why
this is so; and that is what I would like particularly to discuss here.

As one, of course, must expect, Robinson's explanation for this emotional disparity—this "dissimilar effect of the two operas"—lies in the
fact that they come out of and, therefore, reflect (or express) two contrasting world views. *The Marriage of Figaro* expresses the values of the
Enlightenment. "The most important of those values is the conviction
that human beings can overcome the antagonisms that separate them
from one another." Whereas *The Barber of Seville* reflects the cynicism of
an age that had rejected the Enlightenment faith in reconciliation and
withdrawn from an emotional commitment to the elimination of injustice "by a simple effort of mind and goodwill." Rossini's comic masterpiece "is the perfect operatic realization of this mood of intellectual and
emotional retreat. It is relentlessly unserious, displays human vicious-
ness in all conceivable guises, and refuses any kind of psychological or
moral investment." And in that contrast between the optimism of the Enlightenment and the cynicism of the early-nineteenth-century reaction
to it, expressed respectively in *The Marriage of Figaro* and *The Barber of*

Seville, lies Robinson's explanation for the moving quality of the former and the lack thereof in the latter. For "to feel the completeness with which Mozart believed in reconciliation is an exhilarating experience. That, above all else, is why we leave the theater so profoundly moved."

Robinson's account of the reconciliation theme in Mozart's music I find altogether convincing, both in the large and in detail, and I am much inclined to go along with him in saying that this is what the music, not only the libretto, is about, although I think I would prefer to say that the music "represents" reconciliation rather than that it "expresses" it. But where Rossini's music is concerned, I think the situation is somewhat different from the way Robinson characterizes it. To put his argument in a nutshell (I hope not in a caricature), it seems to me that what Robinson is saying is that the shallowness and triviality of Rossini's music—compared, that is, to Mozart's—express the cynicism of the age in which it was written: it is, in other words, about cynicism, triviality, and shallowness, as Mozart's is about depth of feeling and reconciliation. But I think that what he has really shown is merely that, compared to Mozart's music, Rossini's is trivial, shallow, and ornamental. I do indeed agree with the contention that this may (at least in part) reflect the cynicism and shallowness of Rossini's age. But I will not go along with Robinson the rest of the way. It is one thing for music to be shallow, another for it to "express" shallowness or anything else by being shallow. And, in my view, the reason why *The Marriage of Figaro* is moving and *The Barber of Seville* is not is solely because Mozart's music is what it is, deep and unutterably beautiful, while Rossini's is what it is, wonderfully pleasing, titillating, and shallow. It has nothing to do with "content."

In chapter 2 Robinson undertakes to argue that Schubert's two great song cycles, *Winterreise* and *Die schöne Müllerin,* "reflect the unprecedented subjectivity of the romantic movement. This is not merely a question," he observes, "of more emotion, more introspection, or more agonizing. Rather," Robinson continues, "the transformation is structural: the actual location of the drama has been moved from the external world of objects and relationships to the internal one of consciousness."

Again here, as throughout his book, Robinson is determined to make his case by talking about music, not words. Two examples from his analysis of *Die schöne Müllerin* will serve to illustrate his claim "that Schubert's distinctively romantic characterization of the self—as well as his characterization of nature in its relation to the self—is achieved largely though his music."

First, "The miller is an innocent." And Schubert presents this innocence quite simply by writing "innocent" music for the miller to sing. "Musical innocence is thus made to reflect characterological innocence." Just as "children and fools repeat themselves," so Schubert's music does as well, relying heavily on the most repetitive of musical forms, the strophic song. "Thus the strophic form of nearly half the songs in *Die schöne Müllerin* plays an important role in creating our sense of the miller's psychology."

Second, "The miller is a man who yearns." And Schubert conveys this by writing music that yearns, that "reaches." "The harmonic system of Western music provides him with an ideal device for this: the avoidance of the tonic, with its implications of resolution." To instance a case in point:

> The third song, "Halt!" ("Stop!"), marking the appearance of the mill, offers a particularly brilliant illustration of the device. . . . Schubert has taken every opportunity to avoid the home tone of C in the vocal writing. The song is full of upward leaps in which the singer moves from below middle C to above it, the most spectacular being a repeated octave jump (from g to g′) on the word "Himmel" ("heaven") in the fortieth and forty-fourth bars. And perhaps most touching of all, the last line of the song—a question addressed to the brook, "War es also gemeint?" ("Was it so intended?")—is repeated four times, with the "al-" of "also" sustained first on upper D (the second), then on F (the fourth), and finally twice again on D. The effect is superbly heady, in both vocal and emotional terms.

The reader, I think, will have no quarrel with these observations, or with most of the other perceptive insights Robinson provides into Schubert's musical technique for limning the psychological profiles of his two wandering neurotics. And Robinson is, after all, on old and familiar ground here. For music has, since time out of mind, been seen as an icon for psychological states. (More audacious claims are to come when we get to Berlioz's philosophy of history and Verdi's politics!)

But here, as in the case of Mozart, and what is to come, I would prefer to avoid the "express" locution altogether and understand what
Robinson is doing as showing us how music represents or portrays various concepts, ideas, psychological states, what you will. Perhaps not
much hangs on this quibble for most people who will read this book.
Many philosophers, however, will be most uncomfortable with any suggestion that music possesses propositional content. And such a suggestion can, perhaps, be avoided by saying that music represents what is in
the text—longing, or innocence, or whatever—rather than that it expresses ideas about these things. (A painting represents flowers, it doesn't
express opinions about them, is the idea.) Some philosophers may insist
that representations too must have propositional content; but that, at
least, is controversial, whereas there can be no doubt at all that if music
expresses ideas, it expresses propositions.

It is in the third and fourth chapters, dealing with *The Trojans* and
Don Carlo, respectively, that Robinson makes his most seemingly outra-
geous claims for operatic expression. In his treatment of Mozart, Rossini,
Schubert, and (in the final chapter) Wagner and Strauss, he has remained, more or less anyway, within the ambit of "psychology." That is
to say, the ideas musically expressed, or, as I would prefer to say, the
objects of musical representation, have been those having to do with
emotional states of human beings. (Even the Enlightenment theme of
reconciliation manages to fit the mold.) And this, as I have had occasion
to remark before, is more or less familiar and accepted territory for music
to inhabit—has been since Plato and Aristotle, in fact. But when an author tells us that music expresses a philosophy of history, or a political
ideology, it gives one pause.

Nonetheless, even here Robinson has managed to make claims about
music, not words, that are, even when not completely convincing, at least
not "off the wall" either. Berlioz's epic, he argues, "is a musical embodiment of the Hegelian idea of history"; which is to say that "the opera is
constructed according to a grand dialectical pattern." Now, much of
what Robinson has to say in support of this contention, when it has to do
with music, and not with Berlioz's words, has to do with what one might
think of as the external aspects of the work: the orchestration, the

plethora of choruses, the use of the Trojan March as a leitmotiv—all of which, according to Robinson, are meant to represent the "public," the "ceremonial," character of the work. Where the basic musical parameters are talked about, the argument begins to be labored. Robinson's most ingenious observation, in this regard, concerns what he calls the "historical bass." He argues that, at crucial moments in the opera, the instrumental bass takes on an unusual musical prominence, quite the reverse of its usual "musical anonymity": "The bass is released from its supporting role and takes on a life of its own; it assumes a kind of subversive musical independence. The result is to create an impression of forces at work— and on the move—beneath the explicit musical gestures of the characters. In *The Trojans* those forces, I believe, are the impersonal laws of history, which carry the characters toward a destiny that they don't fully understand." The crucial moments where the "historical bass" takes over are those where the ideas of Aeneas' destiny is prominent. For example, in the case of Cassandra, "Berlioz introduces it whenever she speaks in her prophetic mode—in other words, whenever she articulates the opera's historic theme."

Now, someone familiar with the musico-dramatic "language" of opera, particularly the accompanied recitative, might well counter here that what Robinson calls the "historical bass" in *The Trojans* is merely the old and familiar technique, which goes back at least as far as baroque opera seria, of signaling the ominous or important with prominent, frequently unaccompanied, bass passages. (Think of the moment in *Don Giovanni* when Donna Anna first recognizes the murderer of her father; or the "fate" motive in *Carmen*.) Its appearance, then, in *The Trojans*, it might be argued, has no more significance than that, scarcely the metaphysical import attributed to it by Robinson.

But whether or not one is convinced by Robinson's "historical bass," there is no doubt of the real brilliance of Robinson's observation. It is the kind of idea that seems so simple. "Why didn't I think of that?" one is tempted to ask. And if, in spite of its brilliance, one is not entirely persuaded, I suspect Robinson is in a healthy state of skepticism himself. For he warns us that "I cannot of course prove that this musical procedure— a more or less independently moving bass line—has exactly the subliminal connotation I've here assigned to it." And in another place Robinson lets drop the telltale remark that Berlioz may not have intended "the opera's affinities with this major intellectual preoccupation of the age." But when a critic appeals to unintended artistic consequences, I think he is running scared, as well Robinson might in trying to hear Hegel in music. However, when skepticism has had its say, it will not have taken away from the reader the sense of audacity in Robinson's attempt to find philosophy and politics in the purely musical parameters.

In the final chapter Robinson returns to safer ground; and I think the reader will find therefore fewer points to cavil at than in the chapters on Berlioz and Verdi. The point of the chapter is to contrast the treatments of a common theme. For both *Die Meistersinger* and *Der Rosenkavalier* are "about" the generous renunciation, on the part of an aging lover (or potential lover), in favor of a young one, although, of course, the genders are reversed in the two works, Hans Sachs giving up Eva to Walther, the Marschallin giving up Octavian to Sophie. Robinson calls them "operas of romantic sacrifice." And "because the emotional triangles at the heart of *Die Meistersinger* and *Der Rosenkavalier* are so much alike, one is all the more curious to know why the works as a whole should leave such strikingly dissimilar impressions." Robinson's answer, consistent with the general theme of his book, is that "the most interesting source of that dissimilarity . . . is a shift in the general climate of opinion between the late nineteenth and the early twentieth centuries."

On Robinson's view, "Where *Die Meistersinger* is an opera about society, *Der Rosenkavalier* is an opera about the self: its subject, in the last analysis, is human psychology." The great divide is the twentieth century's turn inward. "Nearly all students of our cultural and intellectual life agree that the emergence of an essentially psychological point of view has been the distinguishing feature of the modern era." This contrast is musically symbolized, for Robinson, by the two works' dramatic ensembles, the quintet (in *Die Meistersinger*) and the trio (in *Der Rosenkavalier*). Both are of equal emotional intensity, and both of equal musical worth. "Yet there is an important difference in their dramatic location: Wagner's quintet is followed by the Midsummer Day festival, a scene that has no counterpart in Strauss, and in which the celebration of Hans

Sachs's goodness is transferred from the private to the public realm." But "the Marschallin's sacrifice is . . . an entirely personal affair, and once it has been memorialized in Strauss's great trio there is nothing more to say."

One might remark here that Robinson has really not shown us a musical difference between the quintet and the trio, or between the two operas, but a textual one, and thus has, at least in this instance, failed to carry out his stated purpose of showing in every case how operatic music expresses ideas. For the social as opposed to the psychological view is expressed—or, better, because it is so tenuous, "reflected"—not by any musical quality of either ensemble but merely by the fact that one librettist has provided the composer the text for an ensemble in one place, the other in another. (It is, of course, irrelevant that in the case of *Die Meistersinger* the librettist and composer were the same person.) He has here, as elsewhere in his book, given much musical evidence for his conclusions. But this instance does perhaps show how hard it is, after all, to demonstrate that music "expresses" ideas, and how easy to let the words do the business where opera is concerned.

III

I cannot have done justice, in this brief account of what Robinson is up to, to the richness of his book. It is filled with ingenious observations on various musical features of the operas he discusses, relating them to the intellectual themes of their periods. Some of these observations will strike the skeptical reader as strained. Others will be, I am sure, utterly convincing to anyone. But none of them fails to be fascinating; and many are just downright brilliant.

Further, Robinson's musical observations never merely hold "intellectual" interest for the reader. They invite us to rehear these works with them in mind. And, indeed, as critical observations, that can be their only acid test. But just because these are all invitations to listen, Robinson's book will appeal not only to people who want to think about opera but also to people who want to look, listen, and enjoy. In other words, this is not a book only for professionals. In its appeal to learned and layman alike, it has no recent equal, in my experience, except Joseph Kerman's

Opera as Drama. I know that Robinson will not fail to take that as a high compliment.

Bernard Williams, "Comments on Paul Robinson's *Opera and Ideas*"

There are a lot of points that I should have liked to take up in Paul Robinson's very interesting book, which I like because it extends to opera a serious level of intellectual interest that is taken for granted as appropriate in other dramatic arts but is rarely applied to opera; and also because, even more unusually, it obeys the precept that if you want to understand opera you must trust its music. However, because of the limitations of time, my remarks will be mostly about Wagner and Strauss—about whom Peter Kivy has said less than he has about others—and in particular Wagner.

The work of Wagner's that Robinson considers in his book is *Die Meistersinger,* and he puts it in comparison with *Der Rosenkavalier.* By a technique rather similar to that which he applies to *The Marriage of Figaro* and *The Barber of Seville,* he takes two works that have something in common (in each case, one work greater than the other) and elicits some differences that he associates with differences in their historical circumstances. In considering opera and ideas, Robinson has in mind throughout opera and the history of ideas.

The resemblance that Robinson finds between the Wagner and Strauss works is of course different from that between Mozart's and Rossini's operas; the latter share an author as literary source, the former pair share a structure in their plot, a structure of renunciation. But there is surely another difference, which affects the comparison. Rossini must have known *The Marriage of Figaro,* and that knowledge affected his work in general, but, as Robinson's account brings out, it had little distinctive effect on the *Barber;* while Strauss has *Meistersinger* in mind, as he has Wagner always in mind. This is just one way in which *Rosenkavalier* is immensely historically and stylistically self-conscious, and there are many others, such as the way in which it refers, as has often been remarked, to three different historical periods. There is the time of the action, taken up at least once into the music; the time of the Baron's waltzes; and the time of the work itself, which—as Robinson rightly says—is rather ambivalently revealed in a lot of its music. All this is replicated in the text, which combines elaborately archaic forms of address with pieces of knowing Viennese reflection hardly available to an eighteenth-century Feldmarschallin ("Und in dem 'Wie' / da liegt der ganze Unter-shied").

As Robinson notes, Strauss tries to turn this machinery in the scene of the presentation of the Rose to the expression of simple and naïve goodness and love (as he does in the duet at the end, a cynical and unsuc-cessful attempt to borrow innocence from *The Magic Flute*). Beautiful as it is, I do not myself find this as successful as Robinson does. It fails in the same way as Jokanaan's music in *Salome*, i.e., it is kitsch. The failure is a lot less drastic, because *Rosenkavalier* is all, to some degree, kitsch. I don't go as far as Joseph Kerman's judgment that the Rose scene "has all the solidity of a fifty-cent valentine"; Kerman is a puritan who detests kitsch on principle. But if it is regarded as expressive rather than decora-tive, there is something false about it, because the manifest conditions of its production conflict with what is being expressed.

The point of this is that the vast self-consciousness of *Rosenkavalier* —its exploitation, sometimes engaging, sometimes boring, sometimes disgusting, of its own historical situation—means that it is already quite different from any work of Wagner, above all *Meistersinger*. That is in-deed a difference between 1911 and the 1860s. (It is a difference paralleled in that between Verdi and Puccini, except that Strauss can, above all in *Rosenkavalier,* be seen, if you like, not just as someone who rejected modernism but as a postmodernist avant la lettre, whereas Puccini can't.) The great historical self-consciousness of so much twentieth-century art of course itself puts questions to the history of ideas. But it is this, very general, difference, I think, that overwhelmingly contributes to the con-trast between these works (even if we grant, with Isaiah Berlin, that Wagner himself, in contrast to Verdi, belongs to the "sentimental" or self-conscious type of artist, rather than the "naïve.")

When we take this very general difference into account, we have less reason, I think, to insist on the difference of content that Robinson picks out and tries to explain historically, that *Meistersinger* is social and

Rosenkavalier purely psychological. Society is not denied in the latter; it is merely taken for granted, like hundreds of other things in so knowing a work. In a passage from the libretto that Robinson himself quotes, the remarks of members of society are themselves an important element in the Marschallin's fear of the passage of time.

What is true is that *Meistersinger*, as against *Rosenkavalier*, is not just social but political. In the regrettable passage about German art (which Cosima made Wagner put in against his better judgment) it is indeed explicitly political. At the beginning of his book, Robinson says that he has chosen to consider *Meistersinger* partly because other works of Wagner are too consciously and explicitly related to ideas to bring out the kind of influence or association he wants to illustrate. There is a difference between *Meistersinger* and Wagner's other mature works in some such respect, but I do not think this gets it right. The difference is that the text is less abstract and less explicitly philosophical than, manifestly, that of *Tristan* or most of the *Ring* or—though it again is rather different—*Parsifal;* but this is because the ideas are more directly and unambiguously expressed in the action, which in turn is more locally and concretely political.

Meistersinger is no less a political drama than *An Enemy of the People,* but it is a lot more as well. Robinson has put it the other way round, by making it a psychological story of renunciation with a social setting, but I think this centers Sachs's renunciation too much (the reference to King Mark in *Tristan* at the critical moment in act 3, which Robinson mentions, is in fact deployed, both in words and music, with some wry irony.) Sachs is its hero, but it is essential that it isn't named for him.

Now I would not say that *Meistersinger* is Wagner's most political work—but I think that Robinson should. For he says that Verdi's work is more political than that of Wagner, on the grounds that Verdi often puts before us historically located men of power, while Wagner's works, with the exception of *Meistersinger* (and, I suppose one should add, *Rienzi*), are mostly placed in vaguely medieval or mythological settings. And in this sense *Meistersinger* is closer to a particular political reality than the others. But I wouldn't accept this level of the identification of the political. It seems to me obvious that the most political of Wagner's works is the *Ring,* even though it is determinedly unlocated in history. In order to agree with this one doesn't have to accept Shaw's or some similar reading of it as an allegorical critique of capitalism. Those elements surely exist in it, as Chereau's wonderful centennial production of it—unlike many other such attempts—brought out (not only in its many successes but also in an obvious mistake, that the yet undisturbed Rhinemaidens at the beginning of *Rheingold* should have been represented as already involved in the industrial complex). The *Ring* is basically political just because it is concerned in manifold ways with the exercise of power, its possibilities, limitations, necessities, and costs.

So, of course, as Robinson well brings out, is *Don Carlo,* and it might have been interesting if Robinson had brought his comparative method to bear on King Philip and Wotan. But even in that great work, Verdi subordinates matters intrinsic to the exercise of power to the human, psychological, and ethical interest of the characters involved in it, whereas Wagner, in the *Ring,* deploys an action that is structured in part by the long-range concerns and consequences of power, reaching often beyond the consciousness of particular characters. Wotan is unique in the degree to which these facts, and the associated responsibilities, are represented in his consciousness, alongside more ordinary—one might have said, everyday—concerns.

In fact, Wagner runs extreme risks, both in *Rheingold* and in *Walküre,* in putting together these levels of concern. It has been said that the *Ring* under its world-historical trappings is often only a bourgeois domestic drama, and this criticism, if true, would be deeply damaging; unlike the perfectly correct, and non-damaging, description of *Aida* as a chamber opera with processions. The criticism is false, and the ways in which Wagner holds it at bay would make a revealing study of his skill. He himself said that his art was that of transition, and the musical devices that embody this art are what enable him to move convincingly from domestic to historical or metaphysical preoccupations: one example is the wonderful passage in *Walküre* in which Fricka finally defeats Wotan in their closely argued quarrel over whether Siegmund is to be defended: "Deiner ew'gen Gattin heilige Ehre . . ."

Wagner's many critics, those who hate and in some cases, it must be said, fear his art, will cite just this kind of thing as an instance of his powers as a theatrical showman, a trickster, old Klingsor, as Debussy called him, the original inventor of (the title of a novel by Angela Carter) Dr. Hoffmann's Sexual Dream Machine. But it is hard to sustain this, I think, if one looks carefully at the way in which the junctions between these various concerns are not just concealed by the music but expressed by it, and also represented in the consciousness of, above all, Wotan himself.

Robinson's contrast of *Meistersinger* with *Rosenkavalier* as social to psychological is confined to those two works and is not, I think, supposed to carry over into any larger comparison of the two composers. But inasmuch as he connects this with a change in general consciousness between two historical periods, one would expect it to be more generally revealed. In that light, there is really a problem, since *Tristan*, written just before *Meistersinger*, must surely be one of the most intensely solitary, inwards-turned, unsocial, depth-psychological works ever written. This raises, in fact, a general problem about Robinson's method: if the difference between two works is to be explained in any way in terms of a more general difference between two periods, then the difference has to extend beyond the two works under comparison. A historical difference might of course be focussed more narrowly by its being the case that it shows itself in the way in which *a given subject* is handled at different periods, and I think that is what Robinson has in mind; but then it becomes all the more crucial to identify what the given subject is. It may be that Wagner could have written a more purely psychological version of the story of Hans Sachs if he had wanted to, but he was writing something else. One piece of evidence that he could have written a purely psychological drama of that kind is *Tristan*.

In fact, even *Tristan* has a social dimension, a world outside Tristan and Isolde, but it is exclusively located in relation to them. It plays a part in a more general feature of the work, the way in which its three acts relate differently to time. Each act starts with music off-stage, which provides the basis for the opening musical development. The dramatic content of that music establishes for each act a different relation to time. At the beginning of the first act, the sailor's song, drifting down from high on the mast, looks forward ("Frisch weht der Wind / der Heimat zu"), and the progress of the act is marked by reminders that the ship is rapidly approaching Cornwall, an arrival that Isolde knows she cannot endure. The constant sense of that approaching future holds the act together.

Within this structure, Isolde tells of the past; but her narrative is so placed as to make it clear that it is not merely an expository device; the events are told in this way because Isolde carries them within her, and we have the sense—a sense essentially derived from the music—not so much of being told about the past as of looking within her.

The hunting horns with which the second act begins relate to the present and to what, they pretend, is happening elsewhere. They tell us, as do Brangäne's warnings, of something Tristan and Isolde's music denies, that they are surrounded at that very moment by a world of social and personal relations. After the hideous moment at which that world breaks in on them, Mark's recriminations give voice to those facts, and he gives a complex psychological account of the relations of the three people; but it is barely relevant any longer to the state that Tristan and Isolde have reached.

In the third act, we have Tristan without Isolde, and it becomes finally his drama. It, too, starts with off-stage music, and this relates to the past: *die alte Weise*. Tristan's love is of course associated with death: it is true to a thought Wagner expressed to Cosima, in relation to Siegfried's fear: "The kiss of love is the first intimation of death: the cessation of individuality." But it is essential to the power of this work that Tristan cannot be allowed simply to expire on Melot's sword into *das Wunderreich der Nacht;* he has to pass through knowledge, and his recovery of that is the subject of his great monologue, the climax of the work. That is, above all, why *Tristan,* though its libretto is more textured by vaguely philosophical ideas than any other of Wagner's works, is a psychological work rather than a metaphysical one, and is in fact a drama.

I feel that these points about *Tristan,* and the character of the *Ring* as a political drama, both give the same lesson, that the ideas to which a Wagnerian opera, at least, gives expression have to be understood at a level that lies not just below the libretto but below that of the libretto as musically presented at particular moments. *Tristan* is a psychological drama and not a metaphysical meditation; moreover, it is not a drama of a triangle, of trust and betrayal, but a drama of the self in time, about the loss of self in passion and the recovery of self in memory. The *Ring* is a political drama not in a way that excludes the psychological; its whole aim is to integrate the two (there is an eventual failure of that integration, but that is not the work's failure, it is the failure that it represents). And with each work these features of it come out only in the experience of it as a musical whole.

I do very much agree with Robinson that the power of opera particularly lies at the intersection of the social and psychological worlds, and its capacity to express both at once. As he also says, the way in which ideas are expressed in opera is likely to relate particularly to the images they bear of the self, its relations to others, society, time, and its own history. But, as I am sure he would agree, the exploration of these matters can be carried to further levels, which go still deeper in the right direction, that is to say, into the music.

A last point: with respect to that exploration, I find it odd that he should say, at the end of his book, that the idea of a positivist opera is almost a contradiction in terms. Of course it is true, if it means an opera that declares positivism; but—whatever people say about Wagner and the philosophy of Schopenhauer—that's true of any opera and any philosophy. What is in question is whether any opera could express and mobilize for its dramatic purposes a picture of the self and of human life that bore a revealing relation to the picture of those things given or implied by positivism. I cannot argue it here, but there surely is such an opera— in fact two, the two greatest operas of the twentieth century, *Wozzeck* and *Lulu*.

"Reply to Peter Kivy and Bernard Williams"

I am flattered to be here as the object of this Plenary Session of the American Society for Aesthetics, and, needless to say, I am also flattered by the kind things that Professor Kivy and Professor Williams have said about my book. Their criticisms, furthermore, show that they have read the book as I intended it to be read, or as I hoped it would be read: they precisely identify those moments in my argument that I myself consider most distinctive, and also most debatable.

In my reply I would like to focus on two of those moments. The first is my proposition that ideas are given musical expression, not merely verbal or dramatic expression, in opera. The second is my assertion that those ideas often turn out to be the same or similar to ideas expressed in other contemporaneous cultural documents—novels, poems, philosophical writings, and the like—so that opera in this fashion can be said to reflect intellectual history, indeed to be a constituent of intellectual history.

Both of these propositions share a certain prejudice, whose implications I want to return to briefly at the end. Both are based on an assumption of cultural unity, whether it be the unity of the individual work of art or the larger unity that binds art works together in a cultural age or movement. As I've reflected on this governing assumption of my argument in *Opera and Ideas*, I've been struck by how unfashionable it in fact is. It is an assumption at odds with what I take to be the dominant mood in cultural studies at the present time, where the emphasis is very much on disunity, difference, and, of course, deconstruction. So, if my book represents a fairly radical departure from normal practices in musicology and operatic history, it is at the same time quite old-fashioned—even hidebound—in its broader presuppositions about cultural and intellectual life.

I

The first matter I want to talk about, as noted, is my contention that ideas find expression, or representation, in the music, not merely in the texts, of opera. I must confess that whether or not this contention is true—or whether or not I have been able to show that it is true—it is the only statement about the relation between ideas and opera that holds any interest for me. In recent years opera has become the subject of quite a good deal of what I would call essentially literary analysis—books and articles, often written by professional literary critics, that draw comparisons between opera and the novel, opera and drama, or opera and philosophy. Most of the time these studies turn out to be not about opera at all but about opera librettos. That is, they have little or nothing to say about music—about how, in opera, an idea, a character, or an emotion finds its way into musical language or musical structure. Such is the case, for example, with Peter Conrad's synoptic study of opera, *A Song of Love and Death* (1987), which Philip Gossett criticized in the *New York*

Review of Books for its systematic failure to address the musical characteristics of the operas it discusses. It is also the case with the provocative
book entitled *Opera, or the Undoing of Women* (1979), by the French feminist philosopher Catherine Clement, which argues vigorously, and often
ingeniously, that the great operas are essentially stories of women being
murdered or otherwise done in by men. Virtually the only thing Clement
says about music in opera is that it serves to anaesthetize audiences into
tolerating this misogynist message.

Whatever the value of these studies that examine opera from an essentially nonmusical point of view, they are not the sort of enterprise that
I would ever have launched myself on. From the start my interest in
opera has been essentially musical, probably because I came to know and
love opera simply as an extension of an earlier love of instrumental music. I learned opera largely from recordings, and what drew me to it, and
made me listen to particular works over and over, was precisely the same
mysterious stuff that I found so compelling in symphonies, sonatas, and
string quartets. Of course there was something more, namely, operatic
voices, with their singular and inexpressible charms. But here again my
interest was anything but intellectual, since there is virtually nothing of
intellectual interest one can say about the pleasure to be had from certain
sounds emanating from the throat of a Battistini, a Björling, or a Callas.

I emphasize this unintellectual, largely sensuous, quality of my response to opera in order to explain that when I did come to write an account of the intellectual content of opera, I was interested in the task
only in so far as I could make the argument work at a musical level. Now,
I may well be guilty of forcing the ineffable to speak, when, of course, it
would prefer not to, and I am aware that Wittgenstein, among others,
cautioned against doing so. But, as I say, it seemed to me the only book
worth writing on the subject. So my procedure throughout was to ask
myself with regard to a particular operatic character, or situation, or exchange, or even individual line, "Is this character, situation, exchange, or
line somehow present in the music as well, and if so how?" And I try to
answer that question by talking about such things as melody, harmonic
structure, rhythmic pattern, dynamics, vocal types and effects, and in-
strumentation, and to do so in as nontechnical a fashion as possible.
Throughout the book I employ a vocabulary that, I hope, is accessible to

the literate public, and not simply to those who are musically (or musico-logically) trained. Much of *Opera and Ideas* is thus devoted to the close reading—close musical reading, that is—of individual passages in the works I discuss, always with a view to showing how the music in question might be understood as lending expressive weight to particular ideas.

Now, Professor Kivy complains, albeit gently, that I am over broad in my claims for music's ability to "express" ideas, and that in many instances I would be on safer grounds if I were to speak rather of its "representing" ideas. He cites, by way of example, the different claims I advance for Mozart's *Marriage of Figaro* and Rossini's *Barber of Seville*, the first of which I try to link to the Enlightenment, the second to the early-nineteenth-century reaction against the Enlightenment. If I understand him correctly, the distinction he wishes to draw pertains ultimately to the conscious intention of the composer. He agrees that the Enlightenment ideal of reconciliation is very much on Mozart's mind in composing *The Marriage of Figaro,* and he also accepts, I gather, the particular instances I cite to show how Mozart gives that idea musical expression in the opera—for example, the opening *duettino,* in which the antagonism between Susanna and Figaro is presented as a melodic antagonism, just as their momentary reconciliation at the end of the *duettino* is reflected in a musical reconciliation as well. By way of contrast, he does not believe that Rossini is fully conscious of the cynicism that I say dominates *The Barber of Seville,* and because Rossini is not conscious of it, although the opera may indeed be cynical, it's not really "about" cynicism.

I am prepared to accept this criticism—and to accept Professor Kivy's distinction between expression and representation—but, perhaps because I am not a philosopher (to put it mildly), I don't feel the weight of the distinction quite so strongly as he does. For one thing, I am not sure that Mozart's commitment to "reconciliation" was categorically more explicit than Rossini's commitment to cynicism, and I don't pursue such an assertion with evidence in the book. In general I rather picture the composer, in the cases I talk about, as absorbing and giving expression to ideas in a more or less unreflective fashion, and, with the possible exception of Wagner, I don't see him as a philosopher manqué. He might be able, on occasion, to articulate his ideas in a relatively coherent fashion (one can imagine Mozart, for example, giving a decent lecture on Freemasonry, and hence on the ideas he deploys in *The Magic Flute*). But more often, as I imagine it, the ideas in question remain beneath the level of explicit articulation—remain embedded in particular characters, relationships, and emotions. In other words, I presume that the process of artistic creation moves silently back and forth between conscious and unconscious levels of intention. Professor Kivy seems prepared to accept the notion that a composer may indeed entertain ideas unconsciously, but he insists that, while this fact is of intellectual interest (and thus pertinent to the history of ideas), it lacks aesthetic interest. He may be right, but it is for me a rather fine distinction. The musical cynicism that I find in Rossini's opera—for example, the trivializing coloratura that undermines the construction of character, or the use of mechanical rhythms and rudimentary harmonic repetitions to inhibit meaningful interaction—amounts to something more than Rossini's music being simply "pleasing, titillating, and shallow." The quality is, in my hearing, too systematic, pervasive, and, in some important instances, self-mocking not to carry artistic weight.

But the point I wish to stress—and here Professor Kivy agrees with me—is that *Opera and Ideas* stands or falls on whether the reader finds its *musical* interpretations on balance persuasive. The bulk of my energy in the book is devoted to showing how particular musical procedures underline and enhance the verbal, dramatic, and, of course, intellectual goings-on in opera, and thereby contribute to our sense of the operatic work as an artistic unity.

II

Let me turn now to the second moment of my argument I want to dilate on, my assertion that the ideas I find in opera are the very same ideas that inhabit other more or less contemporaneous cultural documents. At stake here is the higher level of cultural unity that the book aims to demonstrate. I should perhaps point out that, in this contention, I am merely extending to opera a point of view that has become commonplace in the study of the visual arts. Books exploring the affinities between, especially, painting and literature—so-called sister-arts studies—have long been a familiar feature of the scholarly landscape. What I try to do with opera is structurally identical to these sister-arts studies, and I share with them the goal, whether stated or not, of showing that culture is in some sense of a piece—that its various strands are connected with one another.

The discussion of this second issue will allow me to respond more directly to Professor Williams's criticisms, because I think the most telling of them is his suggestion that in treating Wagner and Strauss I have come to grief over this matter of larger cultural patterns. But I should begin by saying that I find myself mostly in agreement with the individual operatic interpretations that Professor Williams offers in his remarks. He is exactly right, it seems to me, in his view of *Tristan und Isolde,* which, like Joseph Kerman, he sees as a drama of the self, whose climax is Tristan's delirium and transfiguration in act 3. Perhaps I view the *Ring* as more evenly divided in its devotion to politics and psychology than he does, but that the cycle is deeply political is undeniable. I will, however, stick to my guns in insisting that *Meistersinger* is legitimately regarded as more social than political, in that it is—or so I argue—an opera about the preservation of community, an opera whose central concern is social cohesion. That social cohesion is shown in the opera to be a creation of art (I compare Wagner's conception here with the ideas of John Ruskin and other similar-minded thinkers in the latter half of the century), a creation that can be maintained only through great personal sacrifice—in this case, the romantic sacrifice made by Hans Sachs.

I suspect Professor Williams and I differ less in our interpretation of Wagner's art than in our estimate of it. I will confess that one of the lesser objectives of my treatment of Wagner in the book is to reduce him to more normal dimensions, to demote him, if you will, from singular genius to ordinary genius. Professor Williams's comments, by contrast, suggest that he is a Wagnerite, by which I mean not merely someone who considers Wagner great but one who considers him uniquely great.

I try to effect my demotion in several ways, all of which place Wagner unceremoniously in the company of other "merely" great composers. First, by comparing *Meistersinger* with *Rosenkavalier,* even though I make clear my strong preference for Wagner's work over Strauss's, I suggest that it is perfectly responsible to consider Wagner and Strauss in the same aesthetic breath. Similarly, I accord Verdi even more attention in the book than Wagner, and I thereby imply that the intellectual interest of an opera like *Don Carlo* is as great as that of any of the Wagner operas, including the *Ring*. (It is the *Ring*, incidentally, about whose merits Professor Williams and I are probably most at odds. For me, as for George Bernard Shaw and Joseph Kerman, it is only a mixed success. I often have the sense that Wagner has bitten off more than he can chew intellectually, and I am far from persuaded of the work's conceptual coherence.) Finally, among my devices for, as it were, regularizing Wagner, I suggest in my discussion of his music that what makes him a great composer is not the creation of some hitherto unknown procedure of combining signature tunes but rather, quite simply, his mastery and elaboration of the compositional techniques inherited by him from his predecessors. Indeed, in my view he is a great composer, above all, because of his ability to create extraordinarily long stretches of music that are structurally unified—that have the effect of sounding almost like a single phrase, passages such as the *Tristan* and *Parsifal* Preludes or the *Meistersinger* quintet. His mastery of musical structure in these moments is equal to Bach's in the B Minor Mass or Mozart's in the second act finale of *Figaro*, and it is surpassed by no other composer.

These, then, are some of the matters of interpretation and evaluation over which Professor Williams and I may differ. But, as noted, I am most troubled about his complaint that I wade into treacherous conceptual waters in arguing that the shift from *Meistersinger* to *Rosenkavalier* reflects a larger intellectual shift from the nineteenth century's preoccupation with society to the twentieth century's preoccupation with the self. He is, of course, absolutely right, although I believe the intellectual historian can't avoid getting his feet wet in those waters, even while trying to keep himself from drowning in them. At stake here is the question of how one talks about intellectual trends, movements, and periods, the question of the spirit of the time, the infamous question of the Zeitgeist. (I have it in mind someday to write an article with the title, "Who's Afraid of the Zeitgeist?") Learning to address this question with appropriate conceptual delicacy is, I believe, the highest art of the intellectual historian.

Professor Williams correctly observes that, although I limit my illustration of a shift from the social to the psychological to the operas under

analysis, not extending it to a more general comparison of the two composers, this limitation has the effect of weakening the explanatory power
of that larger cultural shift. In particular he notes that Wagner's career,
considered chronologically, doesn't fit my pattern at all but in fact seems
to run in the opposite direction. That is, *Tristan und Isolde,* which premiered in 1859, is, as he puts it, "one of the most intensely solitary,
inwards-turned, unsocial, depth-psychological works ever written"—a
characterization with which I fully concur—whereas the more social
work, *Die Meistersinger,* was composed after *Tristan,* being premiered
almost a decade later, in 1868. One might have supposed that in a world
where the Zeitgeist was fully sovereign Wagner would have been obliged
to compose his mature operas in practically inverse order: he should have
begun with the heavily social *Meistersinger,* proceeded to the *Ring* with
its union of political and psychological concerns, turned next to the decidedly more psychological *Parsifal,* and ended his career with what is
clearly his most "modern" opera, *Tristan und Isolde,* in which the figures
representing society (Brangäne, Marke, Kurwenal) are reduced to near
insignificance—indeed, in which they serve merely as points of departure or refraction for the opera's total absorption in the psychic lives of its
title characters.

  This imaginary chronology shows, of course, that the search for cultural unity in the works of a given period has to be pursued in a much
more nuanced and subtle fashion. The unities that the historian posits
are, I think, best thought of as intellectual conveniences, or ideal types.
They are efforts to give expression to the profoundly felt sense that cultural works are not autonomous or discrete but exist in some kind of in-
terrelation with one another, and that chronological proximity is one of
the most important indices of their connectedness. But because they are
merely intellectual conveniences, and not metaphysical structures with
some kind of magical power over the cultural products of an age, they
must always be judged in terms of their relative usefulness. If a sufficient
number of important countervailing instances can be cited, the historical
category will need to be revised; there may even be calls for its complete
abolition, such as Arthur O. Lovejoy issued with regard to the historical
category "romanticism." But, as Lovejoy's case itself illustrates, the
effort to realize such revision or abolition will fail unless the discredited

intellectual convenience is replaced by a more handy one. The effort will fail because such categories are absolutely essential to carrying on any kind of discourse about the history of culture. Their inevitability is perhaps more easily appreciated if we cast our minds backward in time and consider the way we speak of the Middle Ages, the Renaissance, or the Enlightenment—historical categories that, although often challenged and refined, have become indispensable to our intellectual life.

Now, in the matter at hand, I'm not prepared to abandon the proposition that a shift from the social to the psychological is the most helpful way to speak about what happens in European thought and culture as one moves from the nineteenth to the twentieth century. Indeed, there is a quite remarkable consensus among scholars, writing in a number of different disciplines, about the appropriateness of this scheme. Whether one considers the movement from Émile Zola to Marcel Proust, or from Charles Dickens to James Joyce, or from Marx and Engels to Freud and Weber, a similar pattern is manifest.

When I try to make sense of Wagner's overall development as an artist in terms of this larger cultural pattern, I am, not surprisingly, inclined to think of him less as a man of his own age than as, like Dostoevsky, a precursor, an avatar, and, to a considerable extent, a creator of that intellectual and cultural universe that will come into ascendancy with the turn of the century. This line of argument may seem to let me off the hook all too easily, but I believe it simply acknowledges that the cultural patterns the intellectual historian seeks are always chronologically overlapping (they are never neatly bounded), and, more important, that they remain at all times conceptual constructs, to be judged and employed according to their usefulness and economy.

It is precisely against this background of assumptions about how the intellectual historian addresses the issue of cultural unity that I am prepared to cite Wagner's *Meistersinger,* in conjunction with Strauss's *Rosenkavalier,* as an illustration of the shift from the social to the psychological. Given the powerful introspection that dominates so much of Wagner's art, I find it all the more striking that he should nonetheless have devoted one of his greatest operas to an exploration of the question of community. It suggests that even this most psychological of artists was in touch with the dominant intellectual concerns of his age. In *Meis-*

tersinger at least, Wagner abandoned his wonted role of cultural avatar and composed very much as a man of his time.

A great deal still needs to be said on this issue, but I want to mention only one further matter. And that is the suspicion now abroad that the search for cultural patterns or cultural unities involves more serious liabilities than the purely conceptual ones to which I have addressed my remarks so far. Increasingly we hear it suggested that such cultural unities are repressive. Like the putative unity of the individual art work, they are said to represent false "totalizations." As such they discourage us from exploring the ways in which culture is not of a piece but rather a product of tensions and contradictions that are always threatening to explode. Even more damaging—or so it is argued—they serve to exclude voices that don't fit the established unitary pattern, and those voices turn out to be mostly the voices of women, racial minorities, and other nonelite members of society. My own university spent much of last year arguing about precisely this issue, as it considered replacing its required course in the history of western culture with a program that would pay more attention to cultural difference and variety. Finding myself in the middle of the debate and trying to serve as mediator between the two camps, I had frequent occasion to contemplate the essentially conservative intellectual assumptions I had relied on in writing *Opera and Ideas*. As must be evident by now, I'm prepared to defend those assumptions—to argue the case for cultural unity, or at least the intellectual necessity of seeking to detect such unity—but I am vastly more conscious of their precariousness and, so to speak, their untimeliness than I was when I wrote the book.

Finally, let me close by confessing to Professor Williams that, despite my categorical pronouncement on the subject, I did in fact give some thought to the idea of a positivist opera. But I fear that he and I have very different notions of positivism. Most likely he is thinking of the twentieth-century philosophical variety, whereas I had in mind such nineteenth-century figures as Auguste Comte, Herbert Spencer, and Freud's hero Hermann Helmholtz. Hence my candidate for a positivist opera would be neither *Wozzeck* nor *Lulu* but the Olympia act from *The Tales of Hoffmann* (admittedly less a positivist opera than a satire on positivism), or almost anything by Gilbert and Sullivan. Patter songs nearly always put me in mind of positivism. I can't entirely explain the logic of this association, but it is confirmed by the fact that one cannot imagine Richard Wagner, that most unpositivist of composers, even attempting to write one, never mind succeeding.

CHAPTER TWO

Reading Libretti and Misreading Opera

This essay originated at a conference on the libretto at Cornell University in October 1986 and appeared in a collection of papers from the conference, Reading Opera *(Princeton, 1988). It contests the notion that the meaning of an opera can be found in its libretto. It shows how the musical procedures of opera, above all operatic singing, consistently sabotage verbal intelligibility. Put another way, it bolsters my central contention in* Opera and Ideas *that opera remains always a musical phenomenon and that an opera's argument is advanced first and foremost by musical means.*

My observations here are intended as a polemical dissent from certain assumptions informing the essays in this collection and, indeed, informing most operatic criticism that I have read. I take it as axiomatic that polemics should overstate the case, seeking to disturb or provoke, where a more balanced expression of opinion might pass relatively unnoticed. As the reader will ultimately learn, my own convictions are less unorthodox than I like to let on. But throughout the essay I have self-consciously adopted a contrary—not to say contentious—point of view, because the assumptions I examine are, I believe, misguided and largely regrettable.

My theme, which I risk repeating to the point of canonic monotony, is that an opera cannot be read from its libretto. Put differently, a libretto is not a text as we ordinarily understand that term. Because the meaning of opera is at bottom musical—because its essential argument is posed in musical language—any interpretation of opera derived exclusively, or even primarily, from the libretto is likely to result in a misreading.

I have put my proposition in categorical form. Naturally, its truth varies considerably from one operatic tradition to another, from one composer to another, from one work to another, even from one passage to another in the same opera. It is, for example, more true of the operas of the nineteenth century than of those of the seventeenth and eighteenth centuries; more true of Verdi than of Rossini; more true of *Il trovatore* than of *Otello;* more true of concerted passages than of recitative. One of my purposes will be to specify what factors—historical, compositional, and vocal—influence the balance (or, more precisely, the imbalance) between musical and textual elements in the logic of opera.

I intend to pursue this theme largely through what Thomas Aquinas called the *via negativa,* discussing four distinctive aspects of opera that serve to undermine a purely textual approach to it. These are, you might say, the four great operatic enemies of intelligibility, four characteristics of the genre that interfere with our ability to decipher the words and thus limit the interpretative usefulness of any analysis centered on the libretto. But my purpose is not to lament these antitextual forces in opera. Far from it, I am delighted with opera in all its radical musicality. If anything, my object is to liberate opera from the textual fetters that literary interpreters seem determined to impose on it.

The intelligibility of an operatic libretto is inhibited, in varying degrees, by the following considerations: (1) opera is in a foreign language; (2) opera is sung, and much that is sung by an operatic voice cannot be understood; (3) opera contains a good deal of ensemble singing—passages where two or more voices sing at the same time, sometimes to identical words, sometimes to different words—and if one operatic voice is often unintelligible, two or more almost always are; (4) operatic singers must compete with a full symphony orchestra—at least from the nineteenth century onward—and, as every opera-goer knows, the sheer volume of that orchestral sound further limits our ability to make out the words.

Before I examine these factors in detail (and qualify my assertions in certain ways), let me note that I am going to pay no attention to what composers themselves have said about the relative importance of words and music in opera. Scholars and critics love to quote the dicta of Wagner or Verdi or Strauss on this subject. Thus we often read of Strauss's "Golden Rule" for conductors: "It is not enough," he wrote, "that you yourself should hear every word the soloist sings. You should know it by heart anyway. The audience must be able to follow without effort. If they do not understand the words they will go to sleep." The pronouncement might make sense had it been issued by Monteverdi, but coming from Strauss it is merely laughable. Think, for example, of the final trio from *Rosenkavalier* and try, if you can, to square it with Strauss's statement here. By and large such statements are best understood in strategic terms: they represent an effort to persuade singers to be more attentive to the text and conductors to be more considerate of singers. Or perhaps they might be said to reveal the contradictory aspirations of the operatic composer: the impossible wish to be fully loyal to the traditions of both drama and music. But however one interprets them, they are an unreliable guide to what actually happens when language is set to music in opera. Only one source is authoritative in this regard: the operas themselves.

In arguing against the overvaluation of a textual approach to opera—against the usefulness of "reading opera"—I am, of course, doing battle with the imperialistic textualism of today's literary culture. "Text" has in fact become one of the great buzzwords of our time, its only competitor being the equally literary (and equally imperialistic) "discourse." I will readily confess that I find the promiscuous use of these terms annoying even when applied to artifacts that are a good deal more literary than is opera. Indeed, on the grounds that one ought to cherish precision and avoid the clichés of the hour, I make a point of saying "book" or "essay" or "poem" or whatever else might be appropriate, reserving "text" for its legitimate function as a covering term. Students of opera, however, should resist the urge to "textual talk" not just for the sake of intellectual cleanliness but, more crucially, because such talk disfigures the object of their love. They might attend to the example of the art historian Michael Baxandall, whose book *Patterns of Intention* makes exactly the same point with regard to painting: painting, Baxandall suggests, remains at bottom a matter not of words but of images, and historians of painting who reduce those images to language (who interpret them according to a textual model) distort the aesthetic object. Opera, by analogy, is in its essence not a textual but a musical phenomenon, and interpreters of opera, accordingly, should proceed with great delicacy when they come to discuss its textual component.

Let me turn now to my four operatic adversaries of intelligibility in order to specify my claim and examine its implications.

I

The fact that opera is sung in a foreign language is the least significant of the four, but I place it first because in the mind of many, I suspect, it ranks as the most significant. Certainly it is the main inspiration behind the practice of performing operas with supertitles—a subject I will have more to say about later on. And I have no doubt that many opera-goers, especially Americans, believe that the main thing standing between them and the singers' words is the quaint but annoying fact that those words are uttered in a foreign tongue. Yet, important as the foreign-language issue may be, it does not go to the structural heart of the matter.

For one thing, opera is performed in a foreign language only under particular historical and geographical circumstances. The practice is specific to certain times and places. In the three countries that have produced the majority of the works heard in the opera house today—that is, in Italy, France, and Germany—the repertory has always been dominated by native composers, although the domination is more recent in the case of France and Germany. Moreover, since the nineteenth century (and until very recently), in virtually all European countries, works by foreign composers have generally been performed in translation. Needless to say, there have been significant deviations from this norm: in Mozart's Vienna, even operas by indigenous composers were often composed and sung in Italian, as were Handel's operas (though written by a German) in London; and, as every reader of Balzac and Flaubert knows, Italian operas were sung in Italian in mid-nineteenth-century Paris, at least if they were performed at the Théâtre Italien. Nonetheless, for most Continental Europeans going to the opera has not meant, as it did for Dr. Johnson, attending "an exotick and irrational entertainment."

One must also note that until fairly recently most opera singers sang in only one language, namely, their own. Anybody who, like myself, collects historical recordings of opera will be familiar with this phenomenon. And, if the truth must be known, you can become positively addicted to operas sung in the "wrong" language. Likewise, anyone who began attending opera as little as four decades ago will be able to recall some odd residue of this long-standing nativist tradition. As a student in Berlin in the early 1960s, I saw a performance of *Otello* with Renata Tebaldi in which the soprano sang in Italian while the rest of the cast and the chorus sang in German. As a variation on the same theme, there is a notorious pirate recording of Mario Del Monaco singing Don José with the Bolshoi Opera: everybody sings in Russian except the tenor, who alternates between Italian and French.

The proposition that opera is in a foreign language, then, holds true mainly for recent generations in English-speaking countries. And even there opera in translation has sometimes flourished, as at the New York City Opera in the 1950s and 1960s or the English National Opera in the 1970s and 1980s.

Up to now I have considered the foreign-language issue—and its relation to intelligibility—strictly from the standpoint of composers and performers. But it must also be considered from the perspective of listeners, whether live in the theater or at home with their recordings. The important point here is that the foreignness of a foreign language is always a matter of degree. Listeners boast varying levels of competence in a given language, and while the number who enjoy true fluency is probably small, even a rudimentary knowledge will increase a work's intelligibility and therewith the aesthetic weight of its textual component.

In spite of these mitigating factors—the dominance of indigenous operatic works in most European countries, the prevalence of translation, and the linguistic skills of the audience—I would insist that the foreign-language issue is still important, especially in America. When, for example, I attend performances of the operas of Mussorgsky or Janáček —operas that I am very fond of—I can understand virtually nothing of what is said. And I know that the majority of American opera-goers find Italian, French, and German just as mysterious as I do Russian and Czech. Even in Europe, operas are now performed in the original language much more often than they were as little as three decades ago. When I returned to Berlin in the late 1970s virtually every opera, including the Mozart operas, was being sung in the original. Naturally, the proliferation of operatic recordings and the increasingly international careers of major singers have played crucial roles in revitalizing original-language performances. And since this development corresponds, unhappily, with the decline in the study of foreign languages, the result is a situation where the foreignness of opera now constitutes probably a greater barrier to comprehension than it has at any time in the past.

Still, no one who has spent much time listening to opera will delude himself into thinking that opera's being in a foreign language is the fundamental source of its unintelligibility. For one thing, such a listener will have attended too many English-language operas in which passage after passage has defied all efforts at comprehension. In its 1985–86 season, for example, the Metropolitan Opera broadcast performances of *Porgy and Bess* and *Samson* (the latter admittedly not an opera but an oratorio), and, except for the singing of Jon Vickers as Samson, the text of both works was largely incomprehensible. Or, to cite a more absurd example, anyone who was rash enough to buy a ticket to the San Francisco Opera's 1986 production of Gian Carlo Menotti's *The Medium* would have made the surprising discovery that the opera, although, of course, sung in English, had been supplied with supertitles—and from the point of view of intelligibility they were anything but superfluous. So performing opera in one's own language—although there is much to be said for it—in no sense comes to terms with the issue of intelligibility. The matter goes much deeper.

I hope it will be noted that I have not taken sides in the argument over translation in opera. This is not merely because I am of two minds on the issue but, more important, because the really interesting question is why there should be a controversy at all. Such a controversy is, for example, inconceivable with regard to drama, which virtually without exception is performed in translation—even though, as the cliché reminds us, much is lost in the process. So why do we continue to argue about translating opera?

Obviously, we do so for musical reasons. The argument, one might say, pays ongoing tribute to opera's fundamentally musical nature. In the narrower sense, this tribute takes the form of insisting that there is a crucial link between the notes a composer writes and the particular vowels he intends to be sung on those notes. When you change the vowels—as inevitably happens in translation—you change the musical fabric and thus alter the essential character of the work. But there is, I think, a simpler reason why translation has not carried the day (and, indeed, seems to be losing ground): and that is because translation often makes so little difference in the way we experience opera—in the way opera works its effects on us. By far the larger burden of operatic argument is carried by the music, and the music matters most when the burden becomes heaviest. That is why people will sit for hours listening to singing they do not understand, while they would not be caught dead under the same circumstances at a stage play.

II

Operatic singing itself, I wish to suggest, represents the most intractable enemy of intelligibility. It is above all because opera is sung—and sung, of course, in a particular way—that it can at best approximate the level of verbal communication regularly achieved in spoken drama. Furthermore, opera singers are not incomprehensible because their diction is slovenly (although sometimes it is) but because composers write music for them that can be produced only through certain specialized physical procedures, one of whose effects is that intelligibility must, in varying degrees, be sacrificed. In the final analysis, opera is unintelligible for musical reasons.

This is not the place for a lecture on vocal technique, and I am not qualified to deliver one. But let me consider briefly, and necessarily in layman's terms, what operatic singing involves in order to suggest how it serves to undermine comprehension. The most basic demand made on an operatic voice is that it produce an enormous volume of sound. Indeed, a modern operatic voice is distinguished from an ordinary voice not so much by its beauty, flexibility, or even range as by its sheer loudness. This demand increases, moreover, as one moves forward through the repertory of the nineteenth century and the orchestral forces with which

singers must contend grow larger. The first premise of an operatic career, one might say, is the ability to produce a certain amount of noise.

Operatic volume is achieved essentially by putting pressure on the
voice and thereby fundamentally altering the nature of the sound it pro-
duces. One can hear this difference quite vividly by contrasting two
recordings of Eileen Farrell, one operatic and the other popular. When
Farrell sings in a light pop voice (a voice that, in performance, would be
amplified by microphone, as it never is in opera), every word is as clear as
if she were speaking. But when she employs her operatic voice, the large,
penetrating sound she emits often overwhelms the words she is seeking
to reproduce, and the same singer who was so splendidly lucid in Rogers
and Hart's "He Was Too Good to Me" becomes very difficult to understand, despite her excellent diction, in Verdi's "Tacea la notte placida."
This drowning of the words in vocal sound can be explained, technically,
in terms of increased overtones, the distortion of vowels, and several
other particulars that high-pressure operatic vocal production inexorably brings in its wake. For our purposes it is sufficient to note that
words sung in an operatic voice are significantly less understandable than
are words in the spoken voice or the light singing voice. This is a home
truth that all of us know and accept—including Richard Strauss with his
Golden Rule for conductors.

The sheer volume of the operatic voice, then, stands as a mighty
bulwark against intelligibility. It is complemented, so to speak, by the requirement that an operatic voice be able to encompass two full octaves—
a substantially wider range than the normal singing voice encompasses.
Operatic voices, in other words, must be able to sing both lower and,
more important, higher than ordinary untrained voices. (As a point of
reference, "The Star-Spangled Banner," which is notoriously difficult to
sing, encompasses only an octave and a fifth.) The demand for altitude
might be thought of as a variation on the demand for volume, because
from the point of view of the words it has the effect of exaggerating the
distortions created by putting operatic pressure on the voice. When a
singer moves to the top of his or her range (that is, when sopranos, mezzos, and tenors reach the area around top C, or when baritones and basses
reach upward toward top G), words must be sacrificed even more ruth-

lessly than they are lower down in the register. Thus many a singer who is perfectly lucid in the middle of the range becomes incomprehensible at the top. One might say that the amount of nonverbal interference emitted by a voice increases as it approaches the upper register. Moreover, not only singers but conductors and composers as well are absolutely delighted to hear any sound at all when the voice moves into this territory. Nobody is much inclined to quibble about diction on high C.

The crucial thing about high notes in opera is that these altitudinous, incomprehensible tones occur precisely at the moments of greatest dramatic significance, when the text, in theory, ought to matter most. In effect, the musical logic of opera exploits vocal altitude to express particularly intense or significant responses, but that very logic also conspires to undermine the intelligibility of those responses. Opera, in other words, grows inarticulate just when it seeks to say the most important things. Again, it is governed by a musical rather than a textual rationale.

Besides volume and altitude, operatic singing boasts—or ought to —one further characteristic that interferes with intelligibility: what aficionados refer to as "legato." Legato is essentially the singer's ability to sustain the tone inviolate as the voice moves from one pitch to another, or from one syllable to another on the same pitch. In its ideal form, operatic singing consists of an even, uninterrupted column of vocal sound, which undergoes no fundamental alteration in character as it abandons one note to embrace another or as it seeks to articulate different words. In reality, of course, singers achieve greater or lesser degrees of perfection of legato, and a bad singer will chop up the vocal line with aspirates marking each change of pitch or syllable (the tone will stop and start—even if ever so slightly—as the singer attempts to move the voice). But the goal of operatic singing is to achieve the most flawless legato possible.

That legato—that seamless, sustained vocal tone—stands in the service of opera's musical logic. In particular, it abets the composer's object of creating sonic shapes—that is to say, phrases—whose contours will emerge with the same lucidity as they might from a violin or a clarinet. Musical language traffics precisely in such sonic commodities: phrases, one might say, are the basic units of musical expression, and their cumulative weight and configuration constitute the essence of musical argument. Singing, in its effort to contribute to that argument, aims to produce musical shapes that approximate the aural qualities more readily produced by an instrument. Opera singers themselves will often refer to their voice simply as "the instrument," as if it were some alienated, mechanical appendage of the body—a kind of clarinet in the throat.

The significance of this ideal for the intelligibility of opera is vast. Spoken language becomes intelligible only through articulation, that is, through the interruption of sound. Or, put another way, speaking consists of both sound and silence. Singing, by contrast, allows no place for silence; it seeks to eliminate precisely those essential articulations that make language possible in the first place. Singing moves away from words toward vocalise. Indeed, a good deal of operatic singing, especially in bel canto opera, is nothing but vocalise, where the singer sustains the same vowel through a large number of notes. Even when singers try to articulate words, they remain under the more insistent (and opposite) imperative to make their voices into instruments, to bind the notes together, in spite of the words, so that we may hear the real language of opera, the language of musical phrases.

As if this were not enough, we must also reckon with the simple yet awesome fact that the only "singable" sounds are vowel sounds. One cannot produce an operatic noise on a consonant, not even on such accommodating consonants as *l*, *m*, or *n*. In other words, just as the fundamental articulations of language are consistently undermined by the ideal of legato singing, so also the shape or rhythm of language is radically distorted in opera because all the notes in a vocal part are written to be sustained on vowels. In order to be sung—to be rendered musical—words are pummeled and bent so that their vowels are dramatically extended, while their consonants are reduced to mere shadows of their spoken selves. Thus when Radamès sings his final line in act 3 of *Aida*—"Io resto a te"—what we actually hear is a sequence of elongated vowels trumpeted on the tenor's high A. If in speaking we were to redistribute vowels and consonants in the manner in which they are regularly redistributed in opera, our talk would be no less incomprehensible than is much operatic singing. The sovereignty of vowels in singing partly explains why a language like Italian, in which virtually all words end in vowels, is more gratefully operatic than is, say, English, where most words end in consonants.

It will doubtless have occurred to some readers that the generalizations I have just advanced invite all sorts of qualifications. The demands for volume, altitude, and legato do not affect the intelligibility of opera in a uniform way. Rather, their effect is now more or less drastic, now more or less innocuous. Moreover, certain broad qualifications in this area are worth contemplating for a moment, because they help explain why some operas and some operatic roles are more intelligible than others. In particular I wish to call attention to a historical and a sexual variable in this domain.

The first qualification I have already alluded to: operas of the seventeenth and eighteenth centuries are generally more comprehensible than those of the nineteenth century. This is so because, for the most part, seventeenth- and eighteenth-century opera does not demand singing that is either as loud or (in the case of male singers) as high as nineteenth-century opera. As a result, some of the pressure comes off the voice, with the effect that the words are more apt to be understood. Recitative— which disappears from opera after the early nineteenth century—provides the most striking illustration of this process. One might fairly describe recitative as "talk music," since it tends to be set in the middle of the voice and at a reasonable volume (the competition coming not from an orchestra but from a harpsichord), and it also involves very little distortion of the natural ratio between consonants and vowels. Hence recitative—assuming one knows the language—is often as intelligible as spoken dialogue. The operas of the early baroque, of course, were constructed virtually in their entirety from recitative. In his book *Osmin's Rage,* Peter Kivy even argues that Monteverdi's *Orfeo* is not properly an opera at all, because it is governed by literary rather than musical imperatives. In the next generation, the high baroque operas of Handel, consisting as they do of a string of arias separated by recitative, actually gain in intelligibility from what is generally regarded as their undramatic (and unliterary) addiction to repetition. A Handel aria involves as much textual distortion as a representative vocal passage from Verdi or Puccini, but because each phrase is reiterated many times (particularly if the full *da capo* is respected), the listener gets several shots at deciphering the text. I am surely not the only person who has managed to piece together the words of a Handel aria simply by listening very hard to the repetitions.

Intelligibility, then, varies according to a broad historical pattern reflecting changes in the demands made on operatic voices, with the early nineteenth century marking a watershed. A second, and no less important, variable is sex. In general, male voices are more intelligible than female voices. Whatever the reason, all opera-goers know that the sound emitted by a female singer is more apt to overwhelm the words than is the sound emitted by a male singer. Listen, for example, to the splendid 1940 Met recording of *Otello* with Giovanni Martinelli, Lawrence Tibbett, and Elisabeth Rethberg. All three of the principals sing magnificently. The difference is that Martinelli and Tibbett make a good part of the text comprehensible, whereas we can catch only an occasional phrase from Rethberg. That difference, moreover, has nothing to do with the singers' intentions, and everything to do with the fact that the first two are men and the last a woman. Even female singers known for their attentiveness to the words (singers like Maria Callas or Elisabeth Schwarzkopf) are extraordinarily difficult to understand—much more so than an indifferent tenor or baritone—while female singers mainly concerned with producing a smooth and beautiful sound (singers like Joan Sutherland or Gundula Janowitz) are usually unintelligible from start to finish: the words are simply liquefied in a sea of operatic tone.

This almost categorical difference between male and female voices goes a long way toward explaining why certain composers, certain operas, and certain roles are more readily understood than others. Not surprisingly, operas dominated by male voices reveal more of the text than operas dominated by female voices. This is the main source of the relative intelligibility of the Mussorgsky operas (*Boris* and *Khovanshchina* each contain only one important female role), of the later Wagner operas, of Debussy's *Pelléas,* and also of Gilbert and Sullivan (where virtually everyone but the soprano heroine can be understood). Conversely, the same principle explains why we often hear very little of the text in the operas of Puccini and Strauss: both composers have a special affinity for the high female voice. Indeed, Richard Strauss, with his notorious addiction to this voice (which he exploits to glorious effect in the climactic moments of *Salome, Elektra, Rosenkavalier, Arabella, Daphne,* and *Capriccio*), was probably the composer least entitled to promulgate the so-called Golden Rule for conductors.

The overall effect of both the historical and sexual distinctions I have drawn is that intelligibility in opera is an uneven phenomenon. In a given opera, it will vary from passage to passage, indeed from phrase to phrase, depending on whether we are listening to recitative or an aria, whether the singer is a baritone or a soprano, and whether the passage lies low or high. When, at that superb moment at the end of *The Marriage of Figaro,* the Count begs for forgiveness and the Countess grants it, the Count's words, set in the middle of the baritone voice, can be understood by everybody, whereas the Countess's, set in the upper-middle part of the soprano register, are intelligible only to someone who has seen the libretto. This consideration may appear embarrassingly mundane and unworthy of mention in so lofty an aesthetic context as Mozart's great finale. But in fact we ignore such humble matters at the risk of misrepresenting Mozart's actual achievement: for the Countess's forgiveness is realized not verbally but musically. Indeed, even if her words *could* be apprehended, they would not begin to convey the intensity and exaltation of Mozart's musical gesture. The passage illustrates why students of opera who construct their analyses from the text—from "reading the libretto"—will as often as not "misread the opera"—or, perhaps more accurately in this instance, "underread" it.

III

My last two "enemies of intelligibility" will not require such extensive exposition, as they are at once less pervasive and more obvious than the matter of operatic voices. Each represents a further instance of the tension between verbal and musical logic in opera, a tension that is occasionally a source of aesthetic delight but more often simply results in decreased comprehension. Both, furthermore, are exacerbated in the operas of the nineteenth century.

Ensemble singing—my third adversary—is, of course, crucial to the musical logic of opera from Mozart to Strauss, although as the century comes to a close there are important defections from the tradition, notably Musorgsky, Debussy, the mature Wagner, and, to a lesser extent, the Verdi of *Otello* and *Falstaff*. Ensembles generally occur at moments of heightened dramatic interest, and they function as musical center-pieces. Moreover, as everybody knows, when two or more people sing at the same time the words generally suffer. So once again we are con-fronted with an illustration of what is perhaps opera's central paradox: the most important words are often the least likely to be understood.

To be sure, the range of intelligibility in operatic ensembles is fairly broad. At one extreme is the duet for two male voices singing the same text in thirds and sixths (such as one often hears in bel canto opera), where the words can remain exceptionally clear. At the other extreme is the quartet, quintet, or even larger grouping (often supported by the cho-rus), where the characters sing different words set to extremely intricate music, and hardly anything can be deciphered. The singers, in effect, cancel out one another's lines. There are, of course, degrees of intelligi-bility even with this latter pattern. For example, Rossini's ensembles skillfully use repetitions and the strategic liberation of individual voices from the ensemble block to achieve a surprising level of verbal clarity. Rossini is a particularly interesting witness, moreover, because in the act I finale of *L'italiana in Algeri* he satirizes the entire tradition of operatic ensembles by having his characters sing onomatopoetic noises, as if they were instruments rather than voices:

> Din din din,
> Cra cra cra,
> Bum bum bum,
> Tac tac tac.

Rossini's point is splendidly trenchant: what one normally hears in an op-eratic ensemble verges on the instrumental—a confection of homoge-nized, interwoven musical lines, whose inarticulateness grows more pronounced as the music moves toward its climax. "The crowning glory of opera," writes Auden, "is the big ensemble," to which one must add that the coronation is generally mute.

The operatic analyst, then, must approach ensembles with caution. Before assigning particular significance to this or that utterance, he must ask whether the words stand any chance of being heard. More often than not, the answer is No. Even more than is the case for opera as a whole, the logic of ensembles is musical rather than verbal. Admittedly, unintelligibility is sometimes exactly their point. Such is true, for example, of the ensemble in which the second act of *Die Meistersinger* culminates. The piece, of course, represents a civic riot, and the hundred odd lines of poetry Wagner squanders on it are intentionally transformed into verbal chaos by the music. But Wagner's creative exploitation of incoherence is the exception rather than the rule. More representative is the sextet from *Lucia di Lammermoor,* where, once past the solo tenor introduction, very little can be understood, although incomprehensibility is hardly its dramatic point. This wonderful piece works its effect on us in spite of our not understanding what is being said, and it does so almost entirely through musical means.

IV

Finally, we come to the operatic orchestra. Its significance for my topic can be stated very easily: from the point of view of intelligibility the orchestra is simply a source of interfering noise. It stands between us and the words. I can think of not a single instance where the orchestra increases rather than decreases our ability to make out the text. The only conceivable exception would be the verbal associations suggested by certain orchestral effects, such as the ringing of the triangle that Verdi uses to underline Falstaff's allusions to money. But even in such instances the connection between orchestral sound and intelligibility is indirect and, at best, approximate. Judged in strictly aural terms, even these orchestral allusions actually interfere with our ability to hear the words.

Naturally, the great opera composers know how to minimize that interference—how to make the orchestra as considerate of the text as possible. Indeed, intelligibility in opera is often a function of a composer's skill in restraining his orchestra. Or, put more drastically, it is a function of a composer's willingness to sacrifice the sure-fire effects that can be achieved through orchestral volume. Here one could cite Debussy's *Pelléas et Mélisande* as an especially noteworthy example—it being surely among the most orchestrally recessive of all great operas and, accordingly, also one of the most intelligible.

Perhaps we ought to ask why operas are orchestrated at all. Why not just a piano or harpsichord? Or, even better, why isn't the whole thing sung a cappella? The answer has little to do with keeping singers on pitch. Rather, it is because opera would lose its fundamental character without the orchestra. It would become something that it is not. Orchestral sounds give an opera its basic contour—its overarching shape—just as they carry the burden of establishing the distinct mood and flavor of an opera. They do many other things as well—all of them, needless to say, musical. In fact, the question is worth asking only because it reminds us of just how profoundly unliterary opera actually is.

Viewed structurally, orchestral sound bears the same relation to intelligibility as do high notes and ensembles: it asserts itself just when the words are most important. Moreover, in the nineteenth century this essential supporting and shaping sound grew several times more powerful—or, if you prefer, several times noisier—than it had been in the seventeenth and eighteenth centuries. Not only is the nineteenth-century orchestra much larger than its predecessors, but its modernized instruments also produce louder and more incisive sounds. The change is reflected in the increased size of nineteenth-century opera houses, as Michael Forsyth has shown in his study of opera houses and concert halls from the seventeenth century to the present, *Buildings for Music*.

The larger orchestras and larger houses had two effects on operatic singing, both of them detrimental to intelligibility. Especially in the United States, where "barn" theaters have proliferated, singers have had to produce ever greater quantities of sound in order to fill the void, and their efforts in this direction have often resulted in yet further sacrifices in articulation and thus intelligibility. Many opera-goers find performances in medium or small European theaters relatively comprehensible, while the very same singers in a 4000-seat auditorium like the Metropolitan sound altogether wordless. This contrast between the lucidity of the small theater and the opacity of the large is sometimes overrated by devotees of the former (the evidence of recordings shows that theater size is a mitigating, not a determining, factor), but it is nonetheless an authentic distinction. I need hardly point out that it has manifestly elitist implications: opera, it suggests, is for the few; it can maintain its verbal integrity only within the small, aristocratic venues for which it was originally created. It was never meant to be a democratic entertainment.

A second effect of the larger orchestra is that operatic singing itself actually grew louder in the nineteenth century, especially in its closing years. This phenomenon is well known to students of the history of singing. It is associated above all with the emergence of artists like Enrico Caruso and Titta Ruffo, who made decidedly more noise than their counterparts in the previous generation and who were forced by their method of production to let many of the words go by the boards. Still, even the new singers could hardly keep pace with what was happening to the orchestra. If I might paraphrase Malthus, orchestral volume grew geometrically, while singing at best grew arithmetically. When the full Wagnerian or Verdian orchestra is unleashed, it expunges not merely the singers' words but their voices as well. Indeed, at the climactic moments of nineteenth-century opera, whole choruses can be drowned out by the deafening orchestral racket. I hardly need add that no one would wish it otherwise. What is merely interference from a textual standpoint is of the essence of the thing when we view opera in the whole.

V

This concludes my survey of the enemies list. In each instance, as I have tried to suggest, intelligibility is sacrificed to music. Moreover, these sacrifices are not marginal to the logic of opera but central to it. From a consideration of them follows at least one important practical implication for the operatic analyst. The master question for any interpreter of opera must be not What does the text say, but How is the text realized, or at least addressed, in the music? How does it embed itself in the opera's musical fabric? That embedding may not always result in consonance—in an "isomorphism" of text and music—because there are situations in which the music responds to the text by antithesis. But the important point is that an operatic text really has no meaning worth talking about except as it is transformed into music. The failure to come to terms with this hard reality explains why many literary studies of opera hold so little interest for musicologists. Such studies too often treat the language of opera as if it were as transparent as the language of stage drama. They may tell us a great deal about literature or about cultural history broadly conceived (and I have benefited from reading many of them), but so long as they do not speak about music, and about the way words become musical, they are condemned to remain on the periphery of opera—on the outskirts, so to speak, of the operatic village.

Some readers will have noted that these strictures view the question of "reading opera" from a very particular perspective. Everything I have said—about foreign language, operatic singing, ensembles, and the or-chestra—presumes that we should settle the question of operatic intelli-gibility in terms of what can be discerned of the words while seated in an opera house during an actual performance. Or, to use the jargon of con-temporary criticism, I have "privileged" a "house reading" of opera. This is indeed the case. But let me demonstrate my intellectual flexibility —such as it is—by suggesting that I am prepared to consider this read-ing simply one of a number of possible readings, each of which, if it is not equally valid or useful, can at least claim our attention.

I am not sure exactly how many such possibilities exist, but five that I know actually play a role in any opera-lover's experience. The first, of course, is the "house reading" (without supertitles) taken for granted up to this point: hearing the work in the theater and doing one's best to make out the words in spite of the hindrances posed by my four "enemies." A second reading would be opera as heard on record. In terms of intelligi-bility, opera on record differs from opera in the house in only one respect: the solo singers generally have spot microphones on them, thus lending them unnatural prominence and giving the words a better chance of be-ing understood because the relative volume of the orchestra is reduced. A third approach might be termed the "libretto-in-hand reading." This, I suspect, is the way we get to know most operas: while listening to a recorded performance, we follow the text, both in the original language and in the line-by-line translation just to the right, with the effect that many of the words that could not be deciphered by the unaided ear become intelligible. What is going on here, I believe, is in fact a dual process: on the one hand listening, on the other reading, which through years of practice become fused in our minds into a more or less unitary experience. In fact, we become convinced that we actually hear words that are in reality being fed to us by our eyes.

Now, before Wagner the distinction between my first and third readings—between a "house reading" and a "libretto-in hand reading"—may not have been so sharp as it is today. Most important in this regard, before Wagner the house was not darkened during performance, with the result that members of the audience could follow their librettos. Moreover, we know that librettos (often with a translation on the facing page) were on sale at the entrance to the theater and that they were often printed afresh for each new production of an opera. Hence the option of following the text during a live performance was very real, and that option was abetted, so to speak, by stagings that were a good deal more static than those one normally sees today—and thus a good deal less compelling to the eye. It may well be, therefore, that what I have called the "libretto-in-hand reading" is a distinctly post-Wagnerian phenomenon.

A variation on the "libretto-in-hand reading" is the "supertitle reading": we hear the work performed live while a version of the text (in translation) is flashed above the stage. Again, what actually happens with supertitles is that the two processes are carried out more or less simultaneously: reading and hearing. Many people seem to be under the illusion that supertitles serve merely to translate opera out of a foreign language. But that is surely erroneous. As with the "libretto-in-hand reading," supertitles introduce a textual explicitness quite foreign to what one actually experiences in the theater. Perhaps the practice can be refined, but right now it often invites us, for example, to read the text of the Lucia sextet as if it were just as intelligible as the recitative in *The Marriage of Figaro*. Still, providing we are disabused about its actual function, the "supertitle reading" can be defended as a usefully different way to experience opera, or perhaps as a heuristic device. (I will not pretend to have exhausted the pros and cons of supertitles here, only to have related them to the issue of intelligibility.)

Finally, at the opposite end of the spectrum from what I have called the "house reading" stands reading the libretto without listening to anything. This is at once a drastically impoverished and an unrealistically intelligible reading, but it is nonetheless a reading, and one of particular importance to scholars and critics. It shades off, moreover, into all sorts of other textual approaches, which might be usefully lumped together as "approximate or ancillary readings." These would include synopses, recording albums, scholarly books and article, the literary source, even anecdotes recounted on the Metropolitan Opera Quiz.

All five of the readings I have mentioned feed into and inform one another. In other words, we seldom "read" opera one of these ways without being influenced by having read it another way before. Thus, a "house reading" of opera seldom occurs in its purest form. By the time most of us see an opera in the theater, we have listened to it on record with libretto in hand. In some instances we may actually have memorized the text—or large portions of it. At the other extreme, even the most cursory examination of the plot synopsis in the program notes already means that a seemingly virgin house experience has been "textually anticipated."

Because of this complex and, so to speak, layered set of experiences, my earlier pronouncements about operatic meaning must be modified to suit a variety of ways in which opera is actually appropriated. But I would like to return, here at the end, to the archetypal primacy of the "house reading." In spite of the significant role played by readings that draw us away from its purity, I am convinced that it remains at the center of the operatic experience, even after it has been supplemented by more explicitly textual approaches. In fact, those textual readings have a way of receding from consciousness, as we gradually forget the language of operatic texts we once knew—something that never quite happens with the music.

I was reminded of this primitive truth recently when I heard Gounod's *Romeo and Juliet* for the first time in my life. I somehow expected that I would not like the opera, but then a friend happened to give me a tape of the 1947 Metropolitan Opera Broadcast with Jussi Björling. Conrad Osborne calls it "the finest singing of a complete romantic tenor role, beginning to end, I've ever heard," and the singing is indeed so wonderful that I found myself listening to the performance over and over. I listened without a libretto; nor did I consult a synopsis of the opera. I simply indulged myself in the thing itself. I know French well enough, but I found I could make out only a few of the words. Björling was a scrupulous linguist, but the special plangency of his voice (just the quality that makes it for some the most beautiful voice ever recorded) renders his diction less easily understood than that of some lesser tenors.

Of course, my listening benefited from an important extra-operatic source, namely, Shakespeare's play (and its derivatives), which I have read and seen many times. This, along with the odd phrase that I managed to catch, provided me with just enough information to follow the general contours of the plot, identify most of the characters, and get a broad sense of what was being said. Still, the opera compelled my attention, indeed my fascination, above all because of its music. Put simply, I found it extraordinarily beautiful and moving. Later, when I heard a live radio broadcast of the piece from the Metropolitan Opera, some of the charm was lost because the singers, at least by comparison, were so inadequate. But the opera itself still worked its magic. Its music—and, above all, its singing—powerfully conveys the essential ingredients of Shakespeare's play: the unconstrained rapture of young love, the violence of adult hatreds, the sense of doom, the sweet pain of the lovers' simultaneous fulfillment and separation, the agony yet transcendence of their final meeting. Shakespeare's dramatic arc achieves an immediacy in Gounod's music (and in Björling's singing) greater than anything I have witnessed in a performance of the play. As in all good operas, the loss of narrative explicitness is handsomely repaid in emotional resonance. Listening to the piece, I was convinced all over again of how little the words count for in opera. Or perhaps I should say, I was convinced all over again of how much their meaning is a function of their musical embodiment.

But I prefer to end on a more ambiguous—and a more prudent—note. While the words in opera sometimes count for little, they never count for nothing. Even when unintelligible, their existence—or the effort of singers to bring them into existence—is an important component of operatic reality. Above all, they are important as symbols of the human subjectivity that lies at the heart of opera: whether actual or potential, they identify operatic singing as an expression of will. Their willfulness, moreover, is aptly reflected in the extraordinary athleticism of operatic singing: the bulging eyes, throbbing arteries, thickening necks, and reddening faces caused by the effort to produce sounds of impossible volume and extension.

Conrad Osborne makes this connection between the operatic word and human action in his discussion of Björling's singing in *Romeo and Juliet:*

> [Björling's tone] has emotive properties, the power to sadden or to thrill. It has this power in and of itself, independent of the meanings of the words (though not of their sounds). . . . The tone, independent of the word in all these ways, nevertheless bears the word's encoding, which rides within it like a written scroll embedded in richest amber, and sends its messages therefrom with an aesthetic life and finish it could not otherwise know. As we hear the tone sail and arc, swell and fall, we know that all these properties are not simply those of some phenomenon with whose symmetry and gleam Nature has, as they used to say, chosen to astonish us. Instead, they are the deliberate creations of human behavior.

One might argue that this is an artful if eloquent dodge. But it nicely suggests that, while we cannot always understand the words, they remain a significant constituent of our experience. Even when they are unintelligible, their presence identifies the singer as a human actor with specific feelings, giving voice to specific thoughts. This explains, at least in part, why we will not tolerate pure vocalise even in place of words we cannot hear. Indeed, the passion and heartbreak of Björling's singing in *Romeo and Juliet* would largely evaporate if the sound of his voice were dissociated from this particular character, in this particular situation, and, above all, saying—or attempting to say—these particular things. I am inclined to suggest, therefore, that the words in opera are emblems of human volition. As such, they are part of our experience of opera even, as it were, when they are not.

CHAPTER THREE

The Musical Enlightenment:
Haydn's *Creation* and Mozart's *Magic Flute*

This piece originated in two talks I delivered at Stanford in the early 1990s. It is published here for the first time. It interprets two vocal works of the late eighteenth century, Haydn's Creation *and Mozart's* Magic Flute, *as expressions of the European Enlightenment. In Haydn's case the proposition might seem unlikely, since the text he is setting is Genesis. But I argue that Haydn's musical procedures give the oratorio a distinctly deist flavor. Mozart's Masonic libretto for* The Magic Flute *is already an Enlightenment document, but the interest here is, once again, in the composer's musical realization of its ideas. In both cases I also examine the limits of the Enlightenment imagination, especially its treatment of women.*

In this essay I argue that two vocal masterpieces of the 1790s, Haydn's oratorio *The Creation* and Mozart's opera *The Magic Flute,* can be interpreted as artifacts of the Enlightenment. I will have a good deal more to say about *The Magic Flute* than *The Creation,* but by pairing the two I hope to convey the usefulness of viewing musical works from the perspective of intellectual history. I hasten to add that I do not believe that the Enlightenment perspective exhausts the meaning of either work, or even that it offers a privileged reading of their ideological significance. *The Magic Flute* in particular has been interpreted in wildly different ways: in *Mozart and the Enlightenment,* for example, Nicholas Till maintains that it is an expression of Gnostic Christianity. But I am persuaded that hearing these two works as manifestations of the central intellectual movement of the century—that is, of the Enlightenment—is extremely revealing. As is my wont, I will try to make my case by attending to Haydn's and Mozart's music, not just the texts they set.

I

The proposition that Haydn's oratorio *The Creation* (1798) is a document of the Enlightenment confronts an immediate embarrassment. The original source for Baron Gottfried van Swieten's libretto—the Urtext of the oratorio—is, of course, the story of creation in the book of Genesis from the Hebrew Bible. Now, as everyone knows, the thinkers of the Enlightenment—the philosophes—were merciless critics of traditional revealed religion, and if there was one form of revealed religion they hated more than Christianity it was Judaism, just as if there was one religious text they hated more than the New Testament it was the Old Testament. The Enlightenment's conception of God was very different from the willful and jealous figure conjured up in the Pentateuch, just as the Enlightenment's conception of nature was very different from the one embraced by ancient Israel. The Enlightenment's God was a rational being, whose sole responsibility was to create the universe and, even more important, to establish the laws according to which it would work, and then to withdraw discreetly from the scene. Above all, the Enlightenment God was never to interfere in the regular functioning of the natural order: for the eighteenth-century philosophes there were no divine interventions, no miracles, and certainly no Incarnations.

Almost by definition, however, the God of creation must be conceived of as a willful rather than a rational being, because creation, after all, is the ultimate act of will. So the question then becomes, How did Haydn and his librettist deal with this contradiction between the irascible Jehovah of the Old Testament and the deist watchmaker of the eighteenth century? Essentially, I would suggest, they did so by seeking to rationalize, demystify, and finally defang the creator God of Genesis in order to bring Him more into line with the rational God of deism. This transformation, moreover, is largely a musical achievement. One of the musical means Haydn uses to deprive the biblical creator of his awe and mystery is to assign the voice of God to the three archangels, Raphael,

Uriel, and Gabriel—sung, respectively, by a bass, a tenor, and a soprano. All three voices soften and humanize the divine pronouncements, but the tenor and soprano voices in particular eliminate any impression of terrifying patriarchal authority. Similarly, Haydn sets God's words in the least inflected musical language available to an eighteenth-century composer, namely, recitative—a kind of musical prose—which robs the divine utterances of the terror and grandeur that more elaborately composed music might have conveyed.

Of particular interest in Haydn's effort to render both God and nature in a thoroughly Enlightenment guise is the oratorio's first number, the orchestral introduction and chorus meant to depict chaos. Chaos is not a notion dear to the heart of the Enlightenment, and not one it was temperamentally prepared to represent with much conviction. All the preferences of the Enlightenment were for order rather than chaos, and indeed one way to think of Haydn's oratorio as a whole is to say that it exhibits, at great and leisurely length, the natural order that displaces chaos. Nonetheless, chaos must be represented as the terminus a quo, the point of departure, of the creative process. Haydn uses rhythmic irregularity—especially anticipating the beat—as one musical device to depict chaos in the orchestral introduction. He also uses dissonance to the same end. But when all is said and done, Haydn's musical portrait of chaos and the divine void is a fairly tame affair. At least it is tame if we place it against the way composers in the nineteenth century were to represent similar phenomena—not just chaos but the divine presence and other such transcendental essences. Speaking broadly, the nineteenth century believed—in a way that was inaccessible to the Enlightenment—in the power and terror of the transcendental, just as it believed in evil. One thinks, for example, of how Berlioz and Verdi portray the transcendental moment of the final judgment in the spectacular "Tuba mirum" sections of their respective requiems. Or one thinks of the way that Arrigo Boito represents the divine presence in the Prologue, set in heaven, to his opera *Mefistofele*. Or, to take an example that refers properly to chaos, one thinks of the almost Darwinian depiction of the primal ooze that Richard Strauss achieves in the music of his tone poem *Also sprach Zarathustra*, right after the famous brass fanfares with which the piece begins. If you listen to Haydn's "Representation of Chaos" with these later musical images in mind, you see precisely the degree to which he was a man of the Enlightenment.

What interests Haydn in this opening number is not chaos but its overcoming, that is to say, the creation of light. The single most thrilling moment in the oratorio is the sudden fortissimo outburst of the entire chorus and orchestra, in a dazzling C-major chord, on the eighteenth-century codeword "light" in the phrase "And there was light" ("Und es ward Licht"). It is a gesture of profoundest conviction, and, with its resonant dominant-tonic cadence (that most rudimentary and satisfying sequence), it cannot fail to move us with an ideal that Haydn and his century believed in without a hint of ambiguity. As is well known, the same metaphorical code of darkness and light is central to the argument of Mozart's *Magic Flute*. The moment always reminds me of Thomas Mann's wonderful character Lodovico Settembrini, in *The Magic Mountain*, who, of course, is a latter-day spokesman for the values of the Enlightenment and who, when he enters Hans Castorp's sanatorium room, throws on the electric light switch. Light is in fact the central theme of the oratorio. It is wonderfully represented in Uriel's description of the first sunrise ("Der erste Tag entstand. / Verwirrung weicht, und Ordnung keimt empor," "The first day has dawned. / Chaos yields, and order arises"), and it is echoed repeatedly in the emphasis, throughout the piece, on the optical or the "scopic"—on the eye, on sight, on the visual splendor of the created realm.

Admittedly, neither Haydn's text nor his music can explicitly convey the watchmaker God of eighteenth-century deism. That would have been virtually impossible, given Haydn's biblical source. But I think one can make a plausible argument to the effect that Haydn's repeated use of fugue in the choral music of the oratorio, above all in the great choral movements that end all three of its sections, alludes to just such a conception of the deity and his creation. Fugues display an intricacy of moving musical parts that might reasonably be compared to the internal workings of a machine. Moreover, the texts of the concluding choruses nicely support this mechanical image, as they celebrate, in the words of the first of them, the glory of God's "handiwork" ("seiner Hände Werk"). The fugue, one might say, is the composer's handiwork, just as nature is God's handiwork.

The presentation of nature itself in *The Creation* is very much in the spirit of the Enlightenment. It is a nature that is observed and classified, in almost Linnaean fashion. The cataloging intelligence of the eighteenth century, which culminated in Diderot's *Encyclopedia,* is fully on display, as Haydn's delightfully onomatopoetic musical representations lay out the various realms of nature in a lucid sequence before the listener's eye and ear. We are given empirical disquisitions on the weather (storms, wind, lightning, thunder), on water, on plants, on birds, on fish, and on the mammals. This natural order can occasionally be frightening (if in a contained way), but, significantly, Haydn prefers to dwell on nature's pastoral beauty, as in Raphael's lovely description of cattle and sheep in No. 21. Or he dwells on nature's practical uses for human happiness, as in the spectacular coloratura tribute to the plant that benefits mankind with its "healing balm" ("den Wunden Heil") in No. 8. Nature in *The Creation* is not merely orderly and transparent (transparent, that is, to the human eye and to human intelligence); it is ultimately beneficial as well.

Finally, the oratorio also reveals the characteristic limits of the Enlightenment's imagination, although not so drastically as one might expect. The Enlightenment was committed to universalism, which meant, in theory at least, that it believed in the deep equality—in worth—of all human beings. But, of course, it was not yet willing to extend that equality to women. Indeed, precisely because its universalism threatened to undermine traditional distinctions between the sexes, the Enlightenment felt obliged to construct a new language of difference in order to explain why men and women should have dissimilar callings in the world. We have here the beginnings of what, in the nineteenth century, would become the infamous doctrine of separate spheres, the idea that women, as essentially emotional creatures, belong exclusively to the home, while men, as rational creatures, belong to the world of power and action.

We encounter this gendered ideology musically in the second section of the piece when man and woman are created: there man is pronounced "King of nature"—to some aggressive and stately music—while woman—to much more rounded and recessive tones—is seen showering her mate with love, bliss, and contentment. What I find most interesting, however, is the extent to which, in the final Adam and Eve portion of the oratorio, Haydn's music largely ignores (and even cancels out) the invidious sexual division of labor in the text (which associates Adam with Day, Eve with Night) in order to present Adam and Eve as musical equals, singing in parallel phrases, often in harmony with one another, and with neither given musical precedence over the other. Haydn's musical evenhandedness here is all the more remarkable, because we know that Baron van Swieten urged him to compose Adam and Eve's great duet with chorus, "Von deiner Güt', O Herr und Gott," so as to contrast the different feelings appropriate to man and woman by setting Adam's music in the major and Eve's in the minor. But Haydn was true to the deeper impulses of Enlightenment universalism, and, accordingly, he treats Adam and Eve as absolute musical equals. We will find a similar instance of textual misogyny contradicted by musical egalitarianism in *The Magic Flute*.

II

Like Haydn's *Creation*, Mozart's *Magic Flute* also confronts anyone hoping to find the Enlightenment in it with an immediate embarrassment. Certainly the first thing one notices about the piece is that it is a magic opera, a kind of fairy tale, built around a quasi-chivalric rescue story and filled with mythical figures like the Queen of the Night and the sorcerer Sarastro, with magic instruments like Tamino's flute and Papageno's bells, with strange animals and artifacts. The whole is informed by a general sense of unreality light-years removed from the intellectual world of the Enlightenment. We associate the Enlightenment with the celebration of reason and science, with the hatred of superstition, and with a kind of secular humanism, in all of which we recognize the origins of an essentially modern, disenchanted, and realistic view of human beings and the world they live in.

But if the first thing one notices about *The Magic Flute* is that it is a fairy-tale opera—an opera seemingly for children, full of make-believe and silliness—the next thing one notices is that it contains much talk and singing about very serious moral and philosophical issues. Sarastro and his priests go on at great length about reason, wisdom, and truth, about brotherhood, about morality—in a word, about Enlightenment. Indeed the great impediment to getting a firm grip on just what sort of work *The Magic Flute* is stems from its strange juxtaposition of these two worlds: the magical, fairy-tale world, on the one hand, and the morally serious world, on the other. The opera seems a hopelessly confused mixture of the childish and the philosophically earnest. Peter Gay's comment in his recent Mozart biography is typical: "In *Die Zauberflöte*, the listener must struggle to understand—or, perhaps better, to set aside—the plot for the sake of the music."

One attempt to resolve the opera's seeming contradictions is the so-called *Bruchtheorie*, which was embraced by several generations of Mozart scholars but is now out of fashion. English-speaking readers can find it vigorously presented in Edward Dent's study *Mozart's Operas*, originally published in 1913 and revised in 1947. The theory posits that the opera took a change of direction in the middle of its composition. In the original version of the story—which prevails in the first two-thirds of act 1, although its residues can be found throughout the opera—*The Magic Flute*, according to the *Bruchtheorie*, is about the daughter of the good Queen of the Night who has been abducted by an evil sorcerer named Sarastro. The distressed and wronged Queen charges a young prince, Tamino, with the task of rescuing her daughter from Sarastro, which in the course of the story Tamino proceeds to do. To help him in his quest, the good Queen gives him a magic flute, which has the power to make people and animals behave against their wills, and she also provides him with a helpmate in the figure of the bird-catcher Papageno.

In the second version of the story, which the theory imagines simply having been imposed on the original version starting at the first act finale (the scene in which Tamino comes to the temples of Reason, Nature, and Wisdom and is interrogated by the figure of the Speaker, who is, of course, one of Sarastro's priests) the moral positions of the Queen of the Night and Sarastro have been reversed. Now it is the Queen who represents evil and Sarastro who represents good. She stands for all the ugly emotions, in particular vengefulness, and her main purpose in life seems to be to destroy the person and the empire of Sarastro. Sarastro, for his part, is no longer a sorcerer but the High Priest of the Temple of Wisdom. He now stands for everything virtuous. Or, to speak more precisely, he is a complete embodiment of the values cherished by the

European Enlightenment: he represents wisdom, reason, brotherhood, benevolence, moral discipline, and truth-seeking. In this second version of the story, Sarastro has taken the Queen's daughter not for selfish or malign purposes but in order to save the young woman from her own mother—and, of course, to prepare her for marriage to a suitably enlightened and devoted husband.

The notion that there are two incompatible stories underlying the opera helps account for a number of contradictions in the final product. It explains, for example, why the evil blackamoor Monostatos works for Sarastro, instead of for the Queen, as one might expect him to. The connection between Monostatos and Sarastro, the theory suggests, belongs to the original version of the story, although Monostatos ultimately finds his proper home with the Queen. It also explains why the Queen and her Three Ladies, at the beginning of the opera, are able to give Tamino and Papageno the magic flute and the magic bells—those benificent charms that will aid them in their quest and that, in a properly ordered world, ought to belong to the forces of good. Finally, the idea of an originally good Queen explains why her Three Ladies, in the early part of the opera, seem to be enforcers of morality. When Papageno lies about having killed the serpent, they punish him by denying him his usual food and wine and putting a padlock on his mouth, after which they spout a moral platitude about the virtue of truth-telling:

> Bakämen doch die Lügner alle
> ein solches Schloss vor ihren Mund:
> statt Hass, Verleumdung, schwarzer Galle,
> bestünde Lieb' und Bruderbund.

> Would that all liars
> had their mouths padlocked;
> instead of hate, lies, and slander,
> there would be love and brotherhood.

In the final version of the story we would expect to find these noble sentiments in the mouths not of the Queen's ladies but of Sarastro's priests. That they are uttered by the silly and ultimately malevolent ladies is, according to the theory, a residue from the first version of the story, in which the Queen still represented virtue. Of course, the *Bruchtheorie* creates its own contradictions: it is embarrassed by the fact that the three boys who guide Tamino and Papageno—and who are goodly spirits— should be in the employ of the Queen.

Assuming Mozart and Schikaneder did shift directions radically at the finale of act 1, the transformation in the story's moral valence had one supremely important consequence. And that is, if the Queen of the Night is evil and Sarastro good, and if Sarastro has abducted Pamina for the enlightened purpose of saving her from her wicked mother, then the action of the opera can no longer be a quest, on the part of Tamino, to save the daughter from her abductor and restore her to her rightful parent. So, whether by accident or (more likely, I think) because it appealed to Mozart's own moral earnestness and his deepest convictions, the quasi-chivalric quest to rescue a young woman is transformed into a story of enlightenment, of individual growth from error to truth. The opera becomes, in other words, the story not of Pamina's rescue but of Tamino's moral and intellectual development. That development might be said to move from the error of first impressions, through a process of initiation, to a deeper and finally correct understanding of the way things are. In this respect, the fundamental trajectory of the opera is remarkably like that of Jane Austen's *Pride and Prejudice,* the original version of which, we recall, dates from the same decade as Mozart's opera (that is, the 1790s), and which Austen wanted to call "First Impressions." *Pride and Prejudice* shows a comparable intellectual and moral movement on the part of Elizabeth Bennet: a movement from error to truth. Elizabeth begins by forming an incorrect impression of the moral character of Mr Darcy (just as Tamino forms an incorrect impression of the moral character of the Queen of the Night and of Sarastro), and it takes practically the full course of the novel, and a long process of education, before she comes to see Darcy as he truly is.

The main objection to this reading of *The Magic Flute* is that, on the surface at least, there does not seem to be much difference between the way Tamino learns the true story from the way he learns the false one. After all, he is told the first version by the Three Ladies in the opera's opening scene, and he is told the second (and true) version in the third scene by the Speaker. Why should he believe the Speaker any more than he believed the Three Ladies? From a strict epistemological point of view, he is being asked to take both stories "on authority." The only difference between his two authorities is that the first is a group of women (a very touchy issue, to which I will return later), while the second is a man. But, importantly, there are striking musical differences between the two scenes. The Three Ladies tend to cackle and spout, as their music trips along to its regular beat, while the Speaker, with his somber bass, sings in phrases that are slow, rhythmically flexible, and individually shaped to follow the text. These musical differences suggest that the Speaker's version is altogether serious, while that of the Three Ladies is suspiciously lighthearted, even frivolous.

I can't entirely resolve this epistemological difficulty—it remains for me among the problems of the opera—but the important matter is that in the morally revised version (according to the *Bruchtheorie*), Mozart was forced to turn the story into one of individual enlightenment and initiation into truth. Certainly nobody can doubt that truth is among the opera's essential values. It is celebrated magnificently at the moment when Pamina and Papageno are about to be discovered by Sarastro, and Papageno, who is scared to death, asks Pamina, "What will we say to him?" Her answer is a single word, uttered twice, "Die Wahrheit, die Wahrheit" ("The truth, the truth"), and Mozart sets this utterance on two sweeping upward intervals, carrying the soprano to a radiant sustained high F and high G, which, in the way only music can, lend her answer enormous moral weight. One can't hear this passage without knowing that the ideal of truth has deeply engaged the composer. And, of course, it was a cardinal ideal of the Enlightenment.

There is a second transformation that seems to take place at just that point in the story where the moral roles of the Queen of the Night and Sarastro are reversed. And this second transformation is crucial in linking Mozart's opera to the intellectual world of the Enlightenment. At the beginning of the act 1 finale, when Tamino comes to the three temple doors, the ideas of Freemasonry are introduced into the opera in an explicit fashion for the first time. Indeed, from this point on we gradually become aware that *The Magic Flute* is a Masonic opera. Scholars have shown that it is even more thoroughly Masonic than the average operagoer is likely to recognize. There is in fact a large body of interpretive writings, going back into the nineteenth century and culminating in a book by the French musicologist Jacques Chailley (translated into English as *The Magic Flute, Masonic Opera*), that offer, in various levels of detail and persuasiveness, interpretations of the opera in terms of its elaborate Masonic symbols and meanings. Some of these readings are on the speculative side. One nineteenth-century interpretation—that of Moritz Alexander Zille—insists that all the characters can be identified with specific persons and groups that played a part in the history of the Masonic movement in eighteenth-century Austria: Sarastro, according to Zille, represents the scientist Ignaz von Born (a friend of Mozart's and the leading figure of Viennese Masonry); Tamino represents the Emperor Joseph II (a reforming monarch or "enlightened despot" who was generally favorable to the Masonic movement); the Queen of the Night represents Joseph's mother, the Empress Maria Theresa (a devout Catholic, who, siding with the Jesuits and the Church, tried to have the Masons suppressed); while Pamina represents the Austrian people, who need to be rescued from repressive Catholicism by enlightened Masonry.

Carried to such lengths, the Masonic interpretation begins to strain, but the presence of Masonic symbolism and Masonic ideas in *The Magic Flute* is undeniable. Mozart himself became a Mason in 1784, and he appears to have been profoundly devoted to the movement. Masonry represents the key to understanding the deeper meaning of the opera for him.

The literature on Viennese Masonry is substantial and contentious. In general it suggests that the Viennese lodges were divided between esoteric and rationalist branches, and some scholars (such as Nicholas Till) have tried to link Mozart to the former and interpret *The Magic Flute* as a post-Enlightenment work, deeply infused with mystical views, and thus part of the religious revival that marked the beginnings of romanticism. And, in truth, Masonry can be interpreted as a kind of substitute religion, a replacement, emotionally and symbolically, for a moribund Roman Catholicism. In such an interpretation one would stress its preoccupation with secret rituals and magic numbers, and its elaborate hierarchical organization. But all the evidence (marshalled by Mozart's most important modern scholarly biographer, Maynard Solomon) suggests that Mozart belonged to the rationalist branch of Masonry headed by his friend Ignaz von Born. (In an essay published in the *Journal für Freymaurer,* Born wrote: "Is not truth, wisdom and the promotion of the happiness of the entire human race the ultimate purpose of our fellowship? . . . May superstition and fanaticism never desecrate our lodges.") Indeed Mozart appears to have been not just rationalist but, in the best Enlightenment fashion, an anticlerical (like his father), as manifested in the lines he set for the Three Boys at the start of the second act finale:

> Bald prangt, den Morgen zu verkünden,
> die Sonn' auf gold'ner Bahn,
> bald soll der Aberglaube schwinden,
> bald siegt der weise Mann.

> Soon, to announce morning,
> the sun will arise on her golden path.
> Soon shall superstition disappear,
> soon the wise man will conquer.

Put simply, the Freemasonry to which Mozart subscribed is properly thought of as an arm of the Enlightenment, one of its most important practical manifestations, and one that attracted many of the leading critical voices of the century, among them Voltaire, Lessing, Goethe, Haydn, and, of course, the major figures of the American Revolution. Essentially the Masonry in which Mozart believed was an intellectual and social movement that sought to achieve the triumph of reason and nature, of science, and above all of human benevolence and brotherhood —in effect, to realize the fundamental values of the Enlightenment.

III

I am particularly interested in how *The Magic Flute* embodies these values not merely in its text and story but in its music. Music, of course, lacks a mimetic function—or, at least, it has a very restricted mimetic function—so the way in which it conveys meaning in opera is difficult to pin down. Doubtless some listeners will not agree that Mozart's music sends the specific messages that I wish to attribute to it. But I am convinced that there is a kind of musical argument being advanced in *The Magic Flute* and that its terms can be deciphered—up to a point.

I can best make my case by considering the range of characters in the opera. They might be said to exist on four different moral levels, and Mozart composes a distinctive kind of music for each of these moral levels. The first two can be thought of as the pre-ethical levels. These represent human beings before they enter the world of good and evil, before, in other words, the entire Masonic project—the Enlightenment project —is introduced into the drama. Here I will use as examples the music Mozart writes for Papageno and for Tamino (at least in the early going). The second two levels, as one might expect, are expressly ethical: they are the levels of moral choice; they belong to a world where the antithesis between good and evil has become explicit, articulate, and very much to the point. And here I will cite the music Mozart writes for the Queen of the Night and for Sarastro and his priests. In the case of the Queen he writes music that he hopes will convey a sense of conscious malignity; in the case of Sarastro he writes music to convey a sense of goodness. In this fashion music is used to lend resonance to the simple moral antithesis of the story and to raise it to a level of aesthetic power that no one could anticipate from a simple examination of the libretto.

Papageno represents nature, or the natural man. As in Rousseau's use of this idea, he is essentially a pre-ethical being. He exists purely at the level of material reality. Above all he is preoccupied with taking care of his body: with eating, drinking, and sex. Mozart links him expressly to the animal realm. In fact, there is some doubt about whether he is entirely human, and we are perhaps supposed to think of him as half man and half bird (as Tamino hints, much to Papageno's horror, in their first colloquy). His name comes from the German word for parrot, *Papagai*, and, of course, he wears a bird outfit and makes his living as a bird catcher. Most important, throughout the course of the opera he behaves in a distinctly unheroic fashion. The significant thing about Papageno is that he is not destined for an ethical existence. He remains, from beginning to end, resolutely at the level of instinct, of desire, of the simple gratifications of the flesh.

Mozart, in his generosity and broadmindedness, adopts an indulgent attitude toward Papageno. One might say that, in Mozart's enlightened view of humanity, there is space in the world for people who can't rise to the highest intellectual and moral challenges. Put another way, he suggests that a life of material consumption and pleasure-seeking is not to be despised; not everyone is destined to the life of ethical rigor. Yet, when all is said and done, we are left in no doubt that Papageno represents a lower road, a less than full realization of what it means to attain our humanity.

This view of Papageno—tolerant but ultimately patronizing—is perfectly conveyed by the music Mozart composes for his entrance aria, "Der Vogelfänger bin ich ja." What distinguishes this music from that of the rest the opera is, above all, its strophic regularity and harmonic simplicity. We hear a square, symmetrical tune, with only the most rudimentary harmonic changes: except for one venture into the subdominant in its penultimate phrase, it is constructed entirely out of shifts back and forth from tonic to dominant. The melody itself is completely predictable: we sense just where it is going, and in its three verses it simply repeats itself without variation. Moreover, the song's rhythm is utterly regular, even mechanical, and firmly inflected. It is music little disturbed by thought. And yet it is charming and agreeable. It conjures up the affable, carefree world of l'homme moyen sensuel—of an ordinary creature of habit and instinct who is perfectly satisfied to remain true to the essential animal within himself. In act 2 Mozart writes another aria for Papageno, "Ein Mädchen oder Weibchen," whose musical format and ideological import are identical to the first.

Tamino also belongs to the pre-ethical world, at least at the start of the opera. But we sense right away that he has a potential that Papageno lacks. We are thus not surprised, as the opera progresses, that he discovers within himself a capacity to develop on a higher moral and intellectual plane than the lowly bird-catcher.

I would say that the pre-enlightened Tamino belongs to the realm of romance. He is not tied strictly to the desires and demands of the body, as is Papageno, but responds even as a natural man to more refined, more delicate urges. I find it significant in this regard that he falls in love not with Pamina herself but with her portrait—with an image of her face, of her gaze. Pamina appears to him almost as an idea, rather than a material body. Moreover we never sense that the feelings of Tamino and Pamina for one another have a very strong sexual component. In fact, one could make just the opposite complaint: there is, for our modern taste, too little of physical attraction in this love affair, just as one sometimes feels that the body and its demands get shortchanged in the hyperintellectualism of the eighteenth-century philosophes.

Tamino's essentially romantic sensibility—his greater capacity for inwardness, for reflection, and thus his potential for moral and intellectual growth—is beautifully suggested by his opening aria, "Dies Bildnis ist bezaubernd schön," which he sings when the Three Ladies present him with Pamina's portrait. It is, significantly, the next musical number after Papageno's "Ein Vogelfänger bin ich ja," thus setting up an obvious opposition between the two figures. The musical difference between the arias is striking. Tamino's music, in contrast to Papageno's, is complex, nuanced, and organic. There is no jangling melody that repeats itself over and over. Instead the piece is sculpted and seems to change its musical character with each line. Nor is the beat sharply inflected, as it is in Papageno's song. Rather, the music is rhythmically plastic, moving now faster now slower as the sentiments of the text require. The whole has about it an inward excitement and hushed expectancy entirely absent from the happy, satisfied tune sung by the bird-catcher just a few moments earlier.

Before moving to the ethical level of the Queen of the Night and Sarastro, I want to call attention to a further implication of the musical distinction Mozart draws between the world of Papageno and that of Tamino. I've spoken of it as a difference between the world of nature and the world of romance, the first purely material, the second with a distinct implication of the spiritual and the intellectual. But the difference can also be read, without too much difficulty, as a difference of social class. That is, Tamino is an aristocrat, while Papageno is a commoner; Tamino belongs to the elite, Papageno to the great unwashed. The opera, of course, is not at all concerned with the social and economic significance of this distinction. *The Magic Flute* has none of the explicit social awareness of *The Marriage of Figaro* or *Don Giovanni*. Rather, it insists on viewing the difference between Papageno and Tamino as essentially one between two different character types, two different moral constitutions.

But this very insouciance serves to legitimize the hierarchical organization of the social world.

The matter is extremely serious in that it reflects a general weakness in the thought of the Enlightenment, one that Karl Marx, among others, tried to set right in the course of the nineteenth century. The Enlightenment tended to treat the difference between people as matters of individual accident or choice, not as the products of social, economic, or political forces over which the individuals in question had little control. It also tended to find nothing particularly wrong with such differences. Most of us are meant to be Papagenos, a few of us to be Taminos. In this respect the spirit of the Enlightenment is antidemocratic, even though it laid the intellectual groundwork for the democratic political beliefs of the nineteenth and twentieth centuries. Mozart's opera accurately reflects the fact that the Enlightenment's commitment to equality went only so far. For the most part, the thinkers of the eighteenth century were perfectly comfortable with a view of human destiny in which groups of people led lives that were very different from one another in terms not just of their ideals but also of their material circumstances.

I am even more interested in the way Mozart represents what I've called the ethical world—the level of good and evil—in the music of *The Magic Flute*. So let me turn now from Papageno and Tamino to the Queen of the Night and Sarastro (and his followers) in order to suggest how he undertakes this somewhat improbable task.

His general idea of how to portray evil in music is to compose in terms of extremes. The particular extremes he hits on in the case of the Queen of the Night are those of altitude and speed. That is to say, he writes music for her that is extraordinarily high (up to F above high C) and that, at its most characteristic, is also extraordinarily fast. To be precise, he writes for her two coloratura arias, of which the second, "Der Hölle Rache," is the more famous. (Actually only the allegro conclusion of the first aria, "O zitt're nicht, mein lieber Sohn," is a coloratura exercise, but it is made of the same musical stuff as "Der Hölle Rache.") Clearly the intended effect of this coloratura writing is to suggest the Queen's inner emotional turmoil, her burning vengefulness, and I do not doubt that for Mozart himself (and for most eighteenth-century listeners) it succeeded in that object. Yet for listeners shaped by the aesthetic sensibility of the nineteenth and twentieth centuries this musical portrayal of evil comes dangerously close to comedy: the Queen's coloratura antics make us want to laugh instead of inspiring us with terror. (The comic possibilities of the Queen's music are fully realized by the soprano Maria Galvany in her 1906 recording of "Der Hölle Rache," in which the singer ratchets up the tempo and squeaks away like a crazed mouse.) I'm tempted to find in Mozart's choice here something telling about the aesthetic range of the Enlightenment. I would put it this way: the artists of the eighteenth century were not very well equipped to depict evil. Their aesthetic vocabulary was limited, and the darker side of humanity remained slightly out of reach for them. This is a complaint about the eighteenth century that would be voiced frequently in the course of the nineteenth century, starting with the generation of European romantics. And on the whole I think the complaint is just. Without giving in to the verdict that the Enlightenment was hopelessly shallow, I would say that its commitment to reason, to judiciousness, to tolerance, and to the values of humor, articulateness, and benevolence meant that it had to forgo a rich cultivation of the dark, the malevolent, and the dangerous. Such was the price, one could argue, that the philosophes paid for their essential humaneness. And Mozart's music—which is perhaps the most humane ever written—suffers in precisely this regard when we compare it to the music of the nineteenth century. A nineteenth-century composer like Wagner was able to create characters whose music leaves one in no doubt about their essential vileness. The music he writes in the *Ring* for his malignant characters Alberich and Hagen, for example, is as black as anything you can imagine, and there is virtually no chance that one might mistake them for comedians.

There is room for debate, then, about whether Mozart succeeds in painting a musical portrait of evil in *The Magic Flute,* although there is no question that he sought to do so. But I think we can come to just the opposite conclusion with regard to his musical portrait of goodness, and this is in a way much more remarkable. On the whole artists have a harder time portraying good than evil. Think, for example, how much more successful Dante is, in *The Divine Comedy,* in portraying Hell than he is in portraying Heaven. Or think of Milton's greater success, in *Paradise*

Lost, with Satan than with God. Yet Mozart succeeds better than any composer I know of in fashioning music that somehow conjures up a sense of moral goodness. Analysts of *The Magic Flute* have noted this aural fact, although, as one might expect, they have had a hard time explaining how he does it. Dent, for example, speaks of "what we can only call the *Zauberflöte* style, a style easy to recognize, but difficult to describe in words." He hears it for the first time in the music of the Three Boys in the temple scene of act 1—significantly, just as the opera's Masonic theme becomes explicit. It emerges at crucial moments throughout the opera, especially in the second act, and it always seems to convey a distinctly ethical flavor. I'm not sure I can do any better than previous students in explaining how such music works, although I have no difficulty hearing it on those occasions when it emerges from the score. What strikes me as most salient about this music is its extraordinary austerity. In this respect, it is just the opposite of the music Mozart writes for the Queen of the Night, which is, of course, complicated, busy, and quick. The music associated with goodness in the opera, by contrast, is simple, stately, and dignified; it is utterly unadorned, almost naked. It is also music in which one is highly conscious of silence—of the silence that occupies the musical space, so to speak, between sounds. It has a hushed intensity that at times can seem almost unbearable.

Naturally one finds "the *Zauberflöte* style" in the music of Sarastro's two arias, especially the first of them, "O Isis und Osiris." In the case of Sarastro, Mozart is able to draw a further contrast—a purely vocal contrast—with the Queen of the Night, because he has composed the role of Sarastro for an exceptionally deep bass voice, which lies at the opposite end of the vocal compass from the high soprano of the Queen. Generally speaking in opera, the opposition between high and low voices associates high with good and low with bad. But Mozart ingeniously inverts that formula in *The Magic Flute.*

To my ears *The Magic Flute* style is on display even more clearly in the instrumental number with which the second act begins, the March of the Priests, which Mozart apparently composed on the evening before the first performance. The effect of this music is almost uncanny. It is utterly simple, stripped down, laconic. Nothing but the most rudimentary musical gestures remain. Yet its simplicity has nothing in common with the bumptious naïveté of Papageno's music. It is music that suggests a kind of spirituality, but a spirituality that is not in the least ecclesiastical (in the way, for example, that Bach's music is ecclesiastical). It is, in other words, music appropriate to a kind of secular religion, which is, after all, what Mozart's Enlightenment vision ultimately amounts to.

Another example of this sort of music is the famous trial by fire and water, which comes near the end of the opera and which many critics regard as the dramatic and musical heart of the work. One hears the characteristically austere musical manner above all in the passages written for solo flute accompanied by hushed brass and kettle drum—the music Tamino plays as he and Pamina make their way through the two trials. In this number, as in the March of the Priests, the pregnant silences between the flute and tympani utterances contribute significantly to the music's moral intensity.

At the close of the opera Mozart arranges a wonderful confrontation between the two ethical worlds he has conjured up, the world of the Queen of the Night and that of Sarastro. The Queen and her minions come in singing their typically nervous, unsettling music, much of it in the minor, and they give expression to their typically hateful sentiments. By this time Monostatos has joined the Queen's Three Ladies, and together they sing

> Dir, grosse Königin der Nacht
> sei under Rache Opfer gebracht.

> To thee, O mighty Queen of the Night,
> may our revenge be brought as a sacrifice.

Then, with utter suddenness and finality, all of them are plunged into eternal night by the powers of Enlightenment—by the sun whose rays "drive away the night"—and Sarastro and his priests are shown in their final triumph. It is an extraordinarily effective moment on the stage, as darkness gives way to brilliant light, and, of course, in the music as well, where the Queen's forces decline over diminished seventh chords, while Sarastro's rise gloriously on major harmonies in the bright key of E flat. The basic metaphorical dichotomy of the opera—between darkness and light—is given emphatic textual, scenic, and musical expression in these final moments, which mark in effect the triumph of Enlightenment over reaction and inhumanity.

IV

My interpretation of *The Magic Flute* as a progressive and liberating work will be resisted by many modern opera-goers. They will cite two, perhaps even three, stumbling-blocks to considering it a paean to enlightened modernity. I have already mentioned its elitism: its easy acceptance of class differences and a hierarchical conception of society. But the opera's "classism" is largely implicit and won't be noticed by most viewers. Far different are its offenses against the two other pillars of "the modern multicultural triumvirate," race and gender. Here we come up against prejudices that find direct, indeed blatant, expression in the piece. As it turns out, moreover, the opera's racism and misogyny are entirely relevant to a proper intellectual assessment of the Enlightenment. *The Magic Flute* points up the limits of the Enlightenment's imagination— how its vision of universal humanity failed to achieve true universality.

The opera's racism is the lesser of the two impediments, if only because it is confined to the secondary figure of Monostatos. Still, the fact that the opera's sole black character is aligned with the forces of evil and, worse, that the color of his skin is thematically linked to the work's overarching antithesis of light and dark, day and night, is a source of embarrassment to the modern viewer. That viewer will also cringe at Monostatos's stereotypical lubriciousness—at the hackneyed image of the black man who lusts after (and even tries to rape) a white maiden. One might wish to excuse Mozart by arguing that the opera's racism is confined to the dialogue and should therefore be blamed on Schikaneder. But, alas, that is simply not the case: in the nasty little aria he composed for Monostatos, Mozart set bigotry to music and thus fully implicated himself. Here he has Monostatos sing:

> Alles fühlt der Liebe Freuden,
> schnäbelt, tändelt, herzt und küsst;
> und ich soll die Liebe meiden,
> weil ein Schwarzer hässlich ist.

All may feel the joys of love,
trifle, flirt, fondle and kiss;
and I must abstain from love,
because a black is ugly.

To be sure, the music is trivial and comic, but the stain is nonetheless indelible. Ingmar Bergman was so scandalized by Monostatos that, in his film of the opera, he transformed the slave into a large white man and deleted all reference to his blackness from the Swedish translation of the text, including the words of the aria just cited. Mozart's racism, moreover, was anything but anomalous for a Freemason and devotee of Enlightenment: one need think only of the racial views of his fellow Mason Thomas Jefferson or of the infamous three-fifths clause of that quintessential Enlightenment document, the American Constitution.

The opera's misogyny is more widespread and, one might say, structurally significant than its racism. The overarching moral dichotomy of the work equates evil with femaleness (the Queen and her Ladies) and virtue with maleness (Sarastro and his Bruderbund of priests). In this respect, it is a perfect expression of the official misogyny of Viennese Masonry, especially that of its leader (and Mozart's friend), Ignaz von Born. The dialogue is sprinkled with antifeminist pronouncements, as when the Speaker says to Tamino, "A woman does little, chatters much" ("Ein Weib tut wenig, plaudert viel"). Once again, Mozart himself cannot be exonerated, for he set such misogynist sentiments to music, notably in the duet for the First and Second Priests (the two men who accompany Papageno and Tamino as they undergo their ordeals in the second act), "Bewaret euch vor Weibertücken" ("Guard against the wiles of women").

But, in contrast to the opera's racism, its misogyny, one might say, is challenged from within. Above all Mozart's sympathetic and profound treatment of Pamina works against any easy relegation of women to a lesser category of being. Her aria, "Ach, ich fuhl's," exceeds in emotional intensity and musical exquisiteness even the lovely music Mozart writes for Tamino. Moreover, as many commentators have noted, Pamina not only joins her lover in the climactic trials by fire and water but actually takes the lead, and at the end of the opera she is welcomed into the supposedly all-male Brotherhood of Wisdom and Truth. The opera's final stage direction reads: "Tamino, Pamina, beide in priestlicher Kleidung" ("Tamino, Pamina, both in priestly garb").

Even more important, the egalitarian impulse finds expression in Mozart's music, very much as it does in the music of Haydn's *Creation*. Repeatedly Mozart seizes on the opportunity to set his men and women on an equal musical footing. The parallel and symmetrical singing of Tamino and Pamina in the trial by fire and water is a case in point. But, in a way, even more remarkable is the duet celebrating love, "Bei Männern," sung by Pamina and Papageno. Save for Pamina's two cadential runs at the end, the voices are given virtually identical musical assignments: first she sings a line, then he sings one, and finally they join in parallel sixths and thirds, with Pamina's part only slightly more decorated. In the second portion of the duet the parallel singing continues apace, and now the text becomes almost an exercise in political correctness, as the words *Mann* and *Weib* are treated to elaborate symmetrical repetitions that have the effect of denying preferential treatment to either sex. The sung text (as opposed to the written libretto) runs as follows:

> Mann und Weib, und Weib und Mann,
> Mann und Weib, und Weib und Mann
> reichen an die Gottheit an.

> Man and woman, and woman and man,
> Man and woman, and woman and man
> attain divinity.

Perhaps it would be stretching matters to argue that this remarkable exercise in musical (and textual) equality carries a subliminal message about social equality as well, yet I find it intriguing that the opera's only "love duet" should pair these two figures from the opposite ends of the class spectrum. The important point, however, is that, as with the music Haydn writes for Adam and Eve, Mozart the composer is no misogynist.

A BALANCED TREATMENT OF *The Magic Flute* would have to talk about not just the triumph of Enlightenment, as I have in this essay, but also about the Enlightenment's limitations. I would be inclined to argue that those limitations stem from the failure of the Enlightenment to live up to the full logical implications of its own commitment to universal rationality and humanity. Seen from this perspective, the subsequent attack on the injustices associated with race, class, and gender represents the fulfillment of the Enlightenment's ideal, not its repudiation. Significantly—as I have tried to show—both Haydn's *Creation* and Mozart's *Magic Flute* at once display the Enlightenment's shortcomings in their texts and, at least in the matter of gender, transcend them in their music.

CHAPTER FOUR

Fidelio and the French Revolution

Published originally in the Cambridge Opera Journal *(March 1991), this essay argues that Beethoven's only opera,* Fidelio, *embodies the ideas of the French Revolution. It focuses on the transformation the opera undergoes from its domestic beginning (with its comically romantic confusion in a petty-bourgeois household) to its grand political end, in which Beethoven's heroic middle-period style is deployed to celebrate the liberation of imprisoned humanity. The essay contends that this musical and dramatic transformation, which many critics have found clumsy, in fact serves to express the revolutionary idea of moving from an old order to a new one.*

I

Fidelio has always posed difficulties for operatic interpreters. On the literal level it is straightforward enough, much more so, certainly, than its great Mozartian predecessor, *The Magic Flute.* It tells the unproblematic story of a wife, Leonore, who disguises herself as a boy in order to rescue her unjustly imprisoned husband. In the prison she obtains a job with the jailer, Rocco, whose daughter proceeds to fall in love with her. The main action is triggered when the governor of the prison, Don Pizarro, learns that a minister has set out to visit the prison, suspecting that it harbors several "victims of arbitrary force." Pizarro is terrified that the minister will discover one particular inmate, Florestan, who had threatened to expose his crimes and whom the minister believes to be dead (we, of course, have no difficulty recognizing him as Leonore's husband). Pizarro thus resolves to murder Florestan.

In the second act Rocco and Leonore precede Pizarro into the dungeon to dig the victim's grave, and there Leonore ascertains that the condemned prisoner is indeed her husband. When Pizarro descends for the kill he is confronted by Leonore, who tells him he will have to kill Florestan's wife first and pulls a gun on him. At exactly this moment a trumpet call announces the minister, whose arrival dissolves the dramatic situation with breathtaking suddenness: Florestan is rescued, husband and wife are reunited, and Pizarro's tyranny is broken. In the final scene all the prisoners are liberated, Pizarro is banished (presumably to face imprisonment himself), and the minister, learning that his friend Florestan has been saved by his wife's courage, invites her to unlock his chains. The opera ends with a choral tribute to wifely devotion.

Unfortunately, only the bare plot of *Fidelio* boasts the virtues of simplicity, logic, and consistency. Around its clear, if unremarkable, lines have emerged numerous confusions and uncertainties. Most of these focus on inconsistencies of dramatic tone and musical style. Put baldly, the opening scenes belong to the world of eighteenth-century domestic comedy, in which attention is directed to character and human relationships, but by the end of the opera these characters and their predicaments have been utterly forgotten—indeed, the actual figures with whom the opera begins have become almost invisible. Instead, dramatic interest has been lodged in the liberated prisoners, who come to stand for all humanity and express their joy over their new estate. The conventional operatic world of romance, mistaken identity, and intrigue has been displaced by one of ideological celebration. In musical terms, the disciplined classical style of Beethoven's first period, which is the dominant idiom of the opening scenes, gives way to the extravagant musical gestures of his heroic period (the last movement of the Fifth Symphony in particular comes to mind), and there are even anticipations of the choral outbursts of the Ninth Symphony and the *Missa Solemnis*.

The whole, for many critics, is dangerously contradictory—an opera whose conclusion explodes its musical and dramatic premises. Even if not excessively bothered by these anomalies, analysts seem generally uncomfortable with the discrepancy between the simple melodramatic story and the overwhelming emotional burden that Beethoven has imposed on it through his music. Not surprisingly, therefore, virtually every critic of the opera feels the need to interpret it, to ask what *Fidelio* is "really" about, because the music tells us that it cannot simply be about a wife rescuing her husband. In their efforts to account for the discrepancy between subject and form, plot and manner, critics have come to a variety of conclusions. They agree only that the real subject of *Fidelio* must be weighty enough to account for its musical riches and emotional power.

Some of this interpretive energy does not take us very far from the specifics of the plot. Most obvious in this respect have been attempts to link the story to Beethoven's biography, particularly to his long, frustrating, and ultimately unsuccessful pursuit of a wife. The subtitle of Bouilly's original libretto was *L'amour conjugal,* and one needs little hermeneutic daring (or psychological acumen) to explain at least part of Beethoven's emotional investment in the opera in terms of his preoccupation with Leonore, a fantasy figure from the deepest regions of desire, the Immortal Beloved, the idealized mate. A Freudian variation on this theme (suggested gently by Maynard Solomon and heavy-handedly by Editha and Richard Sterba) argues that Beethoven in fact identified with Leonore—that she was for him a means of giving expression to powerful feminine feelings, which were later to find a biographical outlet in his unhappy relationship with his nephew. Alan Tyson offers a more venturesome psychological interpretation when he suggests that Beethoven identified not with Leonore but with Florestan, and in particular that he equated the latter's imprisonment with his own deafness. Just as Florestan is isolated in darkness, Beethoven was imprisoned in silence. Among the attractions of this hypothesis is that it allows us to interpret the opening utterance of Florestan's aria, "Gott! welch' Dunkel hier" ("God! What darkness here"), as a thinly disguised cri de coeur and thus explain, in part, why Beethoven invested it with such incisive musical articulation.

The main weakness of these biographical analyses is that, while they deepen the characters of Leonore and Florestan, they say nothing about the transformation of a simple rescue story into something approaching a myth of universal liberation—the sea change that the work undergoes between its modest domestic beginnings and the communal shout with which it concludes. In other words, the attempt to lend weight to the story through psychological interpretation ignores the opera's sociology, which, if we can judge from the musical attention Beethoven gives it, was anything but peripheral to his concerns. The ideal of marital devotion and the agonies of deafness could have been addressed in a decidedly more intimate format; neither of them requires the liberation of an entire prison, to say nothing of the whole of humanity. And yet it is on precisely this collective material that Beethoven lavishes much of his best music in the opera, from the prisoners' chorus in the first act to the choral apotheosis at the end.

Perhaps we should turn then to interpretations that explore the social or communal dimension of the opera, interpretations that take us beyond the psychological dramas of romantic frustration and deafness. Maynard Solomon, in his influential biography, proposes a Freudian analysis that touches on this domain. His interpretation is rich and more than a trifle confusing, so let me begin by quoting him in full:

> *Fidelio* opens in a Mozartian Eden, a sunlit Arcadia in which a good father (Rocco) seeks to bring about the marriage of his daughter (Marzelline) to the young man she loves (Fidelio). But things are not what they seem. The Eden surface gives way to a darker substratum; the good father is a jailer; Fidelio is Leonore in disguise seeking her husband, Florestan, who lies imprisoned for an unspecified "crime" in a dungeon beneath the ground they walk on. Thus light masks darkness. Marzelline's innocent love unconsciously conceals a forbidden attraction. The good Rocco, protesting, agrees to cooperate in the murder of Florestan by Pizarro as the price of the latter's approval of his daughter's marriage. And Leonore's conjugal fidelity leads her to two conjugal betrayals: of Marzelline, to whom she pledges her love, and of Florestan, whose wife now embraces another. Rocco and Leonore descend into the tomb to prepare Florestan's grave; in a sense, Leonore is cooperating in the murder of her husband. The rescue fantasy is only apparently an inversion of the Oedipus myth: the impulses behind myths of killing and saving are ultimately identical; but in the rescue fantasy the murder (and guilt) is averted by a deus ex machina, here the minister of state, Don Fernando. Florestan's place in the dungeon is now

taken by the evil "father"—Pizarro—and the prisoners (sons) who planned the patricidal crime ascend into the light of freedom while Leonore resumes her sexual identity and receives the plaudits of the multitude for her heroism and fidelity.

Part of the interest of this reading is that it draws attention to what might be called the vertical dimension of the opera: its preoccupation with a world divided between above and below, "surface" and "substratum," light and darkness. But in terms of explaining the collective dimension of *Fidelio,* the most important move in Solomon's analysis is the attempt to link the opera to Freud's patricidal myth in *Totem and Taboo*—that epochal tale of brothers who band together to slay their father and take his place with the liberated women, their mother and sisters. Freud believed that the memory of this primal crime was lodged in the collective unconscious, passed from generation to generation by a kind of psychic Lamarkism. Solomon's interpretation, too, seems to presume such a shared unconscious implication in the idea, at least if it is to account for the power of the opera's collective theme, not only for Beethoven but for his audience as well. The proposition should not be dismissed merely because it can never be proved. Nonetheless one might complain that the emphasis on aggression and guilt fits rather badly with the unambiguously affirmative tone of the opera's conclusion. Solomon could plausibly respond that the affirmations are in fact overemphatic and actually serve to repress the brothers' consciousness of guilt. But his interpretation ultimately comes unstuck over the figure of Pizarro, who makes an improbable father. Beethoven originally wanted to spare Pizarro, and the brief choral episode in which the crowd urges his punishment in the 1814 version of the opera is decidedly inferior to the rest of the finale. Beethoven's heart, one senses, simply was not in this retributive gesture.

Solomon himself does not seem to feel particularly confident about his Freudian reading, because he proceeds to displace it with an entirely different interpretation, although one that again transcends the arena of individual psychology. The terms here are drawn from myth, and one suspects an intellectual debt to Northrop Frye or Sir James Frazer:

> *Fidelio* can be seen as an opera about resurrection as well as rescue. Florestan is not only imprisoned but entombed; Leonore and Rocco descend

with their spades not to dig his grave but to exhume him from his sepulcher. A mythic pattern intrudes here: the dying vegetation god (the meaning of Florestan's name becomes clearer) lies awaiting the arrival of the bisexual goddess (Leonore / Fidelio) and the princely hero (Fernando) to restore him to life and to youth, to mark his passage from the dark ground into the sunlight. The winter god (Pizarro) is slain, replacing Florestan in the tomb, and mankind celebrates the arrival of the New Year with hymns to marriage.

Here the collective element ("mankind") is invoked by linking the narrative, at the deepest level, with the seasonal mythology of an agrarian society, where the rhythms of individual and communal life are at once reflected in and deeply dependent on the cycle of death and rebirth. *Fidelio* thus becomes an opera of germination. Like Solomon's psychoanalytic reading, this mythic interpretation draws its interest from the vertical dimension of the opera—the descent into death, the rise to new life—and, also like the psychoanalytic reading, it is not susceptible of proof. But it is more suited to the affirmations of the finale than is the menacing image of Freud's band of parricides. Solomon finds support in Irving Singer, who also sees the opera as essentially mythic or sacramental, and who likewise stresses its preoccupation with death and rebirth. *Fidelio,* writes Singer (in *Mozart and Beethoven: The Concept of Love in Their Operas*), "is the passion according to Beethoven"; at its heart stands "the mythic rebirth of Florestan, his return to life through his courage and the efforts of an angelic woman."

The appeal of this interpretation is the light it sheds on the collective dimension of *Fidelio.* It makes sense of the opera's inexorable movement from the individual to the community, and it also helps explain the work's deep emotional resonance. But against these virtues one must regret that Solomon and Singer say nothing about the music (they treat the opera as if were no different from a stage play) and that they force us so very far from its manifest content—or, for that matter, from anything that one might reasonably argue Beethoven had in mind. There is about their readings an obvious sense of desperation, of reaching well beyond the textual evidence in order to identify an interpretive register appropriate to the opera's effect.

In the body of this essay I want to argue that a political interpretation of *Fidelio*—and, more precisely, one that links it explicitly to the French Revolution—allows us to avoid the extremes to which Solomon and Singer seem forced. Such a tack deals comfortably with the opera's shift from the individual to the communal, and it also supplies the intellectual freight for which the work seems to beg. But perhaps its chief attraction is that it is supported by evidence from the opera itself. It permits one to argue from the score as well as the libretto—from the musical as well as the verbal record—which, in my common-sensical view, is the hallmark of any good operatic interpretation.

I should not suggest that *Fidelio* has been without its political interpreters. The literature contains countless allusions to its ideological subtext, and one even finds it expressly linked to the French Revolution. But I have come across no sustained attempt to interpret it in terms of the Revolution. Furthermore, an important tendency in recent commentary on the opera's politics—and on Beethoven's political ideas in general—has shifted attention away from the Revolution to the Enlightenment. Once again, the redoubtable Maynard Solomon has been an authoritative figure in this development.

Solomon argues that Beethoven's political views were formed in Bonn during the 1780s, when under Elector Maximilian Franz "the ideas of the Enlightenment virtually became the official principles of the Electorate." In political terms this meant that Beethoven subscribed to an ideal of reform from above—enlightened absolutism—in which a good prince would lead his people toward freedom, brotherhood and peace: "Reliance upon the notion of an aristocratic redeemer remained central to Beethoven's beliefs until his last years." Solomon sees this conviction entering Beethoven's music in a number of places, notably the early *Funeral Cantata on the Death of Joseph II,* the Incidental Music to Goethe's *Egmont,* and the "Eroica" Symphony (Napoleon, the original dedicatee, being for Beethoven, until his disillusionment, another of these princely saviors). Moreover, Solomon doubts that Beethoven was in fact sympathetic to the French Revolution, noting that, "apart from his subscription to a volume of Eulogius Schneider's poems, there is no sure sign of such sympathy on Beethoven's part." In terms of *Fidelio,* Solomon explicitly denies that the opera exhibits revolutionary enthusiasms:

The opera's themes of brotherhood, conjugal devotion, and triumph over injustice are basic to his ideology, but they do not signal his devotion to a Jacobin outlook. On the contrary, the 1798 French libretto by Bouilly that was adapted for Beethoven's use, based on an episode that occurred under the Terror, can be seen as a critique of the Jacobin persecutions of the French aristocracy.

The libretto was indeed based on an incident from the Terror, in which an aristocrat incarcerated in Touraine was saved by his wife. Beethoven, however, knew nothing of this historical derivation, as it was revealed by Bouilly only in his memoirs, published in 1836. Solomon is technically correct when he identifies Florestan as "an imprisoned noble"—we know this from a single reference of Rocco's to "Don" Florestan—but Beethoven virtually ignores such social distinctions in the opera. There are, admittedly, musical residues of the two-couple convention, with its connotations of social elevation and inferiority: Florestan and Leonore, with their *opera seria* style arias, are descended from Tamino and Pamina and from the Count and Countess in Figaro, just as Jaquino and Marzelline are descended from Papageno and Papagena and from Figaro and Susanna. But Beethoven takes remarkably little interest in social discriminations, just as he seems uninterested in specific political convictions, whether conservative or radical. In social and ideological terms the story has been hollowed out, leaving us with such abstract categories as "tyrant," "victim," "victim's devoted wife," "minister," and "prince." Appropriately, *Fidelio* has come to serve as an all-purpose opera of liberation, performed at the Congress of Vienna to celebrate the defeat of Napoleon and at the reopening of the Vienna State Opera after the victory over the Nazis.

By identifying Florestan as an aristocrat, and by linking the opera to its historical source in the Terror, Solomon intends to suggest that it is an antirevolutionary rather than a revolutionary document. *Fidelio* comes to stand to the French Revolution in much the same relation as Burke's *Reflections*. But Solomon is more eager to remove the opera entirely from the revolutionary debate (whether pro or con) and instead to associate its political values with the tradition of enlightened absolutism. He therefore stresses the central role of the minister, the emissary from the "bon prince," whose arrival is signaled by the trumpet call and who holds forth benevolently in the final scene. There is no reason to dispute the presence of this theme in the opera, but the musical and dramatic evidence hardly suggests that it was central to Beethoven's conception. In terms of the amount of time he spends on stage and the music Beethoven composes for him, the minister can only be described as a secondary figure, whom most opera-goers quickly forget. He has no aria, only a few bars of recitative, which are yet further diminished by being set within the heightened choral exclamations of the finale. To make him the ideological centerpiece of *Fidelio* would be to conclude that Beethoven had little notion of how to give his most important ideas compelling musical expression. As we shall see, Don Fernando's princely gesture must be set against the labor, both dramatic and musical, of Leonore in determining where effective agency in the opera resides. In the meantime, arguing that *Fidelio* is an opera about enlightened absolutism involves transforming a dramatically and musically marginal character—really a comprimario—into something approaching the work's protagonist.

II

At the ideological center of *Fidelio* stands the abstract idea of freedom. It is not expressly connected with any particular political movement or social group, nor is it elaborated into particular freedoms such as freedom of speech, religion, or the press. Rather it is freedom tout court. One can identify it with the French Revolution only in the general sense that during Beethoven's lifetime the Revolution became, for virtually all Europeans, the single most important locus of this idea and its realization. Indeed, in 1805 one would need to have been politically illiterate not to know that an opera trumpeting the idea of freedom would automatically be associated with the Revolution, albeit at the highest level of generalization. Moreover, that Beethoven should have appropriated the *idea* of the Revolution rather than its historical reality—that he should have composed *Fidelio* rather than, say, *Andrea Chénier*—is utterly in keeping with the response of his generation of German intellectuals to the phenomenon of the Revolution. The historian R. R. Palmer, in his magisterial *Age of the Democratic Revolution*, documents the way German thinkers and artists transformed the Revolution into categories of mind, discarding its political particulars and elevating it into a grand abstraction. Hegel is the central figure in this development, and there is an unmistakable affinity between Hegel's tribute to the French Revolution as "a glorious mental dawn" in the *Lectures on the Philosophy of History* and Beethoven's paean to liberty in *Fidelio*.

Let us now consider several instances from the opera where the idea finds expression. They were identified more than half a century ago by Ludwig Schiedermair in a monograph entitled *Die Gestaltung weltanschaulicher Ideen in der Vokalmusik Beethovens*. All of these moments are characterized by a heightened musical interest that indicates Beethoven's deep intellectual commitment to the idea.

The first comes in the famous prisoners' chorus. Virtually every commentator on the opera—indeed, virtually everyone who has seen or heard it—recognizes the importance that Beethoven attached to this scene. While present in the original Bouilly libretto, it is, strictly speaking, dramatically gratuitous, thereby calling attention to its ideological character. Leonore begs Rocco to allow the prisoners into the fortress garden while the weather is so lovely, and the jailer accedes to her request. It is, in other words, a transparently symbolical moment.

The word "free" (or "freedom") makes three significant appearances in this scene, and its mantralike repetition over the course of the movement gives it almost leitmotivic weight. It is introduced in the very first verse of the chorus:

> O welche Lust! In freier Luft
> den Atem leicht zu heben!
>
> Oh what joy! In the free air
> to breathe with ease!

The crucial phrase "in freier Luft" is placed at the musical apex of the chorus's opening period. It comes at the culmination of a four-bar crescendo, and Beethoven marks it fortissimo. It is accompanied by a strongly felt ascending figure in the cellos and basses, giving it a firm musical lift—an almost physical elevation appropriate to the elevating idea. The phrase also marks the climax of the melodic and harmonic trajectory of the opening musical gesture: on the word "Luft" the upper voices (tenors) move to their highest note, a sustained G (scale degree 6 of the B flat tonality), and the harmony shifts onto an exalted subdominant—a move that becomes practically a harmonic code for the idea of freedom in the opera. The phrase thus impresses itself on every listener's mind, so carefully has Beethoven underlined it through manipulations of volume, pitch, melody, harmony, and orchestration. Musically italicized in this fashion, it emerges almost as a concept. When the opening couplet is repeated some sixteen bars later, the musical treatment of "in freier Luft" remains unchanged: the phrase is once again firmly located at the center of the melodic and harmonic proceedings.

Next, a single, anonymous prisoner steps forward and sings:

> Wir wollen mit Vertrauen
> auf Gottes Hülfe bauen.
>
> Die Hoffhung flüstert sanft mir zu:
> Wir werden frei, wir finden Ruh!
>
> With trust we will
> build on God's help.
>
> Hope whispers gently to me:
> We shall be free, we shall find rest!

Here the phrase "Wir werden frei" is made the musical crux, and Beethoven deploys virtually the same methods that he had moments earlier to highlight "in freier Luft." As before, the phrase comes at the apex of a gradually ascending melodic line, and the word "frei" itself is given even greater prominence by being set to the highest and longest note the prisoner sings. At the same time, the vocal effort the tenor must exert to produce this relatively high and protracted note lends it a sense of reaching, of aspiration. Most important, this plangent, high-lying phrase is set on repeated upper E's—scale degree 6 of the passage's G major tonality—and the harmony, as with "in freier Luft," shifts to the telltale subdominant with its distinctively Beethovian pathos.

The remaining prisoners respond to their fellow inmate's words in a choral passage of mounting excitement. So great is their emotion that they are reduced at first to broken ideological ejaculations:

Himmel! Rettung! welch' ein Glück!
Freiheit! O Freiheit, kehrst du zurück?

O Heaven! Salvation! What Joy!
O Freedom! O Freedom, will you return?

Beethoven sets these hushed outbursts over evocatively pulsing eighth notes in the strings, and, as we now fully expect, the musical proceedings culminate in the repeated forte cries of "O Freiheit!" The second sounding of the words comes on the longest note in the passage, to an upward interval (from D to E flat), and at a moment of striking harmonic progression, from G major to C minor—the minor subdominant, which creates an even more decisive italicizing effect than the move to the major subdominant in the two preceding episodes. It is a moment of great intensity, in which Beethoven completes what might fairly be described as his musical lecture on the idea of freedom.

When the original chorus is repeated, its opening musical line again climaxes on the phrase "in freier Luft." Now, however, Beethoven asks that the entire passage be sung quietly, for the prisoners have grown conscious of being watched: "Sprecht leise, haltet euch zurück! / Wir sind belauscht mit Ohr und Blick" ("Speak softly, restrain yourselves! / We are observed by ears and eyes"). These terrifying thoughts, which have an almost Foucauldian ring, cast a shadow over the scene, as exhilaration gives way to fear. Freedom has only been imagined. We must await the finale for its realization.

The idea of freedom is again set before us in the concluding F major Poco allegro of Florestan's aria in the second act. The imprisoned husband, in his delirium, imagines he sees his wife as an angel coming to rescue him:

Ein Engel, Leonoren, der Gattin, so gleich,
der führt mich zur Freiheit ins himmlische Reich!

An angel so like Leonore, my wife,
who leads me to freedom in the Heavenly Kingdom!

Here "Freiheit" receives an even more pointed musical treatment than it had in the prisoners' chorus. At the climax the word is repeated no less than eight times within a dozen bars—bars that take less than half a minute to perform. As the final line is sung over and over, Beethoven insists on doubling the phrase "zur Freiheit," almost as if he were lecturing to a particularly obdurate or inattentive audience. The italicizing is musical as well as textual. While the very highest note Florestan sings, a B flat, is reserved for the word "Reich," most of the repetitions of "zur Freiheit" hover in the area of high G, and they are twice sustained for two beats on that altitudinous note. More exactly, the most prominent utterances of the phrase are set midway in a relentlessly ascending vocal line, beginning on F at the top of the staff and moving stepwise through F sharp, G, A, to B flat. The climactic final note lands us in the by-now familiar subdominant, as Beethoven again resorts to his wonted harmonic code. Moreover, for most tenors who sing Florestan, this B flat usually represents the uppermost limit of their range. As a result the passage conveys that sense of reaching, of aspiring, that we heard in the lone prisoner's singing of "Wir werden frei" in the first act. Finally, each of these vocal ascents is marked crescendo, and every conductor I have heard takes the opportunity to increase not merely the orchestral volume but the already brutal pace as well. Beethoven thus manipulates volume, melody, harmony, tessitura, and textual repetition to give the idea of freedom incomparably exalted expression.

The third instance of his preoccupation with the idea comes in the immediately succeeding duet between Rocco and Leonore. The two have descended into the dungeon and are in the process of digging the prisoner's grave. Leonore has not yet been able to determine whether the man is in fact her husband, and, as she seeks to get a better look at him, she sings (aside):

> Wer du auch seist, ich will dich retten,
> bei Gott! Du sollst kein Opfer sein!
> Gewiss, ich löse deine Ketten,
> ich will, du Armer, dich befrei'n!

> Whoever you may be, I will save you,
> by God! You shall not be a victim!
> For certain I'll loose your chains,
> poor man, I will free you!

It is a significant assertion for our understanding of Leonore, because in it she announces her adherence to the humane principles for which her husband has been imprisoned. She is motivated, in other words, not simply by wifely devotion but also by a more impersonal and categorical imperative. The passage has a distinctly Kantian ring to it, and we know that Beethoven admired Kant as a moral prophet. One should also note the reference to chains, which are a recurring material symbol in the opera. When we first see Leonore in the opening act she is returning to the prison with chains she has just bought, and in the final scene her unlocking of Florestan's chains provides the occasion for the most ecstatic passage in the opera, the fugal quintet beginning "O Gott! welch' ein Augenblick!" It is perhaps not inappropriate to hear in these allusions an echo of the famous first sentence of Jean-Jacques Rousseau's *Social Contract:* "Man is born free, and everywhere he is in chains."

Leonore's ideologically loaded pronouncement terminates in the verb "befreien" (to free), which, because Beethoven chooses to repeat the second couplet in order to underline its importance, is sounded twice. The first occasion comes at the end of a melodic line, marked crescendo, that ascends from C in the middle of the soprano's register to a sustained F at the top of the staff. It is a strong, if not especially pointed, musical setting. The repetition of the word, however, is transformed by Beethoven into a grand coloratura display, its significant second syllable stretched out over two and a half bars and carrying the voice over a twenty-four note melisma. The sequence of triplets swoops down nearly an octave from high F and then ascends to a sustained G above the staff. It is the only coloratura writing for Leonore outside the concluding Allegro of her act 1 aria, calling attention to itself by its singularity as well as its length, range, and vocal athleticism. One might complain that it comes dangerously close to preachiness. But Beethoven is never shy about his convictions, and he is fully prepared to risk this sort of musical underscoring. His commitment to the idea of freedom was apparently unqualified.

III

On the evidence, then, freedom is a central concern of the opera, its reigning conceit, deeply embedded in the text and richly articulated in the music. But, as noted, Beethoven's conception of freedom is abstract and categorical. It is linked to no particular historical moment or political agenda. As such, it can be associated with the French Revolution only by way of the now unfashionable invocation of the Zeitgeist—by chronological proximity, as it were. Indeed, one might even argue that linking the opera's liberationist theme to the events of the Revolution violates its universalist spirit and thereby diminishes it.

I wish to propose, however, that *Fidelio* and the French Revolution share a number of important structural affinities, and these affinities lend plausibility to our otherwise only vague suspicion that the two are somehow connected. Almost by definition, affinities never constitute proof, of either authorial intent or historical influence. Rather, their appeal must rest on their ability to illuminate, to explain matters that otherwise seem confused or unaccountable. The identification of affinities between *Fidelio* and the French Revolution provides, I believe, just such a heuristic service.

The most profound similarity between *Fidelio* and the Revolution resides in the conception of historical time they both embrace. Earlier I mentioned that several commentators have drawn attention to the opera's vertical dimension, its preoccupation with above and below, surface and substructure, light and dark. But equally striking is the distinctive horizontal pattern of the opera: its no less obsessive concern with before and after, the beginning and the end, the old order and the new. Indeed, more emphatically than any other opera I can think of, *Fidelio* conveys a sense of historical transformation, of movement from one realm of existence to another, from a defective to a pacified world.

This conception of historical time is precisely the conception that inspired the French revolutionaries. Recent historians of the Revolution such as François Furet and Keith Michael Baker have laid great emphasis on the distinctive historical consciousness of the revolutionaries, finding in it perhaps the deepest source of their extraordinary and unprecedented actions. In Furet's phrase, the notion of a "radical break," a conscious dividing of the historical continuum between the Old Regime (a label invented by the revolutionaries themselves) and the new order created by the Revolution, served as the most powerful agent of revolutionary praxis. The quintessential embodiment of this dichotomous historical consciousness was the new Republican calendar: the institution of the Republic on 22 September 1792, the revolutionaries announced, marked the beginning of a wholly new temporal dispensation, the first day of the Year I. It thereby displaced the birth of Christ as the "break" dividing the old order from the new, the City of Man, as it were, from the City of God.

The literary critic M. H. Abrams sees this same historical conception at work in the poetry and philosophy of the entire generation of European thinkers and artists who came of age in the revolutionary period. In *Natural Supernaturalism* he explicitly identifies the French Revolution itself as the main contemporary source of the idea, which was then internalized in the poetry of Wordsworth and the philosophy of Hegel, among others. The essential feature of this sensibility for Abrams is the notion of history as "right-angled," as sharply divided between two orders, an old and a new, the latter being ushered into existence by a dramatic event or sequence of events.

One distinctive feature of *Fidelio* immediately suggests the pertinence of this conception to an understanding of the opera. I refer to the manner in which its dramatic continuity is sharply interrupted at a single moment in the unfolding of the action, namely, at the arrival of the minister in the middle of act 2. Beethoven acknowledges this moment by bringing the frenetic musical and dramatic proceedings to a sudden halt in order to introduce a solo trumpet call. As countless viewers and critics have observed, it is an intervention of uncanny effectiveness. The unadorned tones of a descending and then ascending B flat major arpeggio, sounded on a single, archaic horn, are like a voice from above. The trumpet call marks an instantaneous and utter reversal of the dramatic situation, an upheaval that the principals (Leonore, Florestan, Pizarro, and Rocco) memorialize in a short but moving chorale. It marks, in other words, the operatic counterpart of the revolutionary Year I, the timeline that categorically separates past misery from future happiness. Significantly, *The Magic Flute*, which shares *Fidelio*'s moral earnestness, boasts no such transformative moment. Tamino's passage from ignorance to wisdom is portrayed as a gradual ascent, a progressive education, in which no single episode can be construed as a turning-point. Only *Fidelio*'s moral trajectory is right-angled.

We see this bifurcated sense of history in *Fidelio* most obviously if we focus on Florestan and the prisoners. The opera begins with them in a state of oppression, and through its dramatic action it brings about their deliverance. Beethoven contrives to draw this antithesis to our attention above all through the prisoners' chorus: the men's melancholy and timorous aspirations create an unforgettable sense of the repressive present, just as their transformation into the jubilant assembly of the opera's final scene marks the institution of a new regime of freedom and brotherhood. But to focus on the prisoners, significant though they are, overlooks a deeper and structurally more compelling link between the opera and the historical consciousness introduced by the Revolution. For it is not just the specific depredations suffered by the inmates that *Fidelio* aims to transcend. Rather, it is the whole order of being that we meet in the opera's opening scenes. The world of Rocco, Marzelline, and Jaquino—the world of bourgeois routine—has been veritably abolished in its concluding chiliastic celebrations. The opera thus depicts the redemption not merely of the prisoners but of the entire social universe to which it introduces us. In its overarching contours, *Fidelio* conforms to the pattern of radical break and right-angledness that Furet and Abrams have identified as the hallmarks of the French Revolution.

Not least among the attractions of this interpretation is that it turns what has generally been regarded as a weakness of the opera into a strength, namely, the putative inconsistency between its beginning and its end. The opera does indeed start in one realm and conclude in another. But we should perhaps contemplate the possibility that this discrepancy is very much to the point. Beethoven has not dawdled in the jailer's household simply because he can think of nothing better to do, or because he must "set the scene" for the significant actions that follow, or even because he is adhering to the conventions of the rescue opera genre. Rather, he is here creating the first term of his grand historical argument, the lapsed world of imperfect beings and relationships that will be utterly transformed in the work's conclusion. We can feel the power of that transformation only if the old order is firmly established in our minds as the terminus a quo of the opera's trajectory.

The sense of moving from an unreconstructed to a redeemed order is in fact the single most powerful impression that *Fidelio* conveys to its audience. This dichotomous experience, furthermore, is as much musical as dramatic. It is perhaps most readily appreciated by considering, in close juxtaposition, the opera's beginning and its end.

Three of the first four numbers in *Fidelio* serve to establish the old regime: the duet "Jetzt, Schätzchen, jetzt sind wir allein" between Jaquino and Marzelline (no. 1), Marzelline's aria "O wär' ich schon mit dir vereint" (no. 2) and Rocco's gold aria (no. 4). The world they depict is neither hellish nor depraved, but it is decidedly egoistic and provincial. It is also tension-ridden, even alienated. The long opening duet is devoted to unpleasant bickering between former lovers. It pits Jaquino's peevish resentment against the cruel annoyance of Marzelline. In the middle of it Jaquino is further angered by repeated knocking at the prison door, thereby drawing our attention to his menial job and his less than gracious fulfillment of it. Marzelline's aria expounds on her infatuation with Fidelio, which we are made to feel is naive and self-indulgent. Rocco, for his part, holds forth with bourgeois satisfaction and pedagogic self-importance on the virtues of money: gold alone, he says, can guarantee a good marriage. In effect, we are introduced to a world of narrow horizons and dim perspectives, a cramped, gray, mindless world of personal antagonism, illusory desire, and selfish materialism—a world sorely in need of redemption.

Beethoven's music for these opening numbers is well suited to convey their shallow sentiment and petty conflicts. It is trivializing music, whose restraint and formality nicely suggest the emotional claustrophobia of the prison household. Some have called it Mozartian, and certainly it has an archaizing flavor about it. But it is Mozart without much spirit. The effect is not bubbly or excited (one thinks of the opening of *Figaro*) but nervous and insubstantial. Perhaps the most distinctive feature of the music is Beethoven's insistence on staccato effects: neither orchestra nor singers are permitted the sort of broad legato expansion that might suggest deep passion or strong conviction. Instead everything is short-breathed and choppy. Sometimes Beethoven even inserts rests between the individual notes of the vocal line, as in the opening phrase of Marzelline's aria. There is a similar feeling of limitation in the harmonic choices, which incline toward automatic alternations of tonic and dominant. Throughout these numbers the singers stick to the middle of their range and rarely venture beyond mezzo forte. The few exceptions, such as the thirteen-bar period in the middle of the duet where Marzelline reflects on her love of *Fidelio,* serve mainly to highlight the prevailing sense of constraint. It all sounds undernourished, especially if we have occasion to make mental comparisons with the powerful and expansive music Beethoven had written less than two years earlier for the "Eroica." Jaquino, Marzelline, and Rocco are untouched by the heroic style, and Beethoven's deliberate withholding of his compositional powers results in their sounding spiritually impoverished.

The contrast with the dramatic and musical language of the opera's conclusion could hardly be greater. Admittedly, the ends of operas are often different from their beginnings, with a larger number of people on stage and the music louder, faster, and more elaborately composed. But Beethoven categorically exceeds the limits of this expectation, especially if we compare his practice with that of the Mozart finales. Where the opera begins with particular characters singing discrete, self-contained musical numbers, it ends with a chorus of undifferentiated individuals, singing what for all practical purposes could be the conclusion of a cantata, a mass, or (significantly) a choral symphony. Instead of half a dozen identifiable figures, we see (in a major opera house) up to a hundred choristers. To be sure, the most important personages from the body of the opera are still on stage, but they have been transformed into a vocal ensemble very much like the vocal quartet that Beethoven uses in both the Ninth Symphony and the *Missa Solemnis* to offset the massed voices of the chorus. That is, the bulk of their singing is devoted not to individual actions or sentiments but to the collective musical articulation of generalized ideas and emotions. Their words are largely interchangeable, and a line originally assigned to one voice will as often as not find itself taken over by the others. The scene is nearly devoid of action, the only important exception—Leonore's unlocking of Florestan's chains—being itself a symbolic rather than a real event. Indeed, there is hardly any reason for the proceedings to be on stage at all, and directors rightly opt for an essentially static deployment of their huge choral forces, who behave exactly as would their robed counterparts standing on risers in a concert performance. They are the secular counterpart of Bach's redeemed chorus of believers.

The scene begins with what amounts to a prolonged orchestral fan-
fare, thirty bars of hammering dotted figures whose essential purpose is
to announce the finale's resolute C major tonality. Beethoven associated
the key with triumph and celebration, as in the last movement of the Fifth
Symphony. The introduction is composed out of almost comically mechanical alternations of tonic and dominant, reaching a deafening intensity between bars 16 and 19, where the entire orchestra screams this
rudimentary antithesis in unison. If it were not so robust and aggressive,
one might almost suspect it of having been composed by Rossini, especially in view of the long crescendo that dominates its first half. The
orchestral music here does not so much set a dramatic scene—in the
manner of, say, Verdi or Wagner—as announce a state of mind, namely,
unqualified affirmation. Any hint of ambiguity or tension has been banished from the philosophical, not to say religious, proceedings about to
get under way.

The orchestral build-up allows Beethoven to march his singers on
stage and array them in a tableau. The stage directions call for the choristers to be divided into two groups, the prisoners and the people, the latter
of whom have been neither seen nor mentioned before in the opera (stage
directors sometimes pretend they are the friends and relatives of the liberated prisoners). In the opening chorus Beethoven maintains the dramatic fiction that these two groups are somehow differentiated: the
two-voiced "Chor der Gefangenen" is set on different lines of the score
from the four-voiced "Chor des Volkes." But the tenors and basses of the
prisoners' chorus sing exactly the same words and notes as the tenors and
basses of the people's chorus. Moreover, throughout the rest of the finale
Beethoven gives up all pretense to verisimilitude and refers simply to
"the Chorus" without qualification. The real purpose of the original distinction was to excuse the introduction of sopranos and altos onto the
stage, thus providing the composer with the full vocal complement
needed to produce the massed choral effects he has in mind. Once again,
dramatic considerations give way to musical ones, which in turn stand in
the service of ideology. The full four-voiced chorus is a more adequate
representative of humanity, which is the finale's real protagonist.

The music it now intones might be described as a kind of all-purpose
shout. The text reads as follows:

> Heil sei dem Tag, heil sei der Stunde,
> die lang ersehnt, doch unvermeint.
> Gerechtigkeit mit Huld im Bunde
> vor unseres Grabes Tor erscheint!
>
> Hail the day, hail the hour,
> long yearned for but unforeseen.
> Justice in league with kindness
> appears at the threshold of our grave!

The mention of the grave is passed over briskly, and the listener is impressed mainly by the repeated outbursts of "Heil sei dem Tag" with its significant allusion to the sunlit open air of the parade ground where the scene is set. The German brings to mind "heiliger Tag," and it is a holy day indeed. We are at the outset of a sacramental act.

The officiating priest is the minister Don Fernando, who now steps forward to deliver his brief monologue:

> Des besten Königs Wink und Wille
> führt mich zu euch, ihr Armen, her
> dass ich der Frevel Nacht enthülle,
> die all' umfangen, schwarz und schwer.
>
> Nein, nicht länger knieet sklavisch nieder,
> Tyrannenstrenge sei mir fern!
> Es sucht der Bruder seine Brüder,
> und kann er helfen, hilft er gern.
>
> The command of the best of kings
> leads me here to you, poor people,
> that I may uncover the night of crime,
> which, black and heavy, enveloped all.
>
> No, no longer kneel down like slaves,
> harsh tyranny, away from me!
> A brother seeks his brothers,
> and gladly helps, if help he can.

Characteristically, Don Fernando turns from a consideration of the dramatic specifics in the first stanza to moral generalization in the second.

His peroration is composed as a dignified recitative, commented on by a woodwind choir. Coming after the noisy assertions of the opening chorus, it marks an unmistakable moment of relaxation. Beethoven takes noted musical interest only in the humane sentiments of the last couplet (which anticipates the apostrophe to brotherhood in the Ninth Symphony). It is set to Don Fernando's most eloquent musical line, which is warmed by doubling in the woodwinds and the reintroduction of the strings. After a final choral exclamation of "Heil sei dem Tag," the couplet is repeated, to identical musical material, thus confirming its ideological importance.

The second large section of the finale, set in A major, is devoted to unraveling the plot. It is the only part of the finale that is truly operatic, in the sense of addressing itself to the resolution of the specific dramatic issues raised by the libretto. The most important thing to be said about Beethoven's response to those issues is that it is thoroughly uninspired, both dramatically and musically. Here, one senses, is precisely the material that Mozart would have developed into a virtuoso display, such as he produced in the finale to the second act of *Figaro*. It is, in fact, ideally suited to such treatment, consisting of a sequence of revelations, clarifications, reunions, and expulsions, for each of which Mozart might have fashioned a brilliant musical realization. Beethoven, however, treats these events in the most perfunctory fashion imaginable. Certain obvious dramatic possibilities, such as the presumed reconciliation of Jaquino and Marzelline, are ignored altogether. For the rest, they are disposed of largely in a narrative for Rocco, who recounts the opera's story for the illumination of Don Fernando. A less dramatic device can hardly be imagined. Beethoven composes this section in an utterly recessive manner, organizing it around an oft-repeated five-note noodling figure in the orchestra, interrupted only by the brief choral outburst that ushers Pizarro off the stage. Transparently he wants to rid himself of these tedious narrative responsibilities with as little fuss as possible, so that he can get on to the important ideological work ahead.

Only Don Fernando's last two lines capture the composer's interest, and that because they belong emotionally and intellectually to the extraordinary musical passage that follows. Beethoven brings the obsessive noodling to a halt, a hush falls over the orchestra, and the minister turns to Leonore in two serene descending phrases:

> Euch, edle Frau, allein
> euch ziemt es, ganz ihn zu befrei'n.
>
> You, noble lady, you alone
> should be the one to set him free.

This is the signal to begin the third section of the finale, the splendid Sostenuto assai in F major. The textual basis for this extended musical episode is not very promising. It consists of a sequence of unspecific emotional ejaculations and theological platitudes:

> O Gott! O welch' ein Augenblick!
> O unaussprechlich süsses Glück!
> Gerecht, O Gott, ist dein Gericht!
> Du prüfest, du verlässt uns nicht.
>
> O God! O what a moment!
> O inexpressibly sweet happiness!
> Righteous, O God, is Your judgment!
> You put us to the test, but don't abandon us.

The first line is intoned by Leonore, the second by Florestan, the third by Don Fernando, and the last by Marzelline and Rocco. But there is no compelling reason for any of these figures to be uttering the particular words assigned to them, and Beethoven quickly abandons any pretense to dramatic appositeness in order to mold his characters into a vocal quintet that sings the whole of the text in a series of overlapping musical repetitions. After their original statement the words become unintelligible, as so often happens in vocal ensembles. But this is of no consequence, because the quintet is a musical, not a textual, event. It is in fact an extended musical tribute to Leonore as an agent of liberation, an angel of freedom.

Nothing in the quintet itself indicates that it serves this function. Indeed, nothing in the text tells us what the quintet is about at all or why Beethoven has lavished such extravagant musical attention on it. Audiences instinctively recognize its importance, but I doubt that they are able to link its solemn and intense music to any precise idea or purpose. Doubtless they feel, in a vague way, that it is somehow appropriate to the opera's lofty sentiments. Its fifty-six bars are dominated by a beautiful arched phrase that Beethoven repeats, either in the voices or on various instruments, no fewer than eight times. It consists of an upward leap of a fourth or a fifth followed by a seven-note descending scale of quarter notes. The soaring upward interval recalls the reaching gesture that Beethoven uses to evoke the idea of freedom in the prisoners' chorus and in Florestan's aria. The cumulative effect of its repetitions is at once mesmerizing and exalted, and the mood it creates can legitimately be described as religious or liturgical. We have reached the heart, one senses, of Beethoven's inspiration.

Scholars have discovered an important hint as to the quintet's meaning for Beethoven. The melody, they have shown, is taken directly from a passage in the *Funeral Cantata on the Death of Joseph II*. In 1924, Alfred Heuss dubbed it Beethoven's *Humanitätsmelodie*. Beethoven used it in the cantata to give musical expression to his vision of human transcendence:

> Exsurgunt, ad lucem,
> revolvitur feliciter orbis circa solum,
> atque sol eradiat fulgore divino.
>
> Then did men climb into the light,
> then did the earth spin more joyfully around the sun,
> and the sun warmed it with heaven's light.

This music clearly had profound philosophical associations for Beethoven. In the context of *Fidelio*, we are able to ascertain its specific import only from Don Fernando's couplet at the end of the preceding section. His lines explicitly name Leonore, the "edle Frau," as the subject of this sonic tribute, and they also specify, with a precision known only to music, that liberation is its theme. The minister's final word—indeed, the significant second syllable to that word—marks the exact moment at which this episode is launched: "befrei'n," the ideological code-word whose repeated musical elaboration in the earlier parts of the opera we have already examined. Here it is italicized even more emphatically than before. At its sounding Beethoven introduces a sudden and breathtaking transformation in the compositional fabric. The tempo is slowed, the meter shifts from common time to 3/4, and, most spectacular of all, the music modulates unexpectedly to F major. Every listener feels the magic of this change. Time seems suspended, and there is a sense of being transported to some remote and ethereal realm, as Beethoven begins his campaign of musical repetitions.

Viewed symphonically, the F major segment of the finale might be compared to the lyrical third movement of the Ninth Symphony. It serves to set off, by contrast, the unbuttoned celebrations of the choral Allegro that follows and brings the opera to a conclusion. There is, furthermore, a specific textual link between this fourth section of the finale and the last movement of the Ninth: it is based on a quatrain whose first two lines are taken, with only slight modification, from Schiller's "An die Freude":

> Wer ein holdes Weib errungen,
> stimm' in unsern Jubel ein!
> Nie wird es zu hoch besungen
> Retterin des Gatten sein.

> He who has won a fair wife
> may join in our rejoicing!
> We can never praise too highly
> A husband's savior.

(The corresponding lines in the "Ode to Joy" are: "Wer ein holdes Weib errungen, / mische seinen Jubel ein" ["He who has won a noble wife, let him mingle his rejoicing with ours"].) The quatrain supplies the basic textual material for a large and complex musical composition, in which the individual phrases are repeated so many times that it makes no sense to count them—or, for that matter, even to listen for them. Save for the occasion when they are sung alone by Florestan, they remain largely unintelligible, set as they are for the massed voices of the chorus or the equally opaque concertato grouping of the vocal sextet (Leonore, Marzelline, Florestan, Jaquino, Don Fernando, and Rocco, who here become simply two sopranos, two tenors, and two basses). Just as in the preced-

ing F major passage, Beethoven's argument in this final section is musical
rather than textual. It is, in effect, an extended essay in musical affirmation, an uninflected expression of joy. The text, one feels, merely supplies
an excuse to add the heft and sonority of a hundred-voice choir to the orchestral goings-on, much as happens in the closing movement of the
Ninth. We have traveled light years from the insipid, textually responsible music of the opera's beginning—traveled, in effect, from the quotidian to the sublime, from the old regime to the new.

THE ATTENTIVE READER will have noticed that, in this contrast between *Fidelio*'s cramped beginning and its expansive end, I have passed
over the so-called canon, "Mir ist so wunderbar," the third number in the
opera and in the minds of many (including myself) the most beautiful
piece in the entire work. The canon represents a challenge to my interpretation of *Fidelio* as the opera of the French Revolution, because its
music conveys the sort of exalted transcendence that we don't hear again
until the finale of the second act and that I want to associate with
Beethoven's musical portrait of a new order of freedom and brotherhood.

Actually, the canon poses a problem even for interpreters who don't
view the opera from the particular historical perspective I do. Its musical
beauties seem unrelated to the thoughts being expressed by the four characters who sing it: Marzelline, Leonore, Rocco, and Jaquino. To be precise, the four characters give voice to their individual thoughts—all of
them are singing "asides"—and in the case of each those thoughts are
very different. Marzelline, who sings first, indulges herself in a happy
fantasy of union with Fidelio; Leonore, who comes in next, expresses
anxious foreboding about Marzelline's infatuation; then Rocco gives
voice to his satisfaction at the prospective marriage between Fidelio and
Marzelline; while Jaquino, who enters last, frets angrily at Rocco's betrayal. Yet in spite of their diverse emotions Beethoven makes no effort
(such as Verdi does in the *Rigoletto* quartet) to differentiate among the
four musically. On the contrary, because it is a canon, all four are given
the identical vocal line, as each repeats the same basic melody.

My hypothesis—perhaps too conveniently—is that the canon is a kind of visionary moment in which we are given a foretaste of the music, and the world, of the future, the music of the opera's conclusion. It is a kind of musical promise, a down-payment, as it were, and has the effect of alerting us near the start of the opera that something much more significant is in store for us than we would be inclined to expect from the trivialities of the opening duet and Marzelline's aria—the only two pieces we have heard up to this point.

Among the most striking features of the canon is the way its music resembles that of the great slow section, marked Sostenuto assai, of the second act finale, the passage beginning "O Gott! welch' ein Augenblick!" Both are set in grave triple meter, both are punctuated by bass pizzicati on the third and first beats of the bar, and both have the same sort of long-breathed, arching phrases, although in the canon this essential legato is created more by the orchestra (especially the woodwinds) than by the voices. Most important, the canon and the slow section of the finale create the same sense of stillness and transfiguration, the same sense of having entered an altered universe. The main difference is that in the canon this stillness gives way gradually to exaltation, as the overlapping vocal lines grow more agitated and are allowed to soar upwards and as the underlying accompaniment becomes more excited, whereas in the Sostenuto assai Beethoven maintains the stillness to the end, because he wants to create the greatest possible contrast with the frenetic movement of the closing Allegro that follows.

The canon, in sum, must be bracketed off from the numbers that surround it. It anticipates the world in which *Fidelio* ends, but it does not fundamentally disturb the opera's bipolar structure—our sense of moving from a discredited past to a redeemed future.

IV

The main affinity between *Fidelio* and the French Revolution is their common right-angled conception of history. But they exhibit an equally remarkable similarity in the way they view the transition from the old order to the new. Admittedly, for both of them the movement from oppression to liberation is categorical and swift. But it is in no sense easy. On the contrary, the passage is marked by anxiety, even despair. It is managed only in the face of opposition and through struggle. Indeed, the revolutionary break is accompanied by violence and profound conflict.

Much of the middle portion of Beethoven's opera is devoted to a dramatic and musical representation of this antagonistic process of transition. We are repeatedly made aware of its heavy psychological costs, particularly in Leonore's frequent expressions of anxiety and in the general intimation of terror that hovers over the action. Beethoven constructs his most concentrated musical portrait of the fear and despair attending the revolutionary struggle in the long orchestral prelude to Florestan's prison aria—a musical essay of symphonic dimensions and intensity. The dark, minor tonality, the piercing brass, and the low moans in the strings, giving way to anxious staccatos, all conspire to create an impression of blackest depression.

The central figure in Beethoven's representation of conflict and struggle in the opera is Pizarro. He is usually thought to be a personification of evil, and in the minds of many he comes dangerously close to comedy in this regard. Even for a conventional rescue-opera villain, he is a decidedly cardboard figure, speaking a melodramatic language that borders on caricature, nowhere more so than in the opening lines of his aria:

> Ha! welch' ein Augenblick!
> Die Rache werd' ich kühlen.
> Dich rufet dein Geschick!
> In seinem Herzen wühlen,
> O Wonne, grosses Glück!
>
> Ah! What a moment!
> I shall have my vengeance.
> Your fate calls you!
> To run him through the heart,
> what bliss, what great joy!

One is tempted to say that Beethoven was not aesthetically equipped to represent evil, certainly not in the persuasive manner of a later artist like Wagner (Hagen is the genuine item, and he seems both psychologically and musically altogether outside Beethoven's orbit). It is a shortcoming he shares with Mozart and, perhaps more generally, with the entire European Enlightenment.

Pizarro is a more impressive achievement if we think of him as the incarnation not of evil but of power. Power, unlike evil, is very much within Beethoven's aesthetic vocabulary. The idiom of the heroic period in particular is ideally suited to its representation. Thus, while Beethoven fails to persuade us of Pizarro's vileness, he is superbly successful at conveying his enormous oppositional force. The libretto is of very little help in the enterprise. Rather, as the embodiment of intense negative energy, Pizarro is strictly a creation of Beethoven's music. It alone convinces us of the formidable obstacles that Leonore must overcome in her mission of liberation.

Beethoven realizes Pizarro in this oppositional sense most effectively in his aria and in the opening music of the dungeon quartet that leads to the opera's climax. In both instances he uses the identical device. He forces Pizarro to plant his voice over and over on the tonic. Not insignificantly, that tonic is the same note in both the aria and the quartet: a D natural, which is the home tone of the aria's D minor key, just as it is of the quartet's D major. The note conveys a sense of power, first, because of the almost compulsive manner in which Beethoven forces his singer to return to it and repeat it and, second, because it lies fairly high in the baritone's range. When the singer is obliged to sustain the note and to emit it over and over again, the effect is decidedly strenuous. We are conscious of his effort, even of a sense of strain. In other words, the vocal power needed to produce Pizarro's reiterated upper Ds is experienced by the listener as a sonic metaphor for personal power.

"Ha! welch' ein Augenblick!" comes about as close as imaginable to being a one-note aria. The way Beethoven sits on upper D in the piece is altogether astonishing. He begins there (on "Ha!") and comes back to it as frequently as decency and the laws of melody will permit. By my calculations Pizarro sings the note forty-nine times. Often the D is unusually prolonged: for two and a half bars on "Wonne" and two and a quarter bars on "Triumph." Pizarro is also apt to hover on the tones half a note below and half a note above D. As a result the musical line is studded with emphatic, sustained C sharps and E flats, which, however, nearly always give way to the inescapable D. Through most of the aria these repeated Ds are sung over an orchestral accompaniment of swirling strings, blaring brass, and rumbling timpani—all playing at full throttle. The orchestral turbulence serves to underline Pizarro's extraordinary energy, and the volume and thickness of the instrumental accompaniment demand that his high-lying trumpetings be consistently loud. It is an exhausting workout for the singer, and few performers can muster the vocal wherewithal to fulfill Beethoven's rigorous demands.

Pizarro's lines at the start of the prison quartet are an even more impressive example of the D principle. The text, once again, seems overblown:

> *(zieht einen Dolch)*
> Er sterbe! Doch er soll erst wissen,
> wer ihm sein stolzes Herz zerfleischt.
> Der Rache Dunkel sei zerrissen!
> Sieh her! Du hast mich nicht getäuscht!
> Pizarro, den du stürzen wolltest,
> Pizarro, den du fürchten solltest,
> steht nun als Ritcher hier.

> *[drawing a dagger]*
> Let him die! But first he shall know
> who hacks his proud heart from him.
> Let revenge's dark cloak be ripped away!
> Look here! You did not confound me!
> Pizarro, whom you tried to ruin,
> Pizarro, whom you should have feared,
> now stands here as avenger.

The work of transforming these implausible utterances into an assertion of power is left to Beethoven's music. All but two of the notes to which Pizarro sings the self-congratulatory fifth and sixth lines of the passage are set on upper D, and the remaining two are on D an octave below. They come, furthermore, at the end of an ascending vocal line that finds him sustaining first C, then C sharp, and finally E, each through two full bars, before settling in to the unparalleled sequence of Ds. As in the aria, this monomaniacal assertion of a single tone (prefaced by its closest neighbors) is set above an accompaniment of singular energy and volume. Pizarro's shouted Ds assume the character of a code. They are the uniquely concentrated expression of his power.

The dungeon quartet that Pizarro initiates with this outburst stands at the heart of the opera's dramatic action. Indeed, it might legitimately be described as "action packed," so compressed is its sequence of happenings. Its eventfulness is all the more striking because it comes in the middle of an opera that is otherwise relatively static—given to rumination rather than drama. Here Beethoven presents his audience with a breathless series of confrontations, physical as well as emotional, culminating in Leonore's "Töt' erst sein Weib!" ("First kill his wife!"). It is a protracted essay in struggle, a distillation of the violent conflict marking the passage from oppression to liberty.

Beethoven succeeds remarkably in embracing the scene's actions within a single musical framework. The music itself is an exercise in unrelenting frenzy. Its violent fabric and headlong pace are interrupted only once—for Leonore's bloodcurdling cry. Throughout, the orchestra remains at an unremitting forte (Beethoven is, along with Verdi, one of the few composers who can get away with this kind of sustained loudness without embarrassment). Rushing strings and fanfares in the brass compete with the ever more excited and strenuous exertions of the singers. Leonore in particular repeatedly assaults the upper register, pounding away in the vicinity of high G (at one point she repeats this note for five straight bars). As the quartet reaches its climax, the individual voices increasingly overlap, singing against one another and creating the effect of a musical shouting match. For the final twenty-one bars, as Leonore and Pizarro utter their threats of mutual destruction, Beethoven jacks up the tempo and alternates vehemently descending runs in the strings with fanfares in the winds and brass. As a piece of sustained musical violence, the quartet might be compared to the first movement of the Fifth Symphony. It is a remarkable instance of Beethoven's skill in the musical realization of heroic struggle.

Throughout the quartet Leonore is unambiguously the central force, the prime mover of the action. Her suitability for this decisive role has been carefully prepared in the earlier scenes of the opera. Virtually from the start Beethoven has conducted a systematic musical and dramatic campaign to empower her—to represent her as an adequate vessel for the extraordinary undertaking that falls to her. This empowering of Leonore, moreover, significantly shapes our understanding of the process of struggle that leads from oppression to freedom. It locates the seat of that transformative action not in the deus ex machina of the absent minister (absent, that is, until the final scene) but in an ordinary human being, a person distinguishable from other persons neither by rank nor by office but only by qualities of character. I am suggesting, in other words, that Leonore represents for Beethoven an essentially democratic principle. The liberating action celebrated in the opera is generated not from above but from below. *Fidelio* is a democratic opera in precisely the same sense that the French Revolution—to invoke R. R. Palmer's authority once again—was democratic: not because it installed or memorialized a particular form of government but because it located significant historical agency in the popular domain. Leonore is the essential agent of the opera's liberating action, just as the Third Estate was the essential agent of the French Revolution. For both Beethoven and the revolutionaries history is viewed from the bottom up.

Leonore is, of course, a woman. What's more, throughout most of the opera she is a woman disguised as a man. We might wonder about the significance of her sex and her male disguise, especially as it affects our view of her as a historically decisive actor. In the current intellectual climate her femaleness and transvestism are apt to prompt excited reflections about the ambiguity or "constructedness" of sexual roles and to invite comparisons with cross-dressed figures in Shakespeare, Mozart, or Richard Strauss. But these temptations should be resisted. The most important thing about Leonore's transvestism is that it interests Beethoven not in the slightest. It is for him nothing more than a necessity of the plot. He systematically rejects every opportunity to exploit it for dramatic or comic effects. Not for a moment, for example, will he titillate us with the sexual ambiguities of Marzelline's infatuation (unless it be in the mercifully deleted duet, "Um in der Ehe," in which Marzelline looks forward to bearing Fidelio's child), even though audiences sometimes ignore his interdiction and give way to fits of nervous laughter. The truth is, Beethoven was a profoundly unsexual artist, with a sensibility of unparalleled austerity. We recall that he disliked *The Marriage of Figaro* and

Don Giovanni because of their salaciousness. His art was desexualized on principle, the purest instance of sublimation, uncompromisingly spiritual and disembodied. Thus *Fidelio*, although an opera about marital devotion, is utterly untouched by eroticism. Significantly, Leonore and Florestan are well past the ardors of the first love. Theirs is essentially a companionship of the spirit, a union based on shared principles rather than physical passion. Leonore, accordingly, is unsexed in the opera. Not a bar of Beethoven's music is devoted to depicting her femininity. It would be unthinkable, for example, for her to reveal the emotional vulnerability of Pamina's "Ach, ich fühl's." In every meaningful musical and dramatic sense Beethoven treats her exactly as if she were a man. More precisely, he treats her as a generic human being. It is her humanity, not her gender or her sexuality, that interests him, and it is as a human being, rather than as a woman, that he makes her the fulcrum of the opera's democratic action.

Let us briefly trace the steps by which Beethoven empowers her in the opera. When, in the opening scene, Marzelline urges Rocco not to take Fidelio into the dungeon because he would be unable to bear the sight of the condemned prisoner, Leonore responds, "Warum denn nicht? Ich habe Mut und Kraft!" ("Why not? I have courage and strength!"). This is no idle boast, and Beethoven takes the occasion to launch a trio (no. 5) in which he provides Leonore with the musical ammunition to back up her claim. Her opening gambit—the trio's second verse—represents the first time she sings alone in the opera, and Beethoven sees to it that she makes a memorable impression:

> Ich habe Mut!
> Mit kaltem Blut
> will ich hinab mich wagen;
> für hohen Lohn
> kann Liebe schon
> auch hohe Leiden tragen.
>
> I have courage!
> In cold blood
> I will dare to go down there;
> for great reward

love can
bear even great suffering.

He takes particular care with the significant opening assertion ("Ich habe Mut"). Save for the violas, playing piano eighth notes, he momentarily silences the orchestra so that the soprano's notes can sound out with uncompromised force. Nor is he afraid of the egoistic display. On the contrary, he sets the opening "Ich" on a confident D. From this moment of unembarrassed self-assertion, Leonore's heroism is never in doubt. The rest of her declaration is composed with athletic brio. The vigor of her musical self-presentation assures us that Leonore does indeed possess the emotional resources for the task before her.

Beethoven confirms this impression, emphatically, in the concluding Allegro of her first act aria. The aria provides us with our fullest portrait of Leonore, and its bracing conclusion establishes her activist credentials beyond doubt. Again, the text is an unembarrassed piece of self-advertising:

Ich folg' dem innern Triebe,
ich wanke nicht,
mich stärkt die Pflicht
der treuen Gattenliebe!

I follow an inner compulsion,
I do not falter,
I am strengthened by the duty
of faithful married love!

The repeated "I's" are fully justified by the energetic music to which the declaration is set. Beethoven begins with an athletic upward E major arpeggio for the soprano, marching her from low E to a stunning G sharp above the staff, from which, on the same syllable ("Gatten"), he drops her over an octave and a half to low B sharp—a baritonal note that any decent Leonore will boom out in chest register—only to carry her (still on "Gatten") up a coloratura scale to C sharp in the middle of the voice. This technical description cannot begin to do justice to what is, in effect, a blatant flexing of the vocal muscles, an unapologetic display of her powers of voice—which the listener readily translates into powers of mind and character. Particularly striking here, as throughout the aria, is Beethoven's juxtaposition of the highest and lowest registers of the voice —the former piercing, the latter growling—in order to suggest Leonore's potent sense of resolve. Before the Allegro is complete he will send her down once again from high G sharp to low B sharp, and in the final phrase he takes her up a fifteen-note run from low E to a thrillingly sustained B natural in alt, the highest note she sings in the opera. It is a show of vocal power such as one rarely encounters in Mozart (Fiordiligi's "Come scoglio" comes closest, and it, of course, is a *mock*-heroic aria). The raucous horn fanfares that accompany Leonore's vehement declaration have a decidedly military flavor and serve to convince us—if any further convincing were necessary—that she is a force to be reckoned with.

I have already mentioned Leonore's disquisition on freedom in the grave-digging duet with Rocco ("Wer du auch seist, ich will dich retten" ["Whoever you may be, I will save you"]). Both musically and textually it is of a piece with the impression we have gained of her from the first act. At its climax, as in that of the aria, Beethoven resorts to coloratura to express Leonore's readiness for action. Furthermore, in the immediately preceding moments we see her engaged in a most unladylike piece of manual labor, namely, shoveling earth, and Beethoven's music nicely conveys the sense of physical exertion this work requires of her. It is a small matter, but it contributes subtly to our sense of her humanity. Her heroism is not limited to rhetorical displays but encompasses bodily labor as well, whether carrying chains or digging a grave.

We are, then, fully prepared for Leonore's courageous and decisive acts in the climactic dungeon quartet where she confronts and ultimately defeats Pizarro. Much of the quartet is in fact composed as a violent musical battle between these two figures, with Pizarro's aggressive high Ds set against Leonore's even more altitudinous and penetrating F sharps, Gs and G sharps. For her most decisive act—when she reveals her identity and challenges Pizarro with "Töt' erst sein Weib!" ("First kill his wife!")—Beethoven interrupts the turbulent musical flow in order to let her stunning imperative ring out unaccompanied into the hall, and he sets it on an unexpected upward interval, E flat followed by a sustained B flat above the staff. That vertiginous B flat is both awkward and punishing for the soprano, and it sums up Leonore's extraordinary initiative with unrivalled conciseness. In the end Pizarro is no match for her, either vocally or temperamentally.

Following the quartet, with the issue now resolved, Beethoven writes the only possible duet for the triumphant Leonore and her liberated husband. "O namenlose Freude" ("O nameless joy") is a duet of surpassing athleticism, in which no distinction is drawn between the muscular upward arpeggios of the soprano and those of the tenor. The two sing as absolute equals—a parity already anticipated by their major arias, which are identical in format and dimension. In effect, the duet recapitulates and summarizes the musical evidence that has been accumulating over the course of the entire opera. Leonore is Beethoven's portrait of humanity in action, struggling in the face of deadly opposition, and ultimately prevailing.

Is BEETHOVEN'S PRISON OPERA, then, a metaphor for the French Revolution? I cannot claim to have demonstrated so conclusively, but I am nevertheless impressed by the structural parallels between the two. By drawing attention to the opera's dichotomous historical vision, its preoccupation with struggle and its democratically empowered protagonist, I hope to have suggested a plausible interpretation linking it to the epochal events of 1789. Perhaps I will be accused of grasping at straws if I remind readers that the Revolution itself began with the liberation of a prison: on 14 July the fortress of the Bastille was attacked by a Parisian crowd, and, after a battle in which more than a hundred civilians were killed, the prison was taken and (as in the opera) all its inmates were released. Ironically, their number contained not a single political martyr, only five convicted felons and two madmen. Yet the revolutionaries insisted on regarding this strategically insignificant victory as the birthplace of their Revolution. They did so, of course, because the Bastille quickly became symbolically freighted: it was for them a metaphor for the old regime, just as its liberation, while practically meaningless, was a metaphor for the new order created by the Revolution itself. In this essay I have argued that we can plausibly read Beethoven's prison opera much as the revolutionaries read the storming of the Bastille: as a symbolical representation of the great political drama with which the modern world began.

CHAPTER FIVE

Verdi's Fathers and Daughters

*This essay originated in a talk delivered to the Leonardo Da Vinci Society in
San Francisco in 1987. A modified version appeared in the programme for Covent
Garden's 1997 production of* Simon Boccanegra. *The essay considers Verdi's
obsession with father-daughter relationships in three of his middle-period operas,*
Luisa Miller, Rigoletto, *and* Simon Boccanegra, *whose greatest music is in fact
devoted to extended duets for fathers and daughters. After examining the biographical roots of this preoccupation, I trace its source to the rise of the modern
nuclear family, with its peculiar passions and tensions, and I connect Verdi's obsession to similar concerns in his contemporary Charles Dickens and his successor
Sigmund Freud.*

I

Arguably the most striking feature of the operas of Verdi's middle
years—from *Luisa Miller* (1849) to *Simon Boccanegra* (1857)—is their
focus on the relationship between fathers and daughters, or, more generally, between parents and children. Irrespective of the importance of the
issue in his literary source, Verdi contrives to make the father-daughter
or parent-child tie the absolute center of our attention. It assumes more
dramatic weight than any other human relationship in these operas—
decidedly more weight, for example, than the traditional operatic tie between romantic hero and heroine. And Verdi also composes his most
profound and adventuresome music to give expression to these relation-

ships. The musical glory of the middle-period operas resides in their beautiful and extended duets for fathers and daughters.

The dramatic and musical importance of this configuration is clearest in *Luisa Miller, Rigoletto,* and *Simon Boccanegra,* whose father-daughter duets I will examine in the second part of my essay. But the same issues are centrally at stake in the two other most important operas of the middle years, *Il trovatore* and *La traviata.* In *Trovatore* it is not father and daughter but mother and son that absorb Verdi's attention, and, as in the father-daughter operas, the relationship between Manrico and his presumed mother, Azucena, is psychologically denser and musically more eloquent than the conventional romantic tie between Manrico and Leonora. I am also persuaded that the bond between Violetta and the elder Germont (her potential father-in-law) in *La traviata* assumes the psychological valence of a father-daughter relationship, and all critics agree that the long duet between them in act 2 is the opera's emotional heart and contains its finest music. (In the duet Violetta sings, "Embrace me as a daughter," and when Germont arrives at her bedside in the last act he responds, "I come to keep my promise and embrace you as a daughter.")

If we narrow our focus to *Rigoletto* and *Simon Boccanegra,* the two middle-period operas that treat the issue most affectingly, we can make some further observations about these relationships. In both operas the father has no significant human bond other than that with his daughter. The mothers of both Gilda and Amelia are long dead—dead, in fact, since the daughter's infancy—and, although their memories figure prominently in the imaginations of both father and daughter, they are absent from the operas. Nor are there any other children in these families. The meaningful emotional world of the operas has been reduced to a single emotional dyad.

Verdi treats father-daughter relationships very much as previous composers had treated romantic relationships: he invests them with all the intensity, passion, and possibility for both happiness and catastrophe that we normally associate with relations between young men and women based on sexual desire. The music of Verdi's great father-daughter duets is indistinguishable from operatic love music, and it is a good deal more powerful than the music he provides for the traditional romantic scenes between men and women in these operas. By setting the music of his fathers for high baritone, moreover, Verdi further narrows the sonic distance between these duets and those for the conventional romantic pairing of soprano and tenor.

Another way to measure the centrality of this subject for Verdi is to cast one's mind back to the operas of Mozart at the end of the eighteenth century and forward to the operas of Puccini at the end of the nineteenth and the beginning of the twentieth. We note immediately that the relationship between fathers and daughters (or, more generally, between parents and children) plays little role in the works of either composer. One can make the case (as does Ingmar Bergman in his film of the opera) for a father-daughter element in the tie between Sarastro and Pamina in *The Magic Flute*, but it's a stretch. (In actuality, of course, Pamina is the daughter of the Queen of the Night, though Mozart's Queen is untouched by parental tenderness.) Donna Anna is obsessed with her murdered father throughout *Don Giovanni*, but Mozart denies them a single musical encounter. There is a genuinely "parental" moment in *The Marriage of Figaro*, when, in act 3, Mozart brings about the splendid reconciliation between Figaro and his newly discovered mother and father, Marcellina and Bartolo. But except for *Idomeneo*, in which the Idomeneo-Idamante relationship recalls that of Abraham and Isaac, the Mozart operas are concerned with different issues, and the matter of parents and children remains on the fringes of Mozart's imagination.

Curiously, the same is true of Puccini. I can think of only two parent-child relationships in the Puccini operas, those between Gianni Schicchi and his daughter, Lauretta, in *Gianni Schicchi* and between Calaf and his father, Timur, in *Turandot*. Again, as with Mozart, Puccini appears largely uninterested in this issue. His operas, in the last analysis, have a single psychological subject, namely, romance: all of them are operas about men and women who pursue various romantic involvements with one another. In effect, the operas of both Mozart and Puccini serve to highlight the extraordinary investment Verdi made in the tie between parent and child.

The only other major opera composer for whom father-daughter relationships claimed equal attention was Verdi's exact contemporary

Richard Wagner. It is a central concern above all in *Die Walküre,* where the relationship between Wotan and Brünnhilde is as deeply felt and richly explored as any of the father-daughter dyads in Verdi, and, somewhat less obviously, in *Die Meistersinger,* where the tie between Hans Sachs and Eva derives much of its pathos, I am convinced, from the elements of a parental bond between these two figures. Significantly, Tristan and Parsifal devote a fair amount of verbal and musical energy to memories of their mother. The relationship between parents and children is very much on Wagner's mind, and in this crucial matter Verdi and Wagner turn out to be surprisingly alike.

Inevitably one wonders why the tie between father and daughter assumed such prominence in Verdi's (as well as Wagner's) musical universe. What is the source of this preoccupation, which gives rise to such magnificent music? Two speculations come to mind, one biographical, the other historical. The biographical speculation is that Verdi was preoccupied with fathers and daughters precisely because he enjoyed no such relationship himself. In other words, he compensated in his artistic imagination for a human tie for which he felt a profound need but that was absent from his own life.

As it turns out, the biographical facts are more complicated, though on the whole they support this explanation. Verdi did have a daughter, by his first wife Margherita Barezzi. He also had a son by Margherita. But the daughter died in 1838, when little more than a year old, and the son died at about the same age a year later. The tragedy of Verdi's early life was not complete until 1840, when Margherita herself died, leaving him alone in the world. Later in the 1840s Verdi began living with the singer Giuseppina Strepponi; indeed, he lived with her until her death in 1897. Although the relationship was regularized by their marrying in 1859, they had no children. (In her recent biography of Verdi, Mary Jane Phillips-Matz has speculated that there was in fact a daughter born in 1851 and placed with foster parents near Verdi's home in Sant'Agata. But the evidence is circumstantial, and, in any event, by that time Verdi's father-daughter fixation was already firmly established.) So Verdi lived out not only a childless life but one presumably haunted by the daughter (and the son) who had died when he was a young man. On this basis one might well argue that the daughters of the operas, and their intense emotional relationships with their fathers, represent a kind of psychic substitute for what was missing in Verdi's own experience.

Of course, this explanation does not account for the similar fascination with parent-child relations in Wagner. (Wagner had three children —a son and two daughters, the first of whom was born in 1865.) Nor does it account for the increasingly central role this concern was to play in many different forms of artistic expression in the nineteenth century. Think, for example, of the way the parent-child relationship also haunts the mid-century novels of Charles Dickens (like Wagner, Verdi's exact contemporary), for whom the danger of becoming an orphan looms as the greatest single threat to human happiness. To be an orphan in the world, as is Pip in *Great Expectations,* is to be without that most fundamental source of wellbeing, the rich, sustained emotional ties to one's mother and father.

This thought brings me to my historical speculation. I believe that the intense concern with fathers and daughters (or, more generally, with parents and children) reflects a structural change in the nature and function of the family during the nineteenth century. Historians such as Lawrence Stone and Edward Shorter have discussed this change and explored its significance. It can be described as follows: whereas the family had earlier been both an economic and a psychological unit, during the nineteenth century it lost most of its economic functions, and as a result, paradoxically, its psychological function became all the more important.

Before the nineteenth century, when most families were rural, they were units of production in which all of the members had economic roles. Children were not simply children but also workers: they were assigned chores in the running of the farm economy. So their father was not just their father but also, for all practical purposes, their employer, their boss. And in the traditional family these economic responsibilities sat comfortably alongside the biological and emotional tasks of reproducing and raising young boys and girls to be adult men and women. Indeed, they reinforced one another.

During the nineteenth century, European society underwent the most profound change in its entire history: it was gradually transformed from a rural into an urban economy, as the old regime, based on the peasant household, was replaced by a commercial and industrial order. Fathers who had once been farmers became urban laborers. And this change—which, of course, happened at different rates in different parts of Europe—meant that the traditional family ceased to be a significant economic unit. More and more, children were only children—not employees as well—and parents were only parents—not in positions of direct supervision over their children. Indeed, the father, at least, was becoming increasingly absent, as he went off every morning to work in the factory.

When these changes occurred, the family—or so historians have argued—became a purely psychological or affective unit. In fact it grew more intensely psychological than it had ever been before. It was, in one famous phrase, a haven in a heartless world, and the cultivation of rich, deeply-felt emotional ties among its members (between husband and wife, and also between parent and child) became its raison d'être. It is this structural transformation, more than anything else, I believe, that explains the rise in the nineteenth century of what might be called the culture of the family, that body of artistic works that explored, with ever more loving exactitude, relationships within the family. In other words, it is this structural transformation that ultimately explains Dickens's preoccupation with orphans and, more important for our purposes, Verdi's (and Wagner's) preoccupation with fathers and daughters. Verdi's great father-daughter duets are, in this view, a reflection, at the highest artistic level, of the new emotional life, the inner life, of the modern nuclear family.

II

Let me follow up my speculative preamble with three musical illustrations. I present them to suggest some of the different ways Verdi examines the relationship between fathers and daughters, in particular how he gives the relationship musical (as opposed to merely textual) life in *Luisa Miller*, *Rigoletto*, and *Simon Boccanegra*.

Luisa Miller is based on Friedrich Schiller's play *Kabale und Liebe*. It is a story of conflict between the old aristocracy and the newly emerging bourgeois or *Bürger* class. Luisa is the daughter of a retired soldier and widower named Miller. She falls in love with the son of a local aristocrat, Count Walter, who, of course, wants his boy to marry a person of his own class. The duet between Luisa and her father is set up in the story when one of Count Walter's henchmen extracts a letter from her saying she had never loved the young man, a letter she writes because the henchman is threatening to have her father killed. In other words, she sacrifices her romantic attachment to the count's son for the sake of her father. In her despair she then decides to commit suicide.

Her father, Miller, cares for nothing in the world other than his daughter's happiness, and he persuades her not to kill herself but instead to go off and live with him. Luisa's and Miller's resolve to depart and spend their lives alone together provides the subject of their duet in the last act. The situation in the opera always reminds me of the union between King Lear and his daughter Cordelia, who, when they are finally reunited toward the end of the play, promise each other joyfully to spend eternity together, even though it will be in prison. Lear says to Cordelia:

> Come, let's away to prison.
> We two alone will sing like birds i' th' cage.
> When thou dost ask me blessing, I'll kneel down
> And ask of thee forgiveness. So we'll live,
> And pray, and sing, and tell old tales, and laugh
> At gilded butterflies, and hear poor rogues
> Talk of court news; . . . (V, iii, 8–14)

The reminder, moreover, is anything but accidental: for years Verdi tried to compose an opera on the subject of King Lear. In 1853 he had Antonio Somma prepare a *Re Lear* libretto, and we know that he intended to write a major duet for just this scene between Lear and the faithful Cordelia. Luisa and her father speak not of going off to prison together but of departing the town to go wandering and poor. But the effect is very much the same.

The music of the duet wonderfully captures the bliss that Luisa and Miller achieve. It is a duet not of ecstasy but of serenity: the pulse is easeful and steady (rather like a slow march, which carries a subliminal suggestion of the two walking together from place to place), and this easefulness aptly conveys their inner satisfaction with the prospect of a life lived only between themselves—no romantic entanglements, no children, not even any friends. They begin by singing their melody separately (to the words "Andrem, raminghi e poveri" ["We'll go wandering and poor"]), but in the middle section of the duet their voices start to join and overlap. By the time the original melody returns the two voices are always united, singing either in harmonious countermelody or in simultaneous phrases, as they repeat variations on the simple four lines of the original text. One might say that their voices are joined as are their souls. Finally, at the very end there is a suggestion of rebirth or transcendence: "Come s'appressi la nuova aurora noi partirem" ("When the new dawn comes we shall depart"), a line they repeat in tenths and octaves. The effect is rather like an elopement.

Rigoletto, based on Victor Hugo's *Le roi s'amuse*, is the most famous of these three operas, and it explores the extreme version—the pathological version—of the father-daughter relationship that we see in its benign form in *Luisa Miller*. In *Rigoletto* the love of father for daughter has become so fierce, so suffocating, that it ultimately destroys the daughter—and, in effect, the father as well, because, as with all these fathers, he has nothing to live for but his daughter. The tragic denouement is managed through a series of melodramatic characters and plot devices, leading to the final scene in which *Rigoletto*, thinking he has arranged for the murder of his daughter's seducer, actually brings about her own murder. At the end of the opera he is presented with a sack by his hired assassin, only to discover that it contains not the infamous duke of Mantua but the dying Gilda. (The episode is the source of many operatic jokes, all of which play on the idea that the soprano who sings Gilda is impossibly large ever to fit into a sack, let alone be carried about by the hunchback *Rigoletto*.)

The ironic thing is that, despite the opera's "message" (which might seem to be about parental oppression), the final scene presents us with the same sort of transcendental romance between father and daughter as we heard in *Luisa Miller*. There is no recrimination or drawing of morals, only a beautiful and tender duet between these two characters, exhibiting the familiar qualities of all the great Verdi duets for father and daughter. Moreover, in contrast to *Luisa Miller*, it has been preceded by two even longer duets for the pair in the opera's first two acts. It marks the musical culmination of an elaborately developed parental romance.

The duet proper begins with Gilda's words "Lassù in cielo, vicina alla madre," through which she conjures up the image of a reunion with her mother in heaven. In effect, she reconstitutes in song the nuclear family that never existed on earth (or in the opera). Her lines, appropriately, are set to a heavenly arc (rising a sixth), supported by high violins. *Rigoletto* then sings a second motive (to the words "Non morir, mio tesoro," "Do not die, my treasure"), which is warm and passionate, and there is a surge of earthly warmth and passion in the lower instruments of the orchestra that accompany him. Finally, as in the *Luisa Miller* duet, the two voices join and overlap one another, creating that union of sounds that is a symbol, I've suggested, for the union of souls. One might say that, for all the ambiguity of its explicit teachings, *Rigoletto* ends in a characteristically affirmative musical rendering by Verdi of the romance between father and daughter, parent and child.

Simon Boccanegra can be viewed as the first opera of Verdi's late maturity in which he turned increasingly to the issues of politics and society. *Don Carlo* (1867) is the most important of these operas, and all of them, in one way or another, are concerned with the role of the political leader, in particular the personal sacrifices the political leader is called upon to make. The title character of the opera is a buccaneer who rises over the course of his lifetime to become doge of Genoa, and he is widely considered the finest of Verdi's roles for the high baritone voice.

The relationship between father and daughter no longer occupies central stage as it so clearly does in *Luisa Miller* and *Rigoletto*. And yet the single most touching moment in all of *Simon Boccanegra* is the recognition scene between Simon and his long-lost daughter Maria, whose mother had died twenty-five years earlier, and who throughout most of the opera—for reasons too complicated to explain here—is known by the name of Amelia. Like Miller and Rigoletto, Simon Boccanegra is a man without a single significant human relationship other than the memory of the dead woman he loved as a young man and the daughter of their union, whom, so far as he knows, he has never seen, indeed, whom he does not even know is still alive.

In the duet Simon and Maria discover one another, and, as in all the Verdi operas of the middle years, they launch themselves on a kind of love duet. It can move us even more profoundly than do the father-daughter duets of *Luisa Miller* and *Rigoletto,* partly because moments of recognition are so emotionally laden (think of the scene between Elektra and Orestes in Strauss's opera), and partly because by 1857 Verdi's compositional technique had become even more secure and effective. In 1881 Verdi revised the entire opera, including important parts of the duet, with the help of Arrigo Boito, and by then his mastery of his craft was as complete as that of only a few composers in the history of Western music.

Let me draw attention to some of the recognition duet's important musical features. First, the opening part of the scene—down to the actual recognition—is, as you might expect, set to music of increasing excitement and anticipation. Then at the moment of recognition the cries of "Father!" and "Daughter!" are punctuated by a huge orchestral outburst and a sequence of modulations, followed by a long decrescendo, over a dominant pedal, that mark the enormous sense of release felt not only by father and daughter on stage but by us listeners as well.

The main portion of the duet (actually the cabaletta of the larger duet) follows, and, like the *Luisa Miller* duet, it is characterized by an easy gait in quarter time, which once again conveys the serenity into which these two individuals fall. As usual, first we hear one voice, then the other, and finally the two joined together in an overlapping and complementary series of phrases (most of them set to the last four lines of Amelia's eight-line stanza), suggesting again the coming together of two separated souls. At the end of the duet Verdi adds something extra. As he had at the beginning, he turns to the orchestra to lend punctuation and emphasis to the vocal lines: there is a short orchestral postlude in which the main melody of the duet is built up into a wonderfully satisfying fortissimo climax (over which Amelia and Simon again issue their cries of "Father!" and "Daughter!"), and just as the orchestra arose so it also subsides into a long decrescendo (dominated by arpeggios in the harp), until at the very end we hear the moving word "Figlia," the first syllable sung on a precarious soft high F, at the top of the baritone voice, the second dropping to the F an octave below. It is the vocal equivalent of a sigh, and it sums up, with extraordinary conciseness, Simon's almost unendurable happiness at the moment of reunion.

LET ME CONCLUDE by mentioning a name that one rarely thinks of in the same intellectual breath with Verdi: Sigmund Freud. Verdi and Freud are joined, profoundly so, as the artistic memorialist and the psychological analyst of the new romance between parent and child. Virtually all Freud's ideas, which date from the last decade of the nineteenth century, can be viewed as an attempt to understand the psychological configurations brought into existence by the modern family, with its overinvested emotional bond between parent and child. Freud's notion of the Oedipus complex, for example, is simply a clinical way of talking about the same reality we see (or, rather, hear) on display in the operas of Verdi's middle years. Even the sexual component of the relationship Freud insisted on so vehemently is, I believe, but barely hidden by the decorousness of Verdi's language, and the real passion that links his fathers and daughters is revealed again and again by the passionate music to which Verdi sets their often quaint words. One might say that Freud stands at the end of the tradition of which Verdi is a major spokesman. Both figures were made possible by the great revolution in the family that took place during the nineteenth century.

CHAPTER SIX

Is *Aida* an Orientalist Opera?

This essay first appeared in the Cambridge Opera Journal *in 1993. It takes is-sue with Edward Said's contention that Verdi's* Aida *is infected with the intellec-tual prejudice Said has famously dubbed "orientalism," a tendentious opposition between the rational, scientific, and progressive West and the instinctual, super-stitious, and backward East. Said's mistake, I argue, stems mainly from his fail-ure to pay sufficient attention to the opera's music, which creates nearly the opposite ideological construct.*

Among the more remarkable events of recent intellectual history is that Edward Said, famous avant-garde literary critic and passionate advocate of the Palestinian cause, has begun to write about music. Moreover, not just about any kind of music but about classical music in the elite (and canonical) European tradition—the symphonies of Beethoven, the op-eras of Wagner, the chamber music of Schubert and Brahms. Several years ago Said took over the music column in the *Nation* magazine, and in 1991 he published a book, *Musical Elaborations,* based on a series of in-vited lectures at the University of California, Irvine.

Most of Said's musical writings have been innocent of the theoretical and ideological concerns that distinguish his literary criticism and his politics. He comes across as a knowledgeable music lover, with a special devotion to the great German composers of the long nineteenth century (from Mozart to Strauss). As it turns out, Said is himself a pianist, who enjoys playing chamber music with friends. I have for some time suspected that music offers him a kind of asylum, a realm of unguarded pleasure, where he can lay aside the heavy burdens of his scholarly and political callings. In a world of pure sound, to which no representative meaning can be attached, he is liberated from the need to be ever watchful for orientalist subtexts or anti-Arab prejudices.

But not always. Instrumental music may be largely without denotative significance, but opera is another matter. Opera weds music to language and hence to literature—and often to politics as well. Thus, not surprisingly, when he has turned his attention to opera, Said has sometimes found himself on more familiar intellectual terrain (where, if I am right in my speculation, music no longer provides the wanted asylum). A case in point is his review of John Adams's opera *The Death of Klinghoffer,* which treats the *Achille Lauro* incident. In general Adams's opera got rather frosty notices from the musical press. Said, however, greeted it with enthusiasm in the *Nation,* partly, one suspects, because of the opera's sympathetic treatment of the Palestinians. An earlier example— and the one I wish to devote my attention to here—is an essay he wrote in 1987 for *Grand Street* on *Aida.* Entitled "The Imperial Spectacle," the essay can fairly be described as an effort to interpret *Aida* as a product of Europe's developing imperialist culture in the nineteenth century. (With only slight modification, the essay was incorporated into Said's 1993 book *Culture and Imperialism.*) In other words, it aims to understand this most famous of Italian operas in terms of Said's theory of orientalism— the theory that the whole of Europe's culture is deeply tainted with invidious representations of the non-European Other.

Said's contention that *Aida* is implicated in Europe's imperial order is in some respects unexceptionable. He draws attention, for example, to the circumstances of the opera's composition. Verdi was commissioned to write the opera by the viceroy (or khedive) of Egypt, Ismail, who wanted an opera by one of Europe's foremost composers for his new opera house in Cairo, which itself had been built in connection with the opening of the Suez Canal in 1869. (Had Verdi refused him, the viceroy was prepared to turn to Wagner or Gounod.) Crudely put, Verdi's opera was to form part of the cultural superstructure of the European presence in Egypt, a presence that reached back to the Napoleonic invasions at the end of the eighteenth century and that, by the time of *Aida*'s premiere in

1871, had transformed Egypt into a semicolony. Indeed, the opera, as Said rightly says, was intended as "an imperial *article de luxe,*" purchased to entertain the European population of Cairo, a population whose real purpose was to administer Egypt as a piece of Europe's overseas empire. With a certain symbolic appropriateness, the new opera house—modeled on the neo-classical opera houses that sprang up throughout Europe in the nineteenth century—was located on the north-south axis dividing the eastern Moslem portion of the city from the western European portion. Naturally, its portals faced westward. On this imperial site Verdi's brilliant operatic display was first seen and heard.

At the same time, *Aida* was, of course, an opera about ancient Egypt and, as such, was intended by Ismail to serve as a significant piece of nationalist propaganda. Verdi seems to have cared nothing for this objective, and, as far as anyone has been able to tell, he never expressed an opinion about modern Egypt, although he was often told that his opera would do much to advance its cultural consciousness. A substantial part of Said's argument depends on his drawing attention to the origins of the opera's story in the richly elaborated traditions of French orientalist scholarship. *Aida* is in fact based on a scenario written by the French Egyptologist Auguste Mariette, a scenario that Mariette urged on Verdi through the offices of their mutual acquaintance Camille du Locle, the director of the Opéra-Comique in Paris. Said views Mariette as driven by the ideological desire to "stage" Egypt for European cultural appropriation. His scenario presents an Egypt that is a locus of satisfactorily grand European origins but, more important, an Egypt that has been orientalized—rendered exotic—so that it can find its properly subordinate place in Europe's imperial imagination. Said makes the ingenious speculation that the settings and costumes Mariette proposed for the opera were directly inspired by the idealized reconstructions of ancient Egypt contained in the anthropological volumes of Napoleon's *Description de l'Égypte,* perhaps the first great document to package Egypt for Europe's imperial consumption. In this fashion the famous scenes of the opera— the Royal Palace in Memphis, the Temple of Vulcan, the Gate of Thebes —are transformed into tableaux vivants from the pages of Napoleon's *Description.*

Of course, any discussion that confines itself to the circumstances of the opera's commission or the origin of its libretto and mise en scène, while illuminating, does not really get us to the heart of the matter. *Aida* is an orientalist opera only if the drama Verdi actually created—under those circumstances and out of those materials—embodies the ideological project Said ascribes to it. Above all, it is an orientalist opera only if its ideological agenda is significantly embodied in its music. For, as Joseph Kerman has shown, in opera the composer is the dramatist. Things that can be identified solely in the text and don't find expression in the music for all practical purposes cease to exist. As we all know, a good deal of what is uttered in opera is incomprehensible, and not merely because it is usually uttered in a language we cannot understand. If *Aida* is an orientalist opera, then, it will have to be because of its music.

AN IMMEDIATE EMBARRASSMENT confronts Said's theory about *Aida:* although the opera does indeed represent an imperialist situation, it is an imperialist situation in which Egypt itself plays the role of aggressor. Verdi's Egypt is an imperial power seeking to subdue its African neighbor, Ethiopia. The opera is set against the background of Egypt's war of conquest against Ethiopia (as well as the guerrilla response of the Ethiopians), and its conventional romantic plot turns on a conflict between desire and patriotism in which a young Egyptian general finds himself in love with an Ethiopian slave, the captured daughter of the King of Ethiopia. In terms of Said's orientalist metaphor, white Egypt ought properly to be equated with imperial Europe, while black Ethiopia stands unambiguously in the role of the imperialized non-European Other. Furthermore, Verdi's sympathies in the opera are wholeheartedly on the Ethiopian side. Egypt is represented as an authoritarian theocracy, tyrannized by its intolerant priesthood, while Ethiopia—"conquered and tormented," in the words of its wily and heroic leader—is repeatedly celebrated as a country of vernal beauty and natural rectitude. In his correspondence, Verdi referred to Egypt as "a land that once possessed a grandeur and a civilization that I could never bring myself to admire." Under these circumstances, Said's contention that *Aida* serves to "stage" Egypt for European imperial consumption begins to look rather dubious. A more natural reading would be to see the opera as an anti-imperialist work, in which the exploitative relation between Europe and its empire has been translated into one between expansionist Egyptians and colonized Ethiopians. Revealingly, when Fascist producers staged *Aida* in Mussolini's Italy, they often presented a blackshirted Radamès subduing Amonasro's Ethiopian hordes, and Amonasro himself became an obvious stand-in for Emperor Haile Selassie, engaged in a bloody anticolonialist war against contemporary Italy.

This antithesis between militaristic Egypt and suffering Ethiopia is not, moreover, merely the dramatic backdrop of *Aida*. It is also deeply embedded in the music Verdi composed to represent the two nations. Egypt is characterized by music that is regular, diatonic, and brassy— music that can be described, I think, as distinctly European, in so far as it finds Verdi relying on the most traditional harmonic, melodic, and rhythmic means to conjure up an impression of power, authority, and military might. Two prominent musical episodes can serve to illustrate this association of Egypt with an aggressively traditional European idiom. The first is the battle hymn, "Su! del Nilo," sung by the king and the high priest, Ramfis, and then by the assembled Egyptians in act 2 as they prepare to send their army into combat against the Ethiopians. The piece is four-square, closed, and classical, its harmonies familiar, and its accompaniment emphatic. Significantly, Verdi himself feared that the tune smacked of the Marseillaise, which puts it firmly on the European side of the imperialist divide. A similar instance is the victory hymn, "Gloria all'Egitto," that the Egyptians sing after they return from thoroughly defeating (indeed enslaving) the Ethiopians. Musically, it is constructed of the same stuff as "Su! del Nilo," only it is even noisier and, appropriately, more triumphalist. Viceroy Ismail was so pleased with this tune that he wanted to adopt it as the Egyptian national anthem, in spite of the fact that it is much too short. One final feature of Verdi's musical treatment of the Egyptians needs to be noted: he typically sets the music for Ramfis and the Egyptian priests within a contrapuntal texture, thereby linking them musically with one of the oldest, most traditional, and most European of musical procedures, associated above all, of course, with the religious music of Bach.

Unlike the Egyptians, the Ethiopians are given no collective musical expression in the opera. Rather their concerns find voice in the two main

Ethiopian characters, Amonasro and Aida. Much of the time, to be sure, Amonasro and Aida sing in an idiom that is not markedly different from the high European style that Verdi uses for all his major characters in the opera. But on a number of significant occasions Aida in particular is allowed to speak of her native country—whose luxurious beauty she contrasts with the aridity of Egypt—and on these occasions Verdi sets her utterances at the polar opposite of the sort of music he writes for his massed Egyptians. Instead of four-square diatonic marching tunes, he composes music distinguished by its sinuous irregularity, its long legato lines, its close intervals, its chromatic harmonies, and its subdued woodwind orchestration, in which the reedy tones of the oboe play an especially prominent part. At such moments Aida's music verges on the exotic. Perhaps the most famous example is her apostrophe to the virgin forests of Ethiopia, as she seeks to persuade Radamès to flee with her back to her native land. It conjures up a world of alien loveliness—the world, I would suggest, of the non-European Other.

Having constructed this antithesis between imperial, Europeanized Egypt and oppressed, orientalized Ethiopia, I should not leave the impression that there is no basis in the opera for Said's claim that *Aida* presents, as he puts it, "an Orientalized Egypt." On the contrary, a not inconsiderable amount of the music associated with the Egyptians is written in the peculiar "oriental" style devised by nineteenth-century European composers—especially French composers—to treat exotic subjects. This oriental music can be characterized in terms of a number of almost clichéd melodic, harmonic, and timbral devices, which I need not describe here and which bear no necessary relation to the actual musical practices of non-European cultures. It's the sort of music we associate with snake-charmers. These conventions were recognized at the time (and can still be recognized today) as denoting the strange, the exotic, in a word the "oriental." They make their significant historical debut in Meyerbeer's *L'Africaine,* which took Europe by storm in the 1860s and left a strong impression on Verdi. They can also be heard in a number of other operas roughly contemporaneous with *Aida,* notably *Carmen, Le Roi de Lahore,* and above all *Samson et Dalila.*

We must, then, consider Verdi's deployment of these oriental conventions in *Aida* in order to assess Said's claim that the opera presents "an Orientalized Egypt." Verdi confines his oriental music in the opera to two functions, both of them ceremonial: he uses it for liturgical exercises and for ballets. None of the main Egyptian characters expresses him- or herself, as it were, orientally. Rather, all of their singing is in Verdi's standard high European mode, as is all the choral and march music he writes for the assembled Egyptian masses. (In purely quantitative terms, the oriental idiom occurs in no more than a tenth of the opera's music.) Nonetheless, the oriental style can be heard in three important liturgical episodes: first, in the great consecration scene in the Temple of Vulcan, where Radamès performs the ritual preparations for the coming battle with the Ethiopians; second, at the beginning of the Nile scene, which opens with priests and priestesses chanting in the Temple of Isis; and, finally, in the last scene of the opera, the tomb scene, where, sealed in a vault below the Temple of Vulcan, Aida and Radamès sing their final duet as the priestesses above are again heard intoning the liturgical chant we know from the consecration scene. A related—albeit livelier—exotic musical language is used by Verdi for the opera's three ballets: the dance of the priestesses in the consecration scene, the dance of the Little Moorish Slaves in Amneris's apartments, and the seven-part grand ballet in the middle of the triumphal scene. In total, there are three liturgical scenes and three ballets for which Verdi composes "oriental" music.

Several considerations, however, undermine any ready or unqualified association of this exotic liturgical and ballet music with the Egyptians. These considerations account for our tendency to hear this music as somehow belonging to a different sonic realm from that normally inhabited by the Egyptians. In some cases the dissociation occurs because the performers in a particular liturgical episode or ballet are either themselves non-Egyptians or are connected with non-Egyptian paraphernalia. Thus, most obviously, the Little Moorish Slaves who entertain Amneris are, of course, captives—like the Ethiopians, they are the victims of Egyptian imperialism—so the exotic character of their dance music hardly serves to create "an Orientalized Egypt." If anything, it has just the opposite effect. Likewise, the dancers in the triumphal scene ballet, while presumably Egyptian, dance around "the spoils of victory" appropriated from the conquered Ethiopians, so that the exotic music of the ballet comes to be associated in our minds less with Egypt than with

Ethiopia. Interestingly, in the famous Berlin production of *Aida* by Wieland Wagner (which I saw in the early 1960s), the whole triumphal scene took the form, as Said accurately records, of a "parade of Ethiopian prisoners carrying totems, masks, ritual objects as elements of an ethnographic exhibition presented directly to the audience," which was part of Wieland's effort to transfer the "setting of the work from the Egypt of the Pharaohs to the darker Africa of a prehistoric age." Furthermore, one should note that all of the opera's exotic music, in both its liturgical episodes and its ballets, is associated with women—to the point that the antithesis between exotic and nonexotic music in *Aida* comes to seem a code as much for gender difference as for national or ethnic difference. Thus the distinctly exotic chant in the consecration scene is sung by a priestess. The succeeding ballet for the priestesses—written in the oriental manner—is, of course, danced exclusively by women. Likewise, the great ballet of the triumphal scene, despite its vigorously masculine music, calls exclusively for ballerinas. Even the dance of the Little Moorish Slaves—already, one would presume, sufficiently feminized by being so described—is also, Verdi says, to be performed by ballerinas. The only oriental music in the opera actually assigned to men is that for the priests in the Temple of Isis at the beginning of act 3 (the Nile scene), and, significantly, their chant again has a feminine association: the priests sing to "Isis, mother and bride of Osiris." At this point one should perhaps observe that all of the archaeological evidence available to Verdi when he composed the opera indicated that the ancient Egyptians had no priestesses, only priests, but Verdi asked Mariette if it might be possible to invent the priestesses, and Mariette—no stickler for authenticity— was only too happy to oblige Verdi with as many priestesses as his heart desired.

Finally, on every occasion when Verdi introduces exotic music into *Aida*, he immediately answers it with music of impeccably occidental credentials. Moreover, these occidental responses are always set in the mouth of some unambiguously *Egyptian* character, either one of the principals (such as Amneris or Ramfis) or the massed chorus of Egyptian citizens and soldiers. It is as if Verdi were unconsciously seeking to inhibit any association of the Egyptians with the oriental—which also explains why, ethnically speaking, *Aida*'s exotic music seems to occupy a kind of no-man's land. I want to cite here just one instance of this dialectic of exotic thesis and occidental antithesis, namely, its first occurrence in the opera. This is the chant of the priestess in the Temple of Vulcan at the start of the consecration scene. The invisible soprano's wailing incantation "in an invented Phrygian mode" (as Julian Budden writes), set above distant harps and supported by female choristers, has many of the musical earmarks of the oriental style, including a repeated grace-note on the flattened second degree, diminished thirds, augmented seconds, and a curling arabesque, all of which, in Budden's words, "color the music with a sense of strange Eastern ritual." But the priestess's melody is immediately answered by a litany of the priests, which is composed in the deeply ingratiating harmonies of the high European idiom. I suppose one might say that it is an instance of "East meets West," except, of course, that all of the singers are Egyptians. Significantly, in my view, the orientalizing singer—the priestess—is female, while the occidentalizing ones—the priests—are male.

The same sort of juxtaposition, in which the exotic East is trumped by the conventional West, occurs in each instance where Verdi momentarily introduces oriental musical effects. Thus the exotic dance of the priestesses in the consecration scene is immediately followed by Ramfis's emphatically diatonic invocation to the gods, a four-square arpeggiated tune with the vocal line firmly supported by pulsating trombones, and the entire consecration scene ends with Ramfis and Radamès trumpeting the priestess's apotheosis to "immenso Fthà" in euphonious thirds, sung at the top of their lungs (and very near the top of the registers as well). Likewise, the dance of the Little Moorish Slaves is immediately followed (and, as it were, ideologically cancelled) by the familiar Western harmonies of Amneris's servants and by Amneris's own sumptuously diatonic invocation of love. The orientalist extravaganza of the triumphal scene ballet—the most sustained stretch of exotic music in the opera—is followed by a repetition of the pompously Westernized victory hymn, "Gloria all'Egitto." Finally, the exotic chant to the goddess Isis at the beginning of the Nile scene—like the dance of the priestesses in the consecration scene of act 1—gives way to a thoroughly Western and warmly ingratiating arioso for Ramfis, inviting Amneris into the temple. Repeatedly, the music of the Occident seems to negate that of the putative Orient.

I do not want to deny that some of this oriental music, as it were, rubs off on Egypt, thus giving substance to Said's contention that *Aida* has the effect of creating "an Orientalized Egypt," one alluding subliminally to the incorporation of nineteenth-century Egypt into the European empire. Under closer examination, however, it is not precisely Egypt that is orientalized by Verdi's exotic music but rather Egypt's imperial victims (the Moors and the Ethiopians), and, among the Egyptians themselves, state functionaries and entertainers, almost all of whom turn out to be women (and thus, presumably, not full-fledged members of Egyptian society). So the ideological import of Verdi's exotic musical gestures in the opera is more complicated than Said allows, and in some respects it seems to be exactly opposite from the construction he insists on.

If we ask what is the source in Verdi's imagination of the ideological universe on display in *Aida*, I would suggest that we look not to Europe's oriental expansion in the late nineteenth century but to the politics of the Italian risorgimento in the 1840s. *Aida* is in fact the last of the operas in which the imprint of Verdi's deep commitment to the risorgimento can still be detected. It is heir to the tradition of operas like *Attila, I Lombardi,* and, above all, *Nabucco,* in which the political repression of Italy by the Austrians is metaphorically represented by the subjugation of the ancient Hebrews under the Babylonians. In Verdi's imagination, Italy was always a colonized country, the victim of Hapsburg imperialism. In writing *Aida,* I would contend, he associated Ethiopia with Italy, just as he associated Egypt with Hapsburg Austria. Likewise, Ramfis and the Egyptian priesthood are products of Verdi's risorgimento anticlericalism; they are equated in his mind with the Hapsburg Catholic hierarchy and the reactionary politics of the Roman papacy. The ideological heart of *Aida,* so to speak, lies in the magnificent outburst of Amonasro in his duet with Aida, where he calls on her to remember her people "conquered and tormented" ("vinto, straziato"). Verdi sets Amonasro's plea on one of those great arching phrases of which he was the supreme master, carrying the voice upward in an arc of passion to a high G flat, and then bringing it back down to rest in the sonic territory from which it began. It is my favorite phrase in the opera—a wonderful opportunity for the high baritone—and it identifies Amonasro and the Ethiopians with all those conquered and divided nations that people Verdi's risorgimento operas of the 1840s and that stand for his own "conquered and tormented" Italy.

In sum, one can make much more sense of the politics of *Aida* if one regards it first and foremost as an Italian opera, rather than an orientalist opera, and if one sees it as the final installment in the tradition of Verdi's political operas reaching back to the 1840s. In spite of its sophistication and refinement, *Aida* is still at heart a traditional number opera, whose musical language looks backward to *Rigoletto* and *Il trovatore* rather than forward to *Otello* and *Falstaff,* just as its politics look back to the risorgimento rather than forward to the fully realized European imperium.

CHAPTER SEVEN

The Wagner Problem

In this essay I suggest that Wagner has been overestimated as an intellectual. His situation is the opposite of the other great opera composers, whose neglected intellectual seriousness has been the underlying theme of all my writings on opera. The essay consists of two parts. In the first (not before published) I trace the history of Wagner's reputation, arguing that the earlier emphasis on his ideas (including German nationalism and anti-Semitism) has yielded to a salutary appreciation of the musical and dramatic skills he shares with his operatic peers, Mozart and Verdi. In the second (which originated as a review in the Cambridge Opera Journal *[March 1995]) I consider the recent attempt by the important opera theorist Jean-Jacques Nattiez to give Wagner a new intellectual profile as a gender-bender, an effort that founders, as do most conceptual interpretations of opera, on its failure to consider the musical (as opposed to the merely textual) evidence.*

The appearance in English translation of Jean-Jacques Nattiez's *Wagner Androgyne* (Princeton, 1993; French original 1990) provides an occasion to consider, once again, Wagner's unique stature in the history of opera. Nattiez calls himself a "musical semiologist," and he holds distinctly irreverent opinions. In the case of Wagner, he aims to show that the figure so greatly admired as a composer and no less greatly loathed as a progenitor of modern anti-Semitism is more properly understood as a sexual theorist, and one of a decidedly postmodern bent. Yet, while the sexual views Nattiez attributes to Wagner are certainly novel, his book ultimately lapses into the old (and, in my view, bad) habit of taking Wagner too seriously as a thinker and not seriously enough as an artist. Where every other important opera composer (most notably Verdi) has been underestimated intellectually, Wagner has suffered exactly the opposite fate: his intellectual claims have been accepted at face value, by friends and enemies alike, and the result has been a distorted picture of his achievement.

I

Wagner's image has undergone a remarkable series of transformations since his operatic career began just over a century and a half ago. There have been three main stages: the literary-philosophical, the political, and the musical. During his own lifetime and into the second decade of the twentieth century he was considered a figure as much of intellectual as of musical history. His prose writings were nearly as well known as his operas, and he exercised a profound influence on extramusical life, above all on the literary symbolists and decadents in France and England. Thanks in large part to Adolf Hitler, Wagner the anti-Semite and rabid German nationalist became the dominant image of the interwar years, despite the existence of a sophisticated left-wing, indeed socialist, interpretation of the operas, notably in George Bernard Shaw's *The Perfect Wagnerite* of 1898. Since the Second World War, Wagner has come to be perceived more and more simply as a great composer, indeed as one of the three greatest (along with Mozart and Verdi) in the history of opera. Doubtless Wagner himself would have balked at so modest an estimate, but his equation with Verdi is now a critical commonplace. The emergence of Wagner the composer, stripped of his intellectual pretensions and ugly political views, has been aided by the Bayreuth stagings of the operas under his grandson Wieland—who reduced them to their bare psychological essentials, thereby allowing the music to work its magic—and by the disinterested scholarly efforts of a generation of musicologists. As a consequence, Wagner has been increasingly embraced by music lovers who care little about him as a thinker or progenitor of National Socialism.

Wagner's enormous intellectual prestige in the nineteenth century now seems almost incomprehensible. Yet many of its seminal figures—

among them Nietzsche and Baudelaire—took him very seriously as a philosopher and poet. His writings—which in the collected edition fill sixteen volumes—have a certain polemical vigor, but for modern readers they are ruined by their exaggeration, their racism, and their bombast. Not surprisingly, the most valuable of the writings are those, like *Opera and Drama* (1851), that examine the fundamental nature of opera. The position Wagner adopts is characteristically extreme: he proscribes all concerted and choral music as incompatible with dramatic truth, a proscription he wisely disregarded in the splendid concerted endings of the first act of *Tristan* and the second act of *Meistersinger*. But his insistence that the music in opera be in the service of the drama remains compelling, and he advanced this doctrine more singlemindedly than anyone before or since.

Still, no responsible student of European intellectual history would now take his amateurish, inconsistent, and largely derivative pronouncements about life and politics as a significant contribution to the history of philosophy or social theory. Strictly as a thinker Wagner was a hopeless third-rater. If the operas did not exist, no one today would bother to read the prose writings. His considerable powers of mind found expression not in his writings but in his operas, which exhibit unparalleled control over musical and dramatic argument. Much the same can be said about his purely literary accomplishments. Without their music the texts have little life beyond the academy. Wagner's language is at its best when it achieves the sort of concise dramatic effect Verdi called "la parola scenica." In other words, Wagner is, along with Da Ponte and Boito, one of the supreme librettists. But that does not make him a poet.

Nor are the operas distinguished by their intellectual content. On the contrary, that content has generally been exaggerated (as in the case of *Tristan und Isolde*) or, where its importance is undeniable (as in the *Ring*), it must be judged largely baleful. Wagner himself made much of his reading of Schopenhauer's *The World as Will and Representation* in 1854, but *Tristan* is far from a Schopenhauerian opera. Its celebration of sexual desire stands at odds with the philosopher's radical asceticism, and, like any opera, it also violates his dictum that music should never be contaminated by language. Wagner's own contribution to asceticism in

Parsifal is more genuinely Schopenhauerian, not least in its misogyny, but *Parsifal*'s obsessive concern with redemption fits badly with Schopenhauer's pessimism and hatred of Christianity.

The *Ring*, alas, is intellectually in earnest. Indeed, its intellectual ambitions keep it from achieving the consistency of musical and dramatic inspiration that distinguishes *Tristan* and *Meistersinger*. Some passages are beyond praise. (Is there anything more perfect than the first act of *Die Walküre?*) But one often has the sense of being lectured at by a mildly incompetent professor of philosophy, who has packed too much material into his course and whose ideas seem always on the verge of collapsing under their own weight and contradictions. The *Ring*'s conceptual shortcomings are underlined by Wagner's abuse of the leitmotif technique, which (as in the irruption of the sword motif near the end of *Rheingold*) verges on the mechanical—the musical equivalent of the textual balloons in a comic strip. How much more discriminating—and hence effective—is Wagner's deployment of the same procedure in *Tristan* and *Meistersinger*. Shaw was right in insisting that the *Ring* begins better than it ends. *Rheingold* is a brilliant anti-capitalist allegory, blessed with economy and wit. But the cycle never recovers from the callow preening and musical brutality introduced by the young Siegfried in the third of the operas.

The political interpretation of Wagner advanced by the Nazis is firmly grounded in the prose writings. At its heart, of course, stands Wagner's anti-Semitism. The locus classicus is the 1850 essay "Judaism in Music," in which Wagner describes the typical "physical appearance of the Jews" that inspires "instinctive revulsion" in gentiles. He also attributes the inability of Jewish composers, like Meyerbeer and Mendelssohn, to create authentic works of art (the Jew's only real talent being for finance) to their cultural rootlessness. As he grew older Wagner's anti-Semitism became more pronounced. It is painfully documented in Cosima Wagner's diaries, which give a day-by-day account of Wagner's activities and remarks from 1869 until his death in 1883. There we may read, for example, how in an 1881 conversation about Lessing's *Nathan der Weise*, Wagner made "a drastic joke to the effect that all Jews should be burned at a performance of *Nathan*." He took particular pride in the thought that his youthful writings had anticipated the more widespread and "scientific" anti-Semitism of the late nineteenth century. Increasingly he held that the only hope for the Jews was to annihilate themselves by conversion to Christianity.

Do the operas reflect this anti-Semitism? In the *Wagner Handbook*, Dieter Borchmeyer advances the traditional view that they are untainted, and that "in all of Wagner's innumerable commentaries on his own works there is not a single statement that would entitle us to interpret any of the characters in the music dramas or any of the details of their plots in anti-Semitic terms." By contrast, Barry Millington, in *The Wagner Compendium*, reflects the growing consensus that Wagner the composer is not so easily exonerated. In 1952 Theodor Adorno argued that, by Wagner's own criteria, the Niebelungen dwarfs who horde gold in the *Ring* are suspiciously Jewish-looking, and that the antithesis between short, dark Mime and blond, athletic Siegfried seems very much like the stereotypical opposition between Jew and German. More recently, in the *Cambridge Opera Journal*, Millington has made a persuasive case for regarding Beckmesser's whining pedantries in the second act of *Meistersinger* as a parody of cantorial singing. The only character Wagner expressly identifies as Jewish—indeed, as modeled on the Wandering Jew—is Kundry, who bears none of the physical stigmata of the Niebelungen but whose baptism in the third act of *Parsifal* seems to embody Wagner's solution to the Jewish Problem.

Surely, however, the most important thing to be said on this subject is that, unlike the prose writings, the music dramas yield anti-Semitic readings only when subjected to aggressive interpretation. The vast majority of opera-goers, I do not doubt, are sublimely oblivious to the idea that Alberich, Mime, and Beckmesser might be Jews or that the operas could be construed as anti-Semitic allegories. Put another way, Wagner's creative genius seems to have protected him from infecting his artistic creations with the hateful views he spouted in his prose works. It is as if they embody only his better self, reflecting a moral sensibility distressingly absent from his writings and his life. Wagner is arguably the most impoverished human being among great artists, yet in Hans Sachs he created one of the most admirable characters in opera, a man who sacrifices his happiness for the sake of his community. Here as elsewhere, Wagner's artistic conscience seems to have been categorically superior to his personal behavior or political convictions.

The musical Wagner who has emerged in more recent years—Wagner as "mere" opera composer rather than philosopher or political guru —remains a formidable figure. The great students of Wagner the musician are Alfred Lorenz, Ernest Newman, and Carl Dahlhaus, who, along with the numerous lesser lights of the international Wagner consortium, have brought us a fuller understanding of his compositional procedures and innovations (above all in the realm of harmony) as well as a more precise sense of his place in the history of music. Judged musically, Wagner shares many of the virtues of the other great opera composers, including his insufficiently appreciated distinction as a melodist. What sets him apart is his ability to encompass large stretches of material into a unified musical argument. One feels the long Wagnerian reach already in *Der fliegende Holländer*, where the Senta-Dutchman duet unfolds in a single musical arch. As Wagner matured, that reach came to embrace whole acts. Thus act 1 of *Die Walküre* remains in the mind's ear as a seamless, hour-long progression from despair to ecstasy. A comparable control over vast territory is displayed in the music of Tristan's delirium. No other opera composer approaches these feats of musical architecture. Wagner's works are the most complete realization of the nineteenth-century's historic evolution from numbers operas to through composition.

Wagner's mastery of large-scale musical structure reflects an artistic discipline unique in history. All of his operas after *Der fliegende Holländer* were conceived in the 1840s and then executed over the course of the next forty years. The composition of the *Ring* in particular bespeaks an almost inhuman capacity for delayed gratification. Wagner wrote the prose sketch for the tetralogy in October 1848. After completing *Das Rheingold, Die Walküre*, and the first two acts of *Siegfried* in the 1850s, he set the entire project aside to compose *Tristan und Isolde* and *Die Meistersinger*. Only after a twelve-year hiatus did he return to the *Ring*, finishing it for the opening of Bayreuth in 1876—which, save for a single performance (insisted on by King Ludwig) of *Das Rheingold* and *Die Walküre* in the early 1870s, was the first time Wagner heard the massive enterprise he had been nurturing for nearly three decades. This unique artistic singlemindedness seems the exact antithesis of the self-indulgence and disarray of his life.

II

The central claim of Jean-Jacques Nattiez's *Wagner Androgyne* can be easily stated. Wagner's thought and art, Nattiez maintains, are androgynous, just as Wagner himself was an androgyne. For most opera-goers, as indeed for most Wagner scholars, the idea will seem immediately preposterous. Nattiez would not be disappointed in that reaction, for he is nothing if not *méchant,* and his book is inspired, at least in part, by the desire to *épater* the Wagnerian bourgeoisie. Moroever, "preposterous" would be the correct response if by androgyny Nattiez meant an ideal of human personality in which sexual differences have been eliminated— an ideal of mannish women and effeminate men. For the most part, how-ever, androgyny serves him as a red (or, better, pink) herring with which to rile or titillate his readers. His actual ideas turn out to be a good deal more conventional.

Nattiez confesses to a weakness for pastiche. And in truth his notion of how to write a book is wildly undisciplined. Rather than an economi-cal presenation of the case for androgyny in Wagner's life and work, he offers a grab bag of ideas and ruminations, many of which have no con-nection with either Wagner or androgyny. The final third of the book in particular wanders indulgently over a vast conceptual terrain, as Nattiez argues with dozens of theorists, from Friedrich Engels to Jacques Der-rida, about questions of interpretation, seeking to position himself to the right of the deconstructionists and to the left of the academic fundamen-talists. Still, he is a lively and genial interlocutor, and, so long as one is not annoyed by his unwillingness to stick to the subject, there is much here that is suggestive and even enlightening.

As far as androgyny is concerned, Nattiez focuses on three moments in Wagner's career, each reflecting, he argues, a different conception of the androgynous ideal. The first is the period of the Zurich writings, es-pecially *Opera and Drama,* and it is represented artistically by the *Ring,* above all the Siegfried-Brünnhilde duet from *Siegfried* (the text of which —though not, of course, the music—belongs to the Zurich period).

Nattiez characterizes this first ideal, oxymoronically, as "male androgyny" and ascribes it to the influence of Feuerbach. The second moment is associated with the Beethoven essay among Wagner's writings and *Tristan und Isolde* among the operas. The ideal now becomes "female androgyny," as the influence of Feuerbach gives way to that of Schopenhauer. The final moment Nattiez calls "asexual androgyny" or "angelic androgyny," and, not surprisingly, it is embodied in *Parsifal,* as well as some of the final writings, although it lacks an explicit philosophical pedigree comparable to Feuerbach and Schopenhauer for the earlier phases.

The first of these—the ideal of "male androgyny"—occupies most of Nattiez's attention. In the theoretical writings he finds the main evidence for this ideal in a sexual metaphor Wagner adopts: the work of art, Wagner writes, results from a fusion of poetry and music, in which poetry is the masculine element and music the feminine element. Poetry, Wagner writes, is the "procreative seed . . . that provides music, that gloriously loving woman, with the subject matter that she must bear." Leaving aside the question of how much interpretive weight one should assign a metaphor—especially in a writer given to metaphorical prolixity and confusion, as Wagner demonstrably was—one might well argue that this particular metaphor is sexually reactionary. Far from suggesting a revolutionary dissolution of the familiar dimorphic categories of male and female—far, in other words, from endorsing androgyny—it in fact serves to shore up the notion of sexual difference, and it does so in the most hidebound fashion by associating maleness with articulate thought and femaleness with wordless emotion. It is of a piece with the separate spheres doctrine of Victorian ideology—historically the most extreme expression ever given to the opposition between male and female capacities—especially when it appears (as it often does in Wagner) in its full-blown nuclear form, where the work of art is identified with the child.

But what of Wagner himself? Does not his sexual metaphor implicate him personally in an androgynous identity in so far as he was both poet and composer, both father and mother of his artistic children? That is indeed the implication Nattiez wishes to draw, but he makes surprisingly little of it and barely explores its psychological significance. Again, assuming we can take this metaphor (among the hundreds, probably thousands, in the Wagner corpus) seriously, what consequences follow for Wagner's conception of himself or our understanding of his deeper motives? Does it imply he wished to transcend the masculinist prejudices of his time, to cultivate a more passive and feminine personality? Does it mean he was consciously or unconsciously homosexual? Nattiez shies away from either of these possibilities, although he lingers over Wagner's intense male friendships with Karl Ritter, King Ludwig II, and Peter Cornelius, whom Wagner hoped to induce to move in with him in 1864 and about whom he wrote: "Perhaps I shall get Cornelius to come. Shall I be able to renounce the 'eternal feminine' completely? Sighing deeply, I tell myself that I ought to wish that I could!—A glance at [Ludwig's] dear portrait helps me again! Ah, the dear young boy! I suppose he must now be everything to me; world, wife, and child!" But Nattiez is inclined to dismiss such talk as "Romantic effusiveness," and he huffily rejects the notion that the Knights of the Grail might represent "a gay community," as has been ingeniously argued by Richard Mohr. He mentions the addiction to silk dressing gowns and the "fascination with women's clothes," but he finds no great psychological significance in Wagner's foppishness or his seductive cultivation of men—themselves often homosexual, as in the case of Ludwig—from whom he had something to gain. "Was Wagner a friend of Dorothy because he conceived of music as a woman?" Ultimately the androgynous identity that seems to follow logically from Wagner's dual role as composer and poet remains an abstraction. We are not asked to abandon our concrete sense of Wagner as one of history's foremost male chauvinists and heterosexual lechers.

The effort to give an androgynous reading to the Siegfried-Brünnhilde duet—the artistic realization, according to Nattiez, of the sexual metaphor adopted in *Opera and Drama*—rests exclusively on an analysis of the duet's text. Nattiez makes two points. The first is that Brünnhilde is given male characteristics while Siegfried is given female ones. Siegfried, he notes, thinks Brünnhilde is a "man in armor" (never mind that the most famous moment in the opera comes precisely when he discovers his error: "Das ist kein Mann!"), and, more important, he compares her hair to "the radiant sunlight's smiling image," which, Nattiez maintains, identifies her with Siegfried even as it feminizes him, because "the sun is

Siegfried himself and, in modern German, the word *Sonne* is feminine."
Once again, a great deal is made to hang on a slender metaphorical reed.
Nattiez's second point is that Brünnhilde expressly claims to be "the
female half of Siegfried" when she sings "Du selbst bin ich." But the
doctrine being asserted here—which also finds expression in the *Tristan*
love duet—is not that maleness and femaleness should give way to some
intermediate form but rather the very different notion that individuality
must be abandoned in the fusion of two souls united in sexual union.
Moreover, precisely because it is a sexual union, and because nothing
suggests that Wagner ever conceived of sexual union in other than heterosexual terms, the abolition of self celebrated in the great love duets
presumes the existence of sexual difference as a necessary condition of
such an experience. The most helpful idea for grasping Wagner's conception is the Hegelian one of *Aufhebung,* in which the higher synthesis
at once overcomes and preserves the components out of which it is fashioned.

To be fair to Nattiez—who is nothing if not resourceful—he does
adduce one piece of documentary evidence that might seem to lend cred-
ibility to his main idea. It comes from neither the operas nor the published writings but a letter of 25/26 January 1854 to August Röckel.
There Wagner opines, "The highest satisfaction of individual egoism is
to be found in its total abandonment, and this is something that human
beings can achieve only through love: but *the true human being is both man
and woman,* and only in the union of man and woman does the true human being exist." The italics are supplied not by Wagner but by Nattiez,
thus lending a whiff of special pleading to his presentation. He insists
that the statement must be understood as a "gloss" on the Siegfried-
Brünnhilde duet but offers no evidence to support that contention. Nor
does he seem to notice that the last phrase ("only in the union of man and
woman does the true human being exist") restores the categorical distinction that the preceding phrase seems to abolish. Above all, he fails to
address the question of what weight we should assign to an ambiguous
sentence in a private correspondence, especially a sentence from a notoriously garrulous writer given to shooting from the hip.

A further embarrassment to Nattiez's interpretation is provided by
the existence of genuinely androgynous characters in the *Ring,* charac-

ters, moreover, toward whom Wagner adopts an attitude of official hostility. The two great androgynes of the tetralogy are not Siegfried and Brünnhilde but Loge and, especially, Mime, who claims to have been both father and mother to Siegfried. My own view is that Wagner is fonder of Loge and Mime than he pretends to be. Certainly he lavishes on them music that I find more ingratiating than the noisy hectoring of the young Siegfried. Perhaps he had a soft spot for androgyny after all. But no one can deny that, both characterologically and musically, Loge and Mime are rendered so as to suggest more than a touch of swishiness, which stands in contrast to the unambiguous sexual orthodoxy of the other characters. We sense the invidious sexual comparison especially in the opposition between Mime and Siegfried in the first act of Siegfried, but it is also present, if more subtly, in that between manly Wotan and epicene Loge in the second scene of *Rheingold*. For Nattiez, however, Mime is not the genuine item. He has simply "tried to pass himself off as androgynous" and is rightly killed by Siegfried, who, along with Brünnhilde, represents "the type of androgyny that is uniquely worthy of the artist of the future."

The love duet from *Tristan und Isolde,* with its elaborate rhetorical exchange of identities ("Tristan du, ich Isolde, nicht mehr Tristan!" "Du Isolde, Tristan ich, nicht mehr Isolde!"), would seem to provide more fertile ground for an androgynous interpretation than the relatively terse "Du selbst bin ich" of the Siegfried duet, although the essential issue remains, I would contend, not androgyny but the loss of self in the erotic other—and, of course, ultimately in death. But Nattiez is mainly concerned to show how the androgynous ideal of *Tristan* differs from that of *Siegfried* in that the active role has been assumed by the female member of the pair—hence "female androgyny." It is Isolde, he insists, "who, from first to last, actuates the lovers' androgynous union." The preeminence of the woman corresponds, appropriately, to the preeminence of music in *Tristan*. Furthermore, it exactly reflects the new theoretical position Wagner adopted in the 1860s and early 1870s, above all in the *Beethoven* essay (which dates from 1870). In *Opera and Drama* Wagner had argued that poetry—the male element—predominated. His critique of Italian opera, for example, rested on its false (and womanish) subordination of drama to music, against which his own manly practice would restore the just authority of the impregnating word. Now, however, he reverses himself. To be sure, music remains a woman, but it is no longer the passive receptacle in which the verbal seed is deposited but rather the "mother" that gives birth to the drama. Music has replaced poetry as the dominant partner, inspiring the poet to fashion words that will express its deep emotional logic. Nattiez sensibly points out that Wagner was driven to this reconceptualization—or this new metaphorical gambit—by the experience of composing *Tristan und Isolde,* when, according to his own endearing account, he permitted himself to be carried away on a flood tide of music: "I completely forgot all my theorizing, . . . since I acted here in total freedom and in utter disregard of every theoretical consideration, so that only during the process of composition did I myself become aware to what extent I had transcended my own system." Nattiez might have added that *Tristan* is a finer work for having been liberated from the procrustean bed of theory that often leaves the *Ring* excessively literary and mechanical. Doubtless Wagner's distinctive achievement cannot be separated from his intellectual pretensions— that is the burden of Thomas S. Grey's closely reasoned argument in *Wagner's Musical Prose* (1995). But he was nonetheless an incomparably greater composer than a thinker or writer, and he is at his most inspired, as in *Tristan,* when he is in the grips of a musical rather than a philosophical idea.

Nattiez seems stuck in his own procrustean bed when he insists on describing the ideal of *Parsifal* as "angelic androgyny." He recognizes that there can no longer be any question of a union of male and female, as in *Siegfried* and *Tristan,* because women have been banished from the all-male world of the Grail. Parsifal, of course, champions celibacy. It is the guilty recantation of a libertine entering male menopause, the sort of renunciatory gesture that has become a wearisome cliché in the lives of former revolutionaries, whether political or sexual. But what possible intellectual purpose is served by calling sexlessness androgyny? And why dignify Wagner's tired conception—which is also, as Nattiez notes, his most anti-Semitic—with the trappings of conceptual coherence by asserting that "*Parsifal* takes the androgynous myth to its logical conclusion." More than any of Wagner's works, *Parsifal*'s greatness is a purely musical affair. In *Richard Wagner and the Synthesis of the Arts* (1960) Jack

Stein shows that it has the shortest libretto and the longest performance time of any of the operas and that all its motifs except one originate in the orchestra rather than the voices. Debussy famously called it "one of the most beautiful edifices in sound ever raised to the eternal glory of music." In no other important opera, unless it be *Il trovatore,* are we so willing to ignore what is being said (and done) in order to bask in the sheer loveliness of the music.

Nattiez's case is damaged, then, by overreaching and insufficient discrimination. It is also weakened by his failure to mount a musical—as opposed to a purely textual—argument for the centrality of androgyny in Wagner. In particular he offers no musical analysis of his chosen passages from the *Siegfried* and *Tristan* duets to suggest how they carry the particular significance he attributes to them. Toward the end of the book, admittedly, he argues that the *Tristan* chord should be regarded as androgynous, because it "belongs potentially to two tonalities, E and A," where E represents Isolde and A Tristan, but this discussion is not related to the crucial passages in the duets. Beyond the question of musical analysis, moreover, Nattiez gives little evidence of having reflected on the actual sounds we hear in the operas. Should he not at least consider the effect on our notions of sexual identity of the radically gendered vocalizing we hear in Wagner, as in nearly all opera? Wagner's sopranos and tenors produce sounds that are unmistakably either masculine or feminine. Virtually every note Siegfied and Brünnhilde or Tristan and Isolde emit, including at those moments when they are claiming to have lost themselves in one another, reminds us of their sexual difference. The aural effect of the duets, I submit, is to heighten, rather than undermine, our consciousness of the male-female dichotomy.

Nattiez does offer musical judgments in his book, but too often they are ham-fisted. Having shown that Alberich's encounter with Flosshilde might be seen as a parody of the duet between Valentine and Raoul in *Les Huguenots,* he fails to note that the passage is nonetheless very beautiful and even a little heart-breaking. Likewise, to describe Alberich's idiom as "ridiculous and grotesque" is to fall victim to Wagner's tendentious conception rather than to listen to the music that, in his artistic wisdom, he actually composes for his dwarf. A similar conceptual prejudice is on display when Nattiez calls Gutrune an "operatic whore"—endorsing

Pierre Boulez's judgment that "everything about Gutrune is light in character, not to say frivolous, both brilliant and empty, thus reflecting the character herself"—on the basis of a comparison between one of her phrases and Auber's *La Muette de Portici,* without noticing the aura of pathetic desperation and innate sweetness that Wagner imparts to her music. In these and other matters Nattiez falls into the familiar trap of an excessive reverence for Wagner the theoretician and writer—the figure in intellectual history—and a corresponding neglect of his skills as a dramatist and above all a composer.

I have been severe in my criticism because of Nattiez's failure to sustain his central thesis. But when he is not riding his androgynous hobbyhorse he often has incisive things to say. He provides a brilliant, if sketchy, reading of the *Ring* as an encoding of Wagner's conception of the history of music, beginning with the Rhinemaidens as the three Greek muses (dance, music, and poetry). Equally impressive is his account of Wagner's evolving notions about the relation between poetry and music in opera, where Nattiez charts a persuasive middle course between Jack Stein's insistence on the volatility of Wagner's ideas and Frank Glass's argument for their consistency. Among the many theoretical and interpretive subjects taken up in the final section of the book, I would single out for praise his effective dismantling of Robert Donington's Jungian interpretation of the *Ring,* which Nattiez shows to be ungrounded in the available documentation and arbitrary to the point of silliness. On the questions of sexual identity and sexual ideals, however, he remains unconvincing. In many matters, musical as well as intellectual, Wagner, as we know, is the great avatar of modernism. Yet when it comes to gender and sexuality he belongs not among the nineteenth-century's vanguard (alongside the Pre-Raphaelites or the Saint-Simonians) but among its unreconstructed defenders of tradition.

CHAPTER EIGHT

Richard Strauss,
Ambivalent Modernist

This brief essay began life as my contribution to a panel discussion, organized by David Littlejohn, in conjunction with the San Francisco Opera's Celebration of Strauss in the summer of 1993. In keeping with the theme of celebration it offers a somewhat guilty defense of Strauss's infamous betrayal of modernism, when, after 1910, he abandoned the astringent musical language of his early masterpieces Salome *and* Elektra *and turned to the ingratiating melodic and harmonic manner (so hated by the theorists and practitioners of atonality) of works like* Rosenkavalier, Ariadne auf Naxos, Arabella, *and* Capriccio.

Let me begin by establishing a suitably modest level of competence. I am not a Strauss scholar, not even a musicologist, although my book *Opera and Ideas* does contain a chapter on *Rosenkavalier*. Rather, I am a European intellectual historian who has been interested in the connection between opera and the history of thought—or between opera and cultural history more broadly conceived.

Seen from this perspective, the most remarkable thing about Richard Strauss is his ambivalent relation to modernism, the dominant cultural movement or tendency of the twentieth century. I don't want to enter upon an effort to define modernism, but I think we all recognize it as having involved a radical break with the conceptual and stylistic assumptions of nineteenth-century romanticism. Modernism has become the common rubric under which we comprehend the literature of Joyce and

Kafka, the paintings of Picasso and Matisse, and the music of Schoenberg and Stravinsky.

In the musical realm modernism entailed, above all, a drastic curtailment of the satisfactions of nineteenth-century melody and harmony, and it tended logically to atonality. Richard Strauss's relation to musical modernism in this sense was spectacularly ambivalent. In the first decade of the twentieth century he was its leading representative, most famously in *Salome* (1905) and *Elektra* (1909). He was the composer who, more than any other, seemed destined to lead music into the modern world. But he then became, in the remaining four decades of his career, the most notorious renegade from the modernist cause. From *Rosenkavalier* in 1911 to the *Four Last Songs* of 1948, he moved inexorably backward into the world of nineteenth-century harmonic and melodic gratifications, a world of glorious euphony. In 1928 he called the works of the arch-modernists Arnold Schoenberg and Ernst Krenek "goat dung."

Because of this betrayal, no composer of the twentieth century has been more reviled by the loyal practitioners of modernism, whether composers or critics. In the latter regard I am thinking particularly of Theodor Adorno, who in 1964 said of Strauss's late music that it "arouses nausea." Strauss's apostasy seemed all the more galling because he was the most lavishly talented of all twentieth-century composers, a man who had the technical wherewithal to be for modernism what Beethoven had been for romanticism. But, according to the critics, he lacked the aesthetic integrity to fulfill his modernist promise. His retreat into the musical past, it is suggested, represented a sell-out to popular tastes, to the forces of reaction, and ultimately to profit. Hence the picture of Strauss as a bourgeois philistine, a vulgar Skat-playing musical profiteer, the German counterpart of Puccini, and ultimately a Nazi fellow-traveler.

Recent criticism (such as the volume *Richard Strauss and His World*, edited by Bryan Gilliam) has argued that the story of Strauss-the-wayward-modernist has become a cliché very much in need of reexamination. But I continue to be persuaded by its fundamental usefulness: as an ideal type or an overarching historical construction of Strauss's career, it still makes a lot of sense to me. Think, if you will, of two contrasting moments in his operas: first, Klytemnestra's long narrative in *Elektra* and, second, the scene of the presentation of the rose in

Rosenkavalier, and recall that these pieces date from within two years of one another (1909 and 1911). Klytemnestra's great narrative is an impeccably modernist exercise, its eerie bitonality and scrupulous avoidance of melody a perfect musical realization of the character's utterly shattered nerves. Two years later, in the presentation of the rose scene, the very same composer overwhelms the listener with a glorious display of diatonicism and a riot of surprising but always gratifying modulations. Moreover, the music of *Rosenkavalier* set the pattern for the future: this is the sort of music we hear again and again in the climactic moments of *Ariadne auf Naxos, Die Frau ohne Schatten, Arabella, Daphne, Capriccio,* and, most seductively of all, the *Four Last Songs.*

Let me concede that the contrast between the modern and the reactionary Strauss can be overdrawn. The later operas have their astringent moments: much the music for the Dyer's Wife in *Die Frau ohne Schatten,* for example, is hardly ingratiating. Conversely, the supposedly modernist works of the first decade of the twentieth century contain more than a few hints of what lies ahead. For me the most telling instance is the final modulation in *Elektra,* where, after nearly two hours of psychological horror set to music of appropriate austerity and violence, Strauss ends the opera with an utterly unearned, cynical, and thunderous C-major chord. I enjoy that triumphalist moment as much as the next listener, but not with a clear conscience.

While I believe, as noted, that the most intriguing pattern in Strauss's career is his about-face with regard to modernism, I disagree with the critics who lament his betrayal. On the contrary, I enjoy the later Strauss operas more than any other music of the twentieth century, and I listen to them far more often than I do to those of other modern composers. I can take satisfaction from Alban Berg and (to a far greater extent) from Benjamin Britten in the theater, where they are undeniably powerful, but at home with my CD player I prefer Strauss. There are few passages in music I find more beautiful, for example, than Ariadne's opening monologue, and to hear a perfect Straussian soprano, such as Gundula Janowitz, trace those glorious sonic arcs is for me among the ultimate operatic pleasures. You might say that if Strauss betrayed modernism, I am inclined to think, so much the worse for modernism—and so much the better for art. Put another way, I believe that he was much wiser than he is given credit for: he turned his back on the twentieth century not because he was a cretin and a materialist but because he knew that modernism offered insufficient musical space for his great gifts as a melodist and harmonist. He was being true to his muse rather than to his time.

I am intrigued by the notion that *Rosenkavalier,* in particular, derives much of its charm and power from the way it "thematizes" (as the literary critics now like to say) the drama of Strauss's career as a composer. There is, I believe, a complex affinity between the problematics of time as they are dramatized in the character of the Marschallin and in the life of Strauss the composer. *Rosenkavalier* is obsessed with time. Not to put too fine a point on the matter, it is an opera about growing old gracefully. How significant, it seems to me, that this story in which the future overtakes the past should find Strauss wrestling, so to speak, with the musical past, as it invades and ultimately overwhelms the modernist idiom of his earlier work. You could say that Strauss pointedly failed to heed the example of his own Marschallin: growing old gracefully, in musical terms, is exactly what he refused to do. Instead, he sought to make the musical clock stand still, even to turn it back. I've speculated, in *Opera and Ideas,* that his fascination with the Marschallin was as much a matter of envy as of identification.

I also think it may be useful to regard Strauss's predicament as merely an exaggerated version of a tension found in many modern composers, and perhaps in modernism itself. One can make a fairly plausible case that modern composers, unlike their baroque, classical, and romantic forebears, are chronically given to musical backsliding, in which they temporarily abandon their usual manner in order to exploit the musical past. Stravinsky's neo-classical phase, above all *Pulcinella,* is only the most obvious example of this tendency. Schoenberg, of course, seems to have been constitutionally immune to the disorder, unless we count his magnificent orchestration of Brahms's Piano Quartet. Before the twentieth century, composers had a completely unproblematic relation to musical history: their work comfortably found its place in a seamless continuum stretching from the musical past into the musical future. You do not find Beethoven suddenly composing in the manner of Bach, or Brahms in the manner of Beethoven. There may be exceptions to this rule, but the only one that comes immediately to mind is the Mozart-like style sometimes adopted by Tchaikovsky, at the very end of the nine-teenth century.

What the typical modernist composer does occasionally, as a kind of musical slumming, Strauss fashions into an entire career, at least after *Elektra*. It makes one wonder whether there is not something unstable about modernism, a kind of built-in contradiction, that leads it to decon-struct in this curious fashion. Perhaps we should even rethink the notion of modernism altogether so as to make this instability, this tendency to escape into the past, part of our understanding of its essential character. In that case Strauss would reemerge not as the great apostate but, in a sense, as the quintessential modernist, the composer who realized more completely than any other the internal contradiction of the modernist impulse.

If this proposal seems frivolous—as little more than playing with in-tellectual categories—I might end with a second possibility. I mentioned earlier the book on Strauss edited by Bryan Gilliam. In its opening essay, Leon Botstein suggests that Strauss can usefully be thought of less as a failed modernist than as a postmodernist before his time. "Strauss," writes Botstein, "prefigures the aesthetics of postmodernism." Post-modernism, of course, has become the category of choice for designat-ing the intellectual and cultural developments of the recent past. There is as yet little consensus as to exactly what postmodernism is, save that it can be understood as a reaction against modernism, which in postmod-ernist discourse is made to sound a good deal more classical, cerebral, and absolutist than it used to appear. But surely among the common de-nominators in nearly all discussions of postmodernism is the suggestion that it rejects essentialism in favor of indeterminacy, pastiche, and, at least in the architectural realm (where the category first emerged), a kind of self-conscious and playful historical eclecticism, which stands in op-position to the austerity, unity, and organicism of the modern.

The reader will doubtless have anticipated how Richard Strauss might now be made out to be a postmodernist avant la lettre (to borrow a phrase I first heard from Bernard Williams, in the symposium repro-duced in chapter 1 of this book). Pastiche, a disdain for the cerebral aus-terities of Schoenberg's atonalism, an eclectic historicism—are these not the very sins of which Strauss has been accused by his modernist critics?

But what were once sins have now been rechristened virtues—or, if they are still sins, at least they have become interesting ones. Perhaps we can at last enjoy the beauties of Strauss's post-*Elektra* masterpieces without feeling any intellectual guilt. No longer are we complicit in some nefarious and vaguely fascist conspiracy against all that is new and progressive and state-of-the-art. On the contrary, we are on the very cutting edge, liberated from the false dogmatism and illegitimate fundamentalism of the modernist claque. I am not sure how long the reprieve will last. Strauss still has lots of enemies: witness Michael Tanner's scathing review of Derrick Puffett's book on *Salome* in the *TLS* a few years back, a review that berates Puffett simply for thinking well of the opera. But I take some solace in knowing that music I have loved virtually from the first time I heard it is now considered, if I may coin a phrase, aesthetically correct.

CHAPTER NINE

The Opera Queen:
A Voice from the Closet

This piece originated as a talk in the Jing Lyman Lecture Series at Stanford in 1994 and was then published in the Cambridge Opera Journal *later that year. (In 1995 it was reprinted, somewhat improbably, in* Socialist Review.*) Marking an obvious link with the essays in the previous section, it offers a speculative answer to the question of why so many gay men are opera lovers. My argument takes its starting point from Wayne Koestenbaum's inspired book* The Queen's Throat. *It focuses on opera's subversion of gender and its affinities with the logic of the closet.*

I

At one point in Paul Rudnick's play *Jeffrey,* the title character, who claims to have slept with 5000 different men, speaks directly to the audience: "I know it's wrong to say that all gay men are obsessed with sex. Because that's not true. All human beings are obsessed with sex. All gay men are obsessed with opera."

The subject of gay men and opera was made intellectually respectable by the publication in 1993 of Wayne Koestenbaum's book *The Queen's Throat,* subtitled *Opera, Homosexuality, and the Mystery of Desire.* Koestenbaum is a professor of English at the Graduate Center of the City University of New York. He is the author of a volume of poetry, *Ode to Anna Moffo and Other Poems,* as well as a critical study of male literary collaboration, *Double Talk*, which examines the erotic aspects of such famous literary partnerships as those between Wordsworth and Coleridge, Freud and Breuer, and Eliot and Pound. He is also a self-confessed opera queen. *The Queen's Throat* is at bottom a series of auto-biographical ruminations—written in a freely associative style—exploring his own infatuation with opera and seeking to understand its connection with his homosexuality. When it appeared in 1993, the book was the subject of major—and largely favorable—reviews in the *New Yorker*, the *New York Times*, and the *New York Review of Books*. If it doesn't finally solve the mystery of why gay men are attracted to opera, its heroic and often poignant self-revelations are the most suggestive thing yet written on the topic. Moreover, they raise profound questions about the modern history of homosexuality, especially concerning how we should think about one of its main institutions, the closet.

I am generally averse to the confessional mode, but I don't see how I can proceed to write about Koestenbaum's book or about gays and opera without declaring my own interests, personal as well as professional, in this topic. I have the sense that it occupies the exact center of my life and my career as an academic. Like Wayne Koestenbaum, I am a gay man who has devoted inordinate time and energy to opera, whether buying and listening to recordings or, after I moved to San Francisco in 1967, going to live performances. Perhaps more remarkable, my scholarly work has revolved around two great themes: sex and opera. My first two books dealt with the history of modern sexual ideas—including ideas about homosexuality—and my next book explored the relation between intellectual history and opera. Perhaps not surprisingly, in reading *The Queen's Throat*, I sometimes felt that Koestenbaum had discovered the hidden key to my existence, a key that I had been either too dim-witted or (God forbid) too repressed to find myself.

There is one further intriguing bit of evidence in this personal story. In 1979 I actually wrote an essay entitled "The Opera Queen" and sent it to the *New Republic*, of which I was then a contributing editor and which had published a number of my essays and reviews. The piece was an attack on opera queens, whom I accused of not liking music. Fortunately, the magazine refused to run the essay, which, although it made some legitimate criticisms of opera queenery (I'll return to them later), came dangerously close to an exercise in self-hatred. Koestenbaum's book has prompted me to revisit the subject in, I hope, a more enlightened vein.

IN WHAT FOLLOWS I am taking as a given that there really is an affinity between gay men and opera. The affinity appears to be most pronounced in Anglo-American culture, and one suspects that its historical roots lie in the distinctive repressions of Victorianism. Needless to say, no statistical study has been conducted—or, in my opinion, is even imaginable—confirming the existence of this affinity. Furthermore, there are heterosexual opera-lovers who rail against the notion, in part, I suspect, because it seems to bring their own sexual identity into question. There are also homosexuals who rail against it, sometimes because they think opera queenery does damage to opera (this was my complaint in the *New Republic* piece) or because they associate the phenomenon with regrettable features of what they call "the gay subculture." A case in point is Bruce Bawer, a conservative gay critic, whose book *A Place at the Table* (1993) attributes the failure of gays to win acceptance to the sexual and stylistic extravagances of the "subculture" and its national leaders. "I don't like opera," declares Bawer solemnly, just as he doesn't like gay parades, leather bars, or bathhouses.

But while I can't prove the existence of a connection between opera and homosexuality, the proposition is supported by such a range and quantity of anecdotal evidence and so widely accepted—by gays and straights alike—that it has achieved the status of a cultural cliché. It was the subject of Terrence McNally's 1989 play *The Lisbon Traviata*, in which the gay characters translate the events of their lives into operatic episodes and whose main figure not only gives a yearly birthday party in memory of Maria Callas but obsesses about getting hold of a pirate recording of Callas's performance of *La traviata* in Lisbon on March 27, 1958. It is also invoked in the AIDS movie *Philadelphia* (1994), in which Tom Hanks, although relentlessly virtuous and butch, is shown too busy listening to Callas recordings to pay attention to his lawyer. Leaving aside the brute empirical question, then, the almost universal acceptance of a connection between gays and opera—its status as what I've called a cultural cliché—begs for explanation.

Before I attempt such an explanation, which will necessarily be highly speculative, we need to clarify—or at least mull over—a central terminological matter, namely, the phrase "opera queen" itself, which, along with Koestenbaum and most others, I am using as a kind of short-hand for the phenomenon. In gay argot the word "queen" has a not so subtly negative connotation. It is used to stigmatize homosexuals judged to be effeminate, often flamboyantly effeminate. In an underground gay lexicon, entitled significantly *The Queens' Vernacular* (1972), we read, "A queen is . . . [a] fellow who plucks his eyebrows." Queens represent that highly interesting sociological phenomenon, a minority within a minor-ity, whose members have suffered social and sexual discrimination within the gay community itself because of their perceived unmanliness. I re-member during the 1970s I thought, only half-facetiously, of founding a movement called "Queens' Liberation," which would draw attention to the hypocritical condescension of many gays toward effeminate men, a condescension based on an internalization of the macho values of the dominant heterosexual culture—what now would be called "heterosex-ism." In a certain respect, it seemed to me, the queen was a political hero, because, unlike the majority of gay men who were so eager to pass, the queen openly challenged the closet, and did so many years before the be-ginnings of Gay Liberation and the ideology of coming out, which date from only two and a half decades ago.

Now, the word "queen" has another meaning, while still at some level retaining the primary connotation of effeminacy. In this second meaning the word carries the generic sense of "devotee," and as such it is used (always with a hint of sarcasm) to designate any distinct proclivity among gay men. The most familiar example of this usage is "drag queen." But it is also employed for sexual preferences, as in "rice queen" for someone fond of Asians. And here, of course, is where we find the meaning of the locution "opera queen": to wit, a gay man, effeminate or not, obsessed with opera.

I have to add that in its strong sense—for example, in the way it is used by Wayne Koestenbaum as a self-designation—"opera queen" de-notes a particular kind of devotion to opera, one not only excessive but also involving a fetishization of opera. That is, the opera queen, like the erotic fetishist, is devoted not to opera in general—to opera as an artistic whole (what Wagner called "drama through music")—but to specific aspects of opera. Above all, opera queens are voice fetishists, preoccupied almost exclusively with operatic singing, as opposed to such other aspect of opera as its musical organization, its dramatic logic, even its stagecraft or scenery. In their response to opera, they home in on particular vocal movements—a single aria or even a single phrase—which are abstracted from the larger musical and dramatic fabric and listened to over and over. Furthermore, opera queens are seldom democratic in their vocal preferences. Typically they are addicted to soprano voices, often to a precise and limited roster of sopranos, of whom Maria Callas is the most notorious. It was precisely this fetishizing sort of opera queen that I complained about in my essay of 1979. A similar objection seems on the mind of one of Bruce Bawer's friends when he regrets the association of gays with opera in the following terms:

> It demeans opera, and it demeans those of us who happen to be gay but who also happen to love opera for itself, not for some psychological boost it supposedly gives us as gay people. To be a gay opera fan is not necessarily to be an "opera queen." Opera is art. I don't respond to it as a gay man who identifies with divas or finds the melodrama wonderfully campy or thinks that the whole thing speaks in some special way to me as a homosexual; I respond to it as a human being who's capable of appreciating beauty.

So the initial difficulty I face in writing about "the opera queen" is that the category is both unstable and ideologically loaded. In the most encompassing sense, it can stand for the general affinity between gays and opera. But strongly construed, it conjures up a narrower phenomenon, as represented by Terrence McNally's Callas devotee in *The Lisbon Traviata* (whom Wayne Koestenbaum calls a "hardcore opera queen") or by Koestenbaum himself. In the past I would have quickly associated myself with the more capacious understanding of the term and distanced myself (rather along the lines of Bruce Bawer's friend) from the fetishizing variety of the species. But I've come to have my doubts about this easy identification, which more and more seems to me implicated in the gender logic of heterosexuality and inseparable from the ideology of the closet. As I proceed, I will probably be guilty of moving inconsistently back and forth between the broader and the narrower meaning of the concept.

II

Perhaps the most important thing to say about the link between gay men and opera is that it is, in the first instance, highly mysterious. There is no obvious connection between attraction to persons of one's own sex and a love of this particular artistic form, which uniquely combines words, music, and stagecraft and of which a distinct form of vocal production— that is, operatic singing—is the most remarkable feature. The hardcore opera queen's obsession with the high female voice—with sopranos—is perhaps even more mysterious. Indeed, one could call it decidedly counterintuitive, in that nothing seems more remote from a gay man's object of desire than the typical operatic soprano, who all too often is middle-aged, matronly, and costumed to accentuate her femininity. How very different, for example, is the equally common phenomenon of the "ballet queen," who, after all, is looking at provocatively dressed and attractive young men, many of whom "in real life" are known or thought to be homosexual. Thus the phenomenon of the opera queen calls for exegetical skill, perhaps even exegetical acrobatics. So strange is it, in terms of obvious or conscious motivations, that it seems virtually to demand the sort of deep explanation offered by psychoanalysis. And here once again, almost against my will, I find myself returning to the autobiographical dimension of my topic. For, alongside sex and opera, much of my scholarly work has been devoted to Freud and the history of psychoanalysis.

The mysteriousness of the connection between gay men and opera is at once highlighted and illuminated by a seeming parallel devotion to opera among lesbians. The lesbian passion for opera is brilliantly analyzed by my Stanford colleague Terry Castle in her book *The Apparitional Lesbian* (1993), especially its final chapter, "In Praise of Brigitte Fassbaender," where Castle explores her own infatuation with the contemporary German mezzo soprano and relates it to earlier instances of "sapphic diva-worship." What's different about the connection between lesbians and opera is that it seems to be based on a direct and logical erotic attachment. In this sense it is analogous to the sexual attraction experienced by gay balletomanes. Speaking in particular of repressed lesbians in the nineteenth century, Castle describes the opera house as "one of only a few public spaces in which a woman could openly admire another woman's body, resonate to the penetrating tones of her voice, and even imagine (from a distance) the blood-warmth of her flesh."

But I must qualify this simple and direct explanation by noting that Castle goes on to discuss the gender ambiguity of her own and most lesbian operatic enthusiams, a gender ambiguity that makes the lesbian version of the phenomenon seem not opposite from but kindred to the gay male version. The typical lesbian opera fan, according to Castle, is devoted to the lower female voice. She is charmed above all by the very lowest notes (referred to in the jargon of singing as the chest voice) of mezzos and contraltos. Moreover, she is especially attracted to so-called "trouser" or "travesty" roles (roles, that is, in which women sing the parts of male characters), such as the pubescent Cherubino in Mozart's *Marriage of Figaro,* or, most provocatively, the teenage Octavian in Strauss's *Rosenkavalier,* who begins the opera postcoitally in bed with the prima donna, in a scene that Castle insists (rightly I think) has a heavy sapphic charge. So what started by looking like a clear-cut matter of sexual attraction turns out to be something more resembling identification—moreover, identification, be it noted, with a singer of ambiguous gender. Indeed, one begins to suspect that precisely the ambiguities of gender, or what is now called gender construction, lie at the heart of the association of opera with homosexuality.

III

Probably the first thought that comes to mind when we ask why gay men are attracted to opera is that it is simply one instance of a more general association of gays with the arts. Seen in this perspective, it is no different from the prominent gay involvement in and enthusiasm for theater, film, the dance, and, to a somewhat lesser extent, the plastic arts, literature, and nonoperatic music. The judgment is doubtless correct, but it begs the question of how to account for this more general affinity, and it also fails to explain the particular intensity of gays' love of opera.

Another explanation might focus on the ironic aspects of opera, particularly its often exaggerated representation of heterosexual passion. Most operas in the standard repertory (the vast majority of which were written in the nineteenth century and thus under the ideological aegis of romanticism) offer such clichéd and exaggerated portrayals of heterosexual love as to be almost self-parodying. Operatic love, because of its extreme conventionality, thus seems a perfect satirical expression of the gay man's aversion to heterosexuality. According to this line of reasoning, the attraction of gays to opera is of a piece with their attraction to the classic movies of Bette Davis and Joan Crawford or to the art of female impersonation, both of which exhibit the same exaggerated version of heterosexual passion. There is something to this explanation as well, but I think it is ultimately peripheral to the main story. Among the great virtues of Wayne Koestenbaum's book is that it testifies to the radical seriousness—the existential seriousness—of the opera queen's devotion. Gays may go to the opera, in part, to laugh at the clichés of heterosexuality and to achieve a certain campy sense of vindication. But irreverence takes us only so far. The attraction of gays to opera, I'm persuaded, goes much deeper than satire.

My own hunch is that the key to this mystery must lie in the phenomenon of operatic singing. Opera is distinguished, above all else, by a particular kind of vocalizing, and I think we have to wrestle with the significance, the implications, of this very peculiar human noise if we hope to make any progress in our inquiry. I'm not confident that I've got to the bottom of the matter or probed its deepest psychic recesses, but I wish to offer some observations that I think at least move toward an explanation.

MY FIRST IDEA is that operatic singing is distinctly sexual. More precisely, it bears such remarkable similarities to sexual expression that it is easily experienced as a metaphor for sex. To begin with, operatic singing involves the mouth and the throat, the primarily erogenous zone after the genitals. Moreover, if we follow the authority of Sigmund Freud, Wilhelm Fliess, and, more recently, Wayne Koestenbaum himself, it is an erogenous zone particularly associated with fellatio and thus, one might say, homoerotically invested. As Koestenbaum writes (with characteristic wit): "The throat, for gay men, is a problem and a joy: it is the zone of fellatio. Not everyone chooses fellatio: gayness doesn't depend on oral sex, and straightness includes it. But sexuality, as a symbolic system of checks and balances, measures and countermeasures, has chosen the throat as a place where gay men come into their own."

At the same time, operatic singing, like sex, is a strenuously athletic activity. Most people who are not singers fail to appreciate the extraordinary physical labor required to produce an operatic sound. Opera singers must be able to emit tones through a two-octave range (a range considerably beyond the ability of untrained singers). Above all, they must sing with enough volume to carry—without electronic assistance —over the assembled forces of a full symphony orchestra and into vast auditoriums, seating up to four thousand people. Opera singing and sex are thus united in their athleticism.

In her book *La Voix et ses sortilèges,* the voice theorist Marie-France Castarède asserts that the sound emitted by an operatic voice is decidedly phallic: it penetrates the body and, in effect, feminizes it. Koestenbaum seems to experience operatic singing in the same way. The voice, he writes, "enters me, makes a me of 'me,' an interior, by virtue of the fact that I have been entered." Rosa Ponselle's tones pierce him like "sabers." Perhaps it is no accident that we speak of a voice "climaxing" on a high note, or compare the ascending and declining vocal trajectory of the typical operatic phrase to the tumescence and detumescence of sexual arousal. There is, in other words, an isomorphism between operatic singing and sexual performance. Moreover the actual sound of operatic singing—which opera fans find so inexplicably beguiling—is itself a form of physical vibration. It is, if you will, the body shaking. In the words of America's greatest nineteenth-century opera queen, Walt Whitman, "I sing the body electric." That vocal electricity, I'm persuaded, is a sublimation or upward displacement (as the Freudians like to say) of the bodily vibrations and tinglings of the sexual act.

Most important, this strenuously produced, erotically charged sound is deployed, in the majority of operas, to give expression to the character's deepest emotions, to say precisely and emphatically just what the character feels, to speak, as it were, the character's profoundest identity. Koestenbaum returns again and again to this phenomenon of "coming out" through the voice, of lyrically shouting one's feelings in a uniquely public fashion—of doing, in effect, precisely what the closeted homosexual cannot do for himself. From this perspective, the secret of gay men's attraction to opera lies in an essentially envious identification with the singer who trumpets his (or, more often, her) deepest sentiments for the entire world to hear, and does so through a form of physical expression (i.e., operatic singing) that alludes to the sexual realities underlying all sentiment. The opera queen is thus linked to the phenomenon of the closet, an association I want to return to at the end.

MY SECOND IDEA begins with the observation that operatic singing is uniquely gendered. That is, operatic vocalizing has the effect of exaggerating the difference between male and female sounds and thus provides us with a heightened sense of sexual dimorphism or gender dualism. My notion here is fairly simple and, I think, incontrovertible. Whereas the speaking voices of men and women differ only slightly—such that when answering the telephone, for example, we are sometimes uncertain whether our interlocutor is a man or a woman—male and female singing voices—at least their *operatic* singing voices—differ radically, so much so that one would virtually never mistake a male singer for a female singer. (There is an exception to this generalization: the countertenor—or, in earlier times, the castrato—who, one might argue, is a male who is not really a male.) A simple musical—and ultimately physiological—fact lies at the base of this difference: female opera singers sing roughly an octave higher than their male counterparts. In a world where gender differences have been systematically questioned and in which the assertion of a categorical distinction between the sexes is subject to heavy critical fire, opera represents a kind of atavism, not just in its nineteenth-century dramaturgy but, above all, in its radically gendered vocalism.

This observation would seem to move us away from rather than toward an understanding of the appeal of opera for gay men, unless, of course, we were to associate it with what I earlier referred to as the campy aspect of opera—the parodic attractions of opera's exaggerated heterosexuality. But, in fact, the radically gendered nature of operatic vocalism actually establishes the premise for two highly interesting transgressions.

The first of these transgressions is that those operatic characters unambiguously identified by their singing as female nonetheless sing as loudly and assertively as do their male opposites. Dramatically women in opera suffer every known form of sexist depredation, but vocally they enjoy absolute parity with men. So opera presents a spectacle in which women are emphatically identified, by the nature of their gendered vocal production, as different—as representatives of what our culture has deemed the inferior sex—yet sing with a physical force and an authority that utterly contradicts the notion of their inferiority.

We ought not be surprised that this particular creature—the transgressive female opera singer—should have become an object of identification for homosexuals. The opera diva, after all, gives the lie to prevailing assumptions about sex and gender. She explodes the system. Small wonder that men whose sexual desires are also stigmatized by that same system of assumptions should find in the diva a kind of spokesperson. There is, I'm saying, an elective affinity between the code of gender and the code of sexual orientation, such that the operatic soprano is able to give voice to the otherwise mute protest of the gay man. I hardly need add that gays are not the only persons for whom operatic singing serves to articulate unspoken (or unspeakable) feelings.

The second transgression I have in mind pertains to a more technical aspect of certain soprano voices, especially those of singers like Maria Callas with whom gay men have most intensely identified. Beyond the gender-bending implicit, as I've suggested, in the sheer robustness of female operatic vocalism, these singers further confound our usual gender assumptions by cultivating a particular style of singing in their low register—in their chest voice. To be precise, they very often sing like men, altering their method of vocal production for the lowest notes so as to boom out tones of unimpeachably masculine authority.

From the first time I listened to Callas (nearly four decades ago) I was most struck by the particular violence of her chest voice. You can hear this feature of her singing in any number of her recordings, but it is spectacularly illustrated by her performance of the aria "Suicidio" in her first recording of Ponchielli's *La Gioconda*, made in 1952, near the beginning of her career. The performance has many interesting and typical features, including the brilliant (but slightly unstable) top notes and the "little-girl" sound Callas adopted to suggest vulnerability. Both of these features are unmistakably feminine and identify the singer, vocally and characterologically, as a woman. Just the opposite is the effect of Callas's fierce dips into the chest register in the aria's low-lying phrases, for example, on the line "Or piombo esausta fra le tenebre!" ("Now I fall exhausted in the darkness!") and above all on the phrase "dentro l'avel" ("in the grave"), where she drives this chest voice up into the middle register (to an F sharp). Here the sound is terrifyingly masculine. Indeed, one fears that such brutal vocalizing must have done irreparable damage to Callas's vocal cords. If I am right in my speculation, the distinct gender ambiguity of this kind of singing holds the key to its homoerotic charms.

MY FINAL IDEA—already hinted at more than once—is that the association of opera with homosexuality is a phenomenon of the closet. It is, I believe, historically tied to the particular situation of homosexuals in the past century, during which a self-conscious gay identity has come into existence, but under circumstances that have required varying degrees of concealment. Wayne Koestenbaum makes this link between the opera queen and the closet axiomatic in his account. It explains the curiously nostalgic tone of his book. He views himself as the last of a dying breed, and he anticipates, almost regretfully, a world in which the abolition of the closet will mean the end of the opera queen. And, of course, it follows logically that if the gender transgressions of operatic singing really have functioned as a disguised form of homosexual protest—if they have served to give voice to homosexual identity—they will cease to perform that function when gays no longer feel the need for disguise. Coming out of the closet may also mean coming out of the opera house, because now we can say and do without subterfuge what before had to be expressed indirectly or metaphorically.

I WANT TO END by suggesting that one of the virtues of Koestenbaum's book is its nuanced, richly ambivalent view of the closet and the role of concealment in the lives of modern homosexuals. In his *New Yorker* review of *The Queen's Throat*, Alex Ross noted, correctly, that the book represents "almost a defense of the closet." These days hardly anyone has a good word to say for the closet, which is routinely dismissed—indeed, reviled—as a hateful compromise with an oppressive reality. But I think a fair-minded account will have to adopt a more complex view of both its attractions and its essential humanity. Concealment has not always or necessarily been destructive. Often it has been simply a gesture of tact toward the feelings, however bigoted, of others, whether friends, family, or colleagues. Moreover, as those of us who are old enough to remember know, the closet had its peculiar charms, as do all forms of concealment, which allows not only for the occasional surprise of revelation (always a choice moment) but also for the undeniable pleasure of having a secret. Finally, the closet gave rise to a number of remarkable cultural forms, including the novels of Henry James. The opera queen, whose days may now be numbered, is not the least of the closet's achievements.

CHAPTER TEN

Homosexuality:
Choice or Destiny?

In this piece, originally given as a talk at the Stanford Humanities Center in 1997, I examine the great debate between "essentialists" and "constructionists" that dominated academic discussions of homosexuality in the 1980s and 1990s. The debate pitted those arguing that homosexuals have always existed (though they have generally been forced to hide their desires) against those who insist that homosexual persons are an "invention" of the past century. I explore the political logic of the two conceptions (the question of which point of view is genuinely progressive, since both lay claim to that title), and I suggest that the opposition between the two positions may reflect differences in age and sex.

I

I want to consider the controversy that has broken out during the past two decades over how we should think about homosexuality. Until recently the controversy was more or less confined to academic circles, but it is now spilling over into a wider arena. The controversy pits what, in the jargon, are called "essentialists" against "constructionists" (or, to speak more precisely, "social constructionists"). The difference between these two points of view is closely related to the old antithesis between nature and nurture. But it is not entirely identical with that older antithesis.

In considering the controversy, I am particularly interested in how the parties to it view the moral and political implications of their respective opinions. Indeed, I want to stress that from the beginning this argument has been conducted with an eye not just to the evidence—whether it be biological, psychological, historical, or philosophical—supporting the one conception or the other but also to the consequences of the debate for the way we think about and treat each other and for the kind of political positions we take, especially with regard to the question of gay rights, which has been much on the nation's mind of late.

My reflections on the controversy between essentialists and constructionists have been heavily influenced by the reading I did to write my book *Gay Lives: Homosexual Autobiography from John Addington Symonds to Paul Monette* (1999). The book is a study of fourteen French, English, and American gay men—most of them artists and intellectuals—who wrote accounts of their sexual lives, from the late nineteenth century to the 1990s. My subjects include Christopher Isherwood and Stephen Spender (among the English), André Gide and Jean Genet (among the French), and Martin Duberman and Andrew Tobias (among the Americans). I found it harder to turn up autobiographies by lesbians and ultimately decided not to include them in the study, but I devoted the summer of 1995 to reading lesbian autobiographies, most of them written by American women in the past three decades, including Kate Millett, Jill Johnston, and Audre Lorde.

One of the matters that especially intrigued me in studying gay autobiographies was the question of sexual identity: how these men and women conceived of themselves as sexual beings. In other words, I read their accounts with a view to ascertaining whether they thought of their sexual preference as a deep-rooted, inalterable, "essential" feature of their identity, or, on the contrary, as something more fluid, subject to change over time, and, within limits, responsive to the exercise of will. Needless to say, I don't mean to suggest that the controversy between essentialists and constructionists can be resolved by an appeal to the evidence of gay autobiographies. The sample is obviously neither large enough nor scientifically assembled, and, in any event, individual experience, as Joan Scott has reminded us, is never definitive. Just like the rest of us, autobiographers can be mistaken. But I find that the testimony of these autobiographies nonetheless supplies rich-textured and suggestive data for thinking about the question.

I believe I can say without fear of contradiction that the majority of gay men in America—perhaps the vast majority—are what might be called "natural essentialists." By that I mean that they are convinced that their sexual orientation is something over which they have no control, something that is built into their hard-wiring, so to speak. They will often tell you that they have been attracted to persons of their own sex from as far back in their lives as they can remember. They will also tell you that no amount of effort on their part to suppress their desires or to redirect them toward women has had the slightest effect on the way they feel. Very often, therefore, the story of their lives—the story they tell themselves (and others) about their past—takes the form of a coming-out narrative: at some point they mustered the courage to face the fact of their homosexuality, to accept it, and to live their lives according to it. For older gay men this decision often involved a great deal of pain and conflict with their families, friends, and colleagues, whereas younger men may have benefited from the historical changes of the past three decades— the decades since Stonewall—and been able to negotiate the coming-out process both earlier and less traumatically than their elders. The coming-out story is the narrative I found over and over again in the autobiographies of American gay men I read. Moreover, many of the relatives and friends of gay men have been persuaded to embrace the same essentialist conception of homosexual identity.

In the more recent past this essentialist way of thinking about homosexuality has received an intellectual boost from certain discoveries—or perhaps I should say, more accurately, hypotheses—made by biological scientists, hypotheses that have received considerable attention in the media. The two best known scientists working on the biological origins of homosexuality are Simon LeVay and Dean Hamer. Simon LeVay studied the part of the brain known as the hypothalamus (which is generally linked to sexual behavior). He found that this region of the brain is typically smaller in gay men (or presumably gay men, his sample having come from men who had died of AIDS) than in straight men, in fact closer in size to the hypothalamus in women. If Simon LeVay can be loosely associated with "the gay brain," Dean Hamer's study has become popularly linked with the notion of "the gay gene," because Hamer was able to show an unusually high prevalence in gay men of certain genetic markers (known as Xq28), located near the tip of the long arm of the X chromosome. Hamer's study, as I understand it, is more sophisticated scientifically than LeVay's, and he has been very careful to state that the gene in question cannot be considered the "cause" of homosexuality, first because it is not present in all gay men but also because even where it is present Hamer believes it is only a contributing (or predisposing) factor.

What I find particularly interesting is the way these—and other— scientific studies of homosexuality have been greeted, especially by gay people. Probably no one will be surprised to learn that those gay men whom I have called "natural essentialists"—and who, I say, constitute the majority of the gay male population in America—have tended to embrace these scientific findings as a confirmation of their own conception of themselves and the way they experience their sexual identity. The notion that sexual orientation has a biological basis seems to fit perfectly with their own powerful sense that their desires are something over which they have no control, something that, as I said earlier, is built into their hard-wiring. The notion of biological determinism—or some sort of biological influence—also has an obvious political appeal to these gay men. If homosexuality is innate, they reason, it cannot be condemned morally or prohibited politically. Or, to state the matter somewhat more precisely, it is, they say, unreasonable and un-American to discriminate against individuals who are simply affirming and acting upon an identity that they did not choose but that belongs to the very structure of their being. The biological argument, in other words, makes discrimination against homosexuals seem very much like discrimination against blacks: it penalizes people not for what they do but for what they are.

I should perhaps note that the argument from biology represents the strongest, most emphatic, version of the essentialist point of view, but essentialism is not identical with biologism. One might, for example, hold that, while not necessarily genetic, homosexuality is firmly imprinted by very early psychological experience—an argument favored by Freudians, for example—so that a gay person experiences his sexual orientation as something deep, enduring, and inalterable. This viewpoint (which might be called psychological determinism), although perhaps weaker than biological determinism, is still very much an essentialist position.

Interestingly, Simon LeVay's study of the hypothalamus was inspired by the very political and moral considerations that make the biological argument attractive to so many gays. That is, Simon LeVay is himself a homosexual, and he sees his scientific work as contributing to the fight against discrimination. Moreover, LeVay and other gays are confirmed in this conviction by the evidence supplied by their enemies—by homophobes and opponents of gay rights—who typically assert that homosexuality is not a state of being but a willful and regrettable choice. My favorite instance of this perspective was supplied by Dan Quayle during the 1992 presidential campaign, when he was asked a question about homosexuality and responded, "My viewpoint is that it's more a choice than a biological situation. . . . I think it is a wrong choice." Similarly, the lead proponent of the anti-gay amendment in Colorado offered the following comment to the *New York Times:* "'From up until the time I was in the eighth or ninth grade, I didn't really like girls, wasn't interested in them. . . . If I had [had] a counselor who was predisposed in that way, he could easily have convinced me: "You're one of us. We like guys.'"

But not all gay people have reacted with enthusiasm to the new scientific studies. Right from the start there has been a minority of cautionary or nay-saying voices. And here we move to my other camp of controversialists, the social constructionists. In the most immediate sense these individuals have objected to the scientific studies because of the potentially repressive use to which their so-called findings might be put. Like the genetic teachings of the Nazis, they say, Simon LeVay's gay brain or Dean Hamer's gay gene raises the prospect of genetic engineering being used to wipe out homosexuals. For example, so-called gay fetuses—that is, fetuses with a small hypothalamus or with an Xq28 gene—could be systematically aborted by parents who don't want to have gay children. Or perhaps future research will lead to the development of techniques that allow surgeons to alter the organ or the gene in question so as to turn the potentially homosexual child into a heterosexual child. These fears, of course, make sense only if you actually believe that the organ or the gene does in fact cause homosexuality, which the social constructionist denies. I am inclined to think, however, that those who argue in this fashion are moved less by such repressive prospects than by their conviction that homosexuality is not in fact an essential condition—whether determined by biology or anything else—but rather an identity that is historically contingent, a way of being in the world that is variously permitted or prohibited in different societies and at different times, and that exists as a more or less fluid possibility in a far larger number of lives than most people think.

II

Social constructionism originated in a series of historical studies, inspired by the work of Michel Foucault, all of them contending that "the homosexual" is, in effect, an invention of the last century or so. The proposition can be examined, in a particularly aggressive form, in a book written by the classicist David Halperin, a book that bears the significant title *One Hundred Years of Homosexuality* (1990). The contention, I hasten to add, is not that there were no individuals before the late nineteenth century who indulged in homosexual acts or experienced homosexual desires. That would be patently absurd. Rather, social constructionism insists that before the late nineteenth century (when, in fact, the term "homosexual" was coined—coined by doctors and sexologists, who also, of course, coined the term "heterosexual" at the same time) no individual conceived of his essential identity as that of being a homosexual person, an individual for whom the desire to have sex with someone of the same sex constituted a central and enduring component—a defining component—of his self.

What's at stake here, I'm convinced, is how we picture the mental life of people a century or more ago who happened to engage in homosexual acts or experience homosexual desires. What are we to think of, say, Michelangelo, or Winckelmann, or Whitman, or any of those long-ago persons for whom we have good reason to believe that they committed such acts and felt such desires? The automatic inclination of the modern gay man is to project his own experience onto these "predecessors," to imagine them as having the same self-conception as we do today, but to imagine further that, because of the social prohibition on homosexuality at the time or because of internalized homophobia, they could not embrace and proclaim that identity. In other words, the modern gay man pictures them as being in the closet.

An important early work of gay scholarship, John Boswell's *Christianity, Social Tolerance, and Homosexuality: Gay People in Western Europe from the Beginning of the Christian Era to the Fourteenth Century* (1980), portrays the situation of gay men in the Middle Ages in just this fashion. That is, Boswell argues that a significant gay subculture existed in the Christian Middle Ages, especially within the Catholic Church, but that its participants were forced to hide their inclinations and develop an elaborate coded language in which to communicate with one another. Not surprisingly, Boswell's book has been one of the main targets of the social constructionists' criticism.

Rather than regarding such individuals as closeted gays, the social constructionists argue, we must imagine an entirely different state of mind. We should picture instead a world in which performing homosexual acts or having homosexual desires did not lead to the conviction that one was a homosexual person. Put another way, these acts were taken much less seriously from a psychological point of view than they are today; they were simply one possibility among a variety of different ways in which individuals behaved sexually. They did not become part of a person's psychological core—or self-conception—but remained more casual, contingent, and marginal activities into which the person entered from time to time.

One might legitimately wonder what brought about the changes, roughly a century ago, leading to the "invention" of the modern homosexual person. No consensus exists among social constructionists about this issue of historical causation. A lot of them—taking their signal from Foucault—are inclined to see it as the work (perhaps one should say the dirty work) of the turn-of-the-century psychologists and sexologists who invented the term, figures like Richard von Krafft-Ebing, Havelock Ellis, and Sigmund Freud. But others—who doubt that mere intellectuals could exercise such influence—have looked for the cause in the industrial and urban revolutions of the nineteenth century, which brought young men together, separated from their families, in anonymous cities. Another variation on this theme (one I happen to like) sees the origins of the homosexual in the emergence of the modern nuclear family, with its tight, emotionally intense triangle of father, mother, and child. Here the assumption—and it is a very Freudian assumption—is that this nuclear family created dangerous emotional ties between mother and son that, by way of complex reaction, may have stimulated homosexual inclinations.

The more general point the social constructionists wish to make when they speak of the late-nineteenth-century invention of homosexuality is that sexual desire is a highly malleable phenomenon. Above all, it is a phenomenon that has to be interpreted or, in their preferred formulation, "constructed" by the individual before it can become anything so complex as a sexual identity. Moreover, as the individual proceeds to make such interpretations—such constructions—he does so with the intellectual resources made available to him by the society and the age in which he lives. Hence his sexual identity can be said to be "socially constructed." If a society does not include in its repertory of possible identities the notion of "a homosexual person," then no isolated individual is going to be able to fashion such an identity for him- or herself. That is why many social constructionists put such great emphasis on the importance of the turn-of-the-century sexologists, those scientists who in fact created the category of "homosexual person" and thus made it available for people to adopt as an identity. In any event, the important matter for the constructionist is to think of sexual identity as something socially and historically contingent and thus, as least in theory, changeable. The implication, clearly, is that the will—human volition or human agency—has a role to play in the process, even though it is limited in the choices it can make by the possibilities available in a given society. I should add that social constructionists are loath to admit that their position commits them to any such voluntarism, but I think it necessarily does.

III

Another way, or register, in which the battle between essentialists and constructionists has been waged involves the question of bisexuality. The contestants in the argument over bisexuality are not always the same players, and they don't necessarily use the same language, but, it seems to me, the identical issue is at stake. For the typical gay man in contemporary society—who, as I said earlier, is a natural essentialist—bisexuality is a kind of dodge. It is the equivalent, in the sexual realm, of what the Marxists used to call false consciousness. That is, the modern gay man is inclined to suspect that someone who claims to be bisexual simply lacks the courage to accept the fact of his homosexuality. Bisexuality becomes a kind of weasel category, a way of fooling oneself (and one's peers as well). Put differently, for the modern gay man you are not bisexual simply because you happen to be able to have sexual intercourse with women. If bisexuality exists at all (and they tend to doubt it), it ought to indicate a desire for the opposite sex that is no less imperious than the desire for the same sex. It also ought to mean that one's sexual fantasies are as apt to be populated by women as by men.

By way of contrast, for the adepts of bisexuality—such as the Harvard English professor Marjorie Garber, who has published a large analysis and celebration of bisexuality, *Vice Versa: Bisexuality and the Eroticism of Everyday Life* (1995), in which she speaks of the present as "the bisexual moment"—sexuality is profoundly fluid and tractable. It is able to assume different forms at different times in a person's life. And it is more amenable to the influence of will and imagination than is allowed by rigid essentialists, who insist that we come in only two fundamental varieties, homosexual and heterosexual.

A fascinating example of this disagreement over bisexuality is provided by the poet and critic Stephen Spender, whose autobiography *World within World* (1951) is among the texts I examine in *Gay Lives*. One of the book's central episodes is Spender's highly decorous account of his romance with a young working-class man, whom he calls Jimmy Younger and whom he followed to Spain during the Civil War. Spender doesn't hide the fact that the relationship was sexual, but he gives a very antiseptic account of it. Moreover, Spender eventually married (in fact he married twice) and produced a family. In the autobiography he gives a kind of theoretical explanation for the ultimate failure of his romance with Jimmy Younger and why he turned to women:

> We had come [up] against the difficulty which confronts two men who endeavor to set up house together. Because they are of the same sex, they arrive at a point where they know everything about each other and it there-

fore seems impossible for the relationship to develop beyond this. . . . My relationship with Jimmy had therefore made me realize that if I were to live with anyone it could not be with a man. Through this very relationship I began to discover a need for women, to think about them, to look for them.

He continues:

Love for a friend expressed a need for self-identification. Love for a woman, the need for a relationship with someone different, indeed opposite, to my-self. I realized that self-identification leads to frustration. . . . The relation-ship of a man with the 'otherness' of a woman is [by contrast] a relationship of opposite poles. They complete, yet never become, one another.

In 1993 the gay American novelist David Leavitt, who was born in 1961, published a novel, *While England Sleeps,* based on the Jimmy Younger episode in Spender's autobiography. David Leavitt changed the story in two significant ways, which might be said to have transformed the bisexual protagonist of the memoir into a full-fledged homosexual. First, he supplied the episode with intensely graphic sexual encounters, so that what I've called Spender's decorous romance becomes a raunchy erotic adventure. The gentle "friend" of the autobiography is turned into a willing, indeed an eager, recipient of anal intercourse. The effect of this sexualizing of the story is to make us feel the raw intensity of Spender's desire, which he had dismissed so offhandedly with his airy talk of "self-identification" and "otherness." After you read these scenes you are disinclined to believe that anything so ecstatic could be easily abandoned. Second, Leavitt gave his protagonist an unambiguously gay identity. As Leavitt wrote later, in defending the novel when it was at-tacked by Spender—for plagiarism and for supposedly being porno-graphic—"In sharp contrast to *World within World,* my hero [whom he calls Brian Botsford], once he arrives in Spain, never doubts where his loyalties must lie. And where Spender renounced his homosexuality in favor of what he called 'the normal'—he married twice—Botsford ends up uninhibitedly and unapologetically gay." One might say that David Leavitt has given Stephen Spender the essentialist treatment. He refuses to take seriously Spender's claim to have changed his mind.

Now, there are two further pieces of evidence in this story that I find most revealing about the debate I've been discussing. The first is that Marjorie Garber takes up the Spender-Leavitt controversy in her book *Vice Versa* and mounts a spirited defense of Spender's bisexuality against the demand—dare I say?—for "sexual correctness" in the Leavitt novel. Garber doesn't approve of Spender's tendentious contrast between homosexuality and so-called normal sex, but she views his different sexual choices at different moments in his life as perfectly authentic.

The second piece of evidence is supplied, in turn, by a review of Marjorie Garber's book written for the *New Yorker* by Edmund White. Edmund White is probably the most admired gay novelist of his generation (which is also my generation). He is the author of a two-part autobiographical account of the evolution of his sexual consciousness from the repressed fifties into the liberated seventies, a quintessential coming-out narrative in which the events of Stonewall mark a significant watershed. He is, again, what I would call a "natural essentialist." Yet he gives Marjorie Garber's book a remarkably sympathetic review (in contrast to the snooty dismissal issued by Frank Kermode in the *New York Times*), which concludes with a striking passage of autobiographical revisionism:

> I must confess that Garber's very multiplication of examples browbeat me into wondering whether I myself might not have been bisexual had I lived in another era. When I was a young man, in the sixties, before the beginning of gay liberation, I was always in therapy trying to go straight. I was in love with three different women over a ten-year period, and even imagined marrying two of them. But after the Stonewall uprising, in 1969, I revised my thinking entirely: I decided I was completely gay and was only making the women in my life miserable. Following a tendency that Garber rightly criticizes, I denied the authenticity of my earlier heterosexual feelings in the light of my later homosexual identity. After reading *Vice Versa,* I find myself willing to reinterpret the narrative of my own personal history.

What one has in this passage—if you can believe it—is a staunch essentialist preparing to take a social-constructionist turn—or perhaps I should say coming out of the social-constructionist closet.

IV

I would like to conclude with three considerations that I think may help us understand why some people have landed on one side of this argument while others have landed on the opposite side. I make no excuse for the speculative character of my ideas.

My first observation is that social constructionists tend to be more radical than essentialists. Generally speaking, their political views are to the left of those of essentialists, and they often link their critique of the sexual order to a broader critique of society as a whole. On the specific matter of sexual politics, they detest what they regard as the minimalist argument, made by essentialists, that homosexuals ought to be tolerated mainly because they have no choice about their sexuality. That plea seems to them hatefully abject. It implies that despising homosexuality is perfectly all right so long as you concede that there is nothing that can be done about it. It puts gays in the position of seeming to beg for indulgence, rather like the shuffling black stereotype of yore.

Instead of an obsequious plea of tolerance, social constructionists, I sense, are eager to confront their straight antagonists—to proclaim that they have nothing to be ashamed of, that they don't need to apologize for their lives by appealing to the inexorable force of biology or early conditioning. As a civil right, the choice to love a person of the same sex ought to enjoy full legal protection no matter what its cause or even if the person is acting on pure whim. Likewise, the constructionist spurns trying to ingratiate himself with straights by assuring them there is no need to fear their children will be converted to homosexuality by gay relatives, gay teachers, or gay celebrities. The historian John D'Emilio, an early and influential constructionist, is a case in point. In 1983 he wrote:

> *There are more of us* than one hundred years ago, more of us than forty years ago. And there may very well be more gay men and lesbians in the future. Claims made by gays and nongays that sexual orientation is fixed at an early age, that large numbers of visible gay men and lesbians in society, the media, and the schools will have no influence on the sexual identities of the young, are wrong. . . . To be sure, this argument confirms the worst fears and most rabid rhetoric of our political opponents. But our response must be to challenge the underlying belief that homosexual relations are bad, a

poor second choice. We must not slip into the opportunistic defense that society need not worry about tolerating us, since only homosexuals become homosexuals.

I'm sure the reader will be as intrigued as I am that the radical John D'Emilio is arguing the same position—from a structural point of view—as the conservative Dan Quayle, who, it will be recalled, said that homosexuality is a choice. D'Emilio and Quayle seem to disagree only about whether the choice is good or bad. It is one of those classic instances of the two ends of the political spectrum coming together, at least at the level of theory.

My second observation is that there is something of a generation gap between essentialists and constructionists: constructionists are usually younger. They tend to be post-Stonewall, while their opposite numbers typically grew up and experienced their coming-of-age in a more repressive era. Sometimes these younger people choose to call themselves "queer" instead of "gay." Indeed, "queer" often implies adherence to a constructionist viewpoint.

I suspect that this generation gap has a clear historical logic. Older gays needed to feel very strongly about their sexual identity before they could muster the psychological wherewithal to pursue that identity in a hostile world. You didn't become a gay man in the fifties or sixties without having gone through a good deal of agony and confronting an equal amount of adversity, which means you didn't do it without your sexual desires being intense, unrelenting, and unambiguous. By contrast, in the much more hospitable climate of the 1980s and 1990s, a young person's homoerotic desires did not need to be nearly so singular, so uniquely focused, to be pursued. Such a person might very well have homosexual experiences that seem like chosen adventures rather than the forced and reluctant acceding to uninvited impulse. Although I would not go so far as to call post-Stonewall gays "natural constructionists" or "innate bisexuals," I do think that the quite remarkable historical changes of the past two decades have introduced a new dynamic into gay identity.

Finally—and this observation will have been anticipated by the reader who has been paying attention to my pronouns—I think there is a marked difference between the way men and women experience homosexuality. Lesbians are more likely to find that the constructionist interpretation makes sense of their lives than are gay men. I noted this difference particularly in the autobiographies I read for *Gay Lives*. Virtually all the lesbian autobiographers went through a long period, lasting often into their thirties, in which they led heterosexual lives and seemed to have had little or no awareness that they were unsatisfied. This pattern contrasts dramatically with the out-of-the-closet narratives in the male autobiographies, where homosexual desire announces itself early and unambiguously and where the problem is simply to acknowledge it and act on it. You even hear people speaking of "political lesbians," meaning women who seem to be straight for much of their lives but then, out of feminist conviction or sympathy, "decide" to become lesbians. The poet Adrienne Rich has proposed the notion of a "lesbian continuum" to describe the way in which feminist sympathy shades off into same-sex eroticism for many women.

Arguably this difference is rooted in more general differences between male and female sexuality (and here I betray my lingering essentialism). I'm thinking particularly of Alfred Kinsey's findings about the very dissimilar patterns of sexual aging in men and women. Men, according to Kinsey, reach the high point of desire (and even performance) before they are eighteen, after which those desires taper off over the rest of their lives. By contrast, women's sexual feelings emerge more gradually, reach a kind of plateau in the late twenties, and remain there often well into the fifties. The moment of crisis in a gay man's life usually comes during adolescence; the crisis for lesbians often happens much later.

Obviously I'm speaking about a tendency, not a hard-and-fast rule. Many lesbians, especially of the older generation (and here I would recall my second observation), consider their sexual orientation a deep and lasting part of their identity. Still, just as there is a generation gap there is also, I'm convinced, a gender gap that helps explain the opposition between essentialists and constructionists.

I OUGHT NOT END without declaring my own allegiance in this matter. I guess I would describe myself as a recovering essentialist. I think there is a good deal to be said for the historical and cultural arguments advanced by the social constructionists. But I'm not yet fully prepared to give up the notion that factors over which we have no control—probably biological factors, certainly psychological factors—play a role in sexual orientation. Perhaps more important, I suspect that "homosexuality" is not a single phenomenon: hidden beneath this covering term are individuals and groups whose sexual stories differ significantly. I suspect further that the role of biology and early conditioning are more important in some instances than in others—more important for men than for women, more important for certain men than for others. On my radical days I would confess to a high tolerance for the constructionists' political conviction that homosexuality doesn't have to be biologically or psychologically determined to be defended. But on my more prudent days I'm inclined to think that the essentialists, who advocate gay rights on the grounds that you can't legislate against nature, have the better argument. Their case may sound defensive, but it is more likely to persuade a reluctant public to do the right thing. And if I have my nose to the political winds—which are rather smelly right now—I think the old-time essentialists are about to stage a political comeback. Indeed, they already have, in the person of Andrew Sullivan, a former editor of the *New Republic*, whose influential book *Virtually Normal* (1995) makes the case for gay rights (or, in Sullivan's quaint view, the right to marry and the right to join the army) entirely on essentialist grounds and casts the social constructionists into outer darkness. Another example is Bruce Bawer, the author of *A Place at the Table* (1993), who in 1997 wrote in the *Advocate* (a national gay and lesbian newsmagazine), "The truth [is] that homosexuality is a widespread, naturally occurring orientation that cannot be willed, wished, prayed, argued, or moralized out of existence." Finally, and most impressively, there is Bruce Bagemihl, whose *Biological Exuberance: Animal Homosexuality and Natural Diversity* (1999) supplies the essentialist cause with a massive body of evidence gathered from among three hundred species of mammals and birds. The argument is far from settled—in all likelihood it will peter out in some sort of compromise—but I believe the scales have been slightly tipped in the essentialist direction. Time will tell.

CHAPTER ELEVEN

Sex Studies and Sex Books:
Four Reviews

A good deal of my intellectual labor over the years has gone into book reviewing, which I consider a serious academic and civic responsibility. Here I have gathered four reviews (which appeared in the New Republic, Psychology Today, *and the* New York Times Book Review*) on the subject of human sexuality. I use them to draw a distinction between what I call "sex studies" and "sex books." Sex studies are statistically serious (although not immune to conceptual criticism) and hence a source of genuine information, while sex books merely retail titillating anecdotes with a view to turning a profit. Of the four books discussed below, the first two are sex books, the second two sex studies. The landmark work of Alfred Kinsey, which I examined in* The Modernization of Sex, *serves as my point of reference in assessing all four books. The reviews, I would suggest, provide a snapshot of what passed for sexual wisdom in the late twentieth century.*

1. Shere Hite, *The Hite Report on Male Sexuality* (1981)

We apparently have need of a distinction between two kinds of writing about human sexuality: sex books and sex studies. Shere Hite's publication about the sexual lives of American men serves to illustrate that need, one might say, graphically.

Like its hugely successful predecessor, *The Hite Report: A Nationwide Study of Female Sexuality* (1976), the new report is a sex book pretending to be a sex study. It stands in relation to a true sex study much as a coffee-table art book stands to a scholarly monograph on art history. It makes many statements about the sexual behavior and attitudes of American men, but those statements are no more reliable than the things one hears from drinking companions, one's barber or hairdresser, or Dear Abby. Some of the statements could well be true, but the reader has no way of telling.

The book is a statistical disaster area. Its inadequacies in this respect are too numerous to catalogue, and I will mention just the most glaring. The report's "findings" are based on questionnaires. But out of the 119,000 questionnaires distributed, only 7,239 were returned. One needs little imagination to guess what kind of man responded to questions such as: "Do you like mouth-anal contact?" or "Do you like to be rectally penetrated? By a finger? By a penis? How does it feel?" or "Do you enjoy cunnilingus with a woman?" The farm vote, one suspects, was not well represented. (The percentage of respondents with college degrees was twice the national average.) Indeed, Hite's questionnaires seem to have found their way mainly into the hands of the sexual avant-garde. To the extent that I can make sense of the garbled statistical information at the end of the volume, it would appear that nearly half of Hite's replies were secured from men who had read or heard of her earlier books, who answered versions of the questionnaire reprinted in magazines like *Penthouse,* or who knew about Hite from her appearances on television and radio, in magazines and newspapers. No sensible person would compare this book to Alfred Kinsey's monumental studies of 1948 and 1953, *Sexual Behavior in the Human Male* and *Sexual Behavior in the Human Female,* both of which boasted a much richer empirical base and a truly sophisticated statistical technique.

Even if one were to make the outrageously generous assumption that the report's 7,239 questionnaire responses came from a representative sample of the American population, the book would remain scientifically worthless because of its chronic imprecision. To be sure, there are some desultory tables in the appendix, but they bear faint and infrequent relation to the generalizations in the body of the report. The text itself is almost innocent of numbers. Its assertions typically take the form of "Most men . . . ," "Many men . . . ," "Some men . . . ," "Other men . . . ," "A few men . . . ." Unwisely, Hite allows just enough percentages or fractions to slip into the text to expose her extraordinary carelessness.

Consider "many." I was able to find the word associated with specific percentages on three occasions:

24%—the "many men" who enjoyed anal penetration and sometimes included it in their masturbation

43%—the "many boys" who had had sex with other boys

83%—the "many men" who, while demanding an orgasm for themselves, could enjoy sex even when their partner failed to achieve one

Thus "many," in Hite's usage, stretches from just under one-quarter to more than three-quarters of the population, and, accordingly, all her assertions in which "many" is not further specified (that is, all but the three instances cited here) are hopelessly elastic. What, for example, is one to make of her statement, "Many men had their first intercourse with a prostitute"?

The crucial phrases "some men" and "a few men," both of which appear dozens of times in Hite's book, are treated even more cavalierly. I found "some," like "many," associated with percentages three times:

.7%—the "some men" who masturbated by water massage

6%—the "some men" who had raped a woman

20%—the "some men" who had always liked and practiced monogamy

The last group, although designated by the same adjective, is 29 times larger than the first. So in Hite's population of 7,239, "some" could mean as few as 50 or as many as 1,450 individuals.

The greatest range of all is encompassed by "a few." I detected the following associations:

.3%—the "few men" who sometimes masturbated by self-fellation

1%—the "few men" who masturbated "by pushing their penis down, holding it between their legs and grinding or rotating their hips"

3%—the "few" who said they wanted less intercourse

8%—the "few" whose happiest times had been spent with other men

20%—the "few" single men who said they would like to live with a woman but not marry

Given this spectrum of possibilities, how is the reader to interpret, say, the statement, "Quite a few men who were single were also celibate"?

Unfortunately, the mere insertion of percentages would not be enough to salvage Hite's amorphous text. Its weaknesses go beyond imprecision to the level of structural incoherence. Typically, Hite will pose a question—legitimate enough in its own right—to which she then gives every conceivable answer. The reader is left knowing no more at the end of the discussion than at the beginning. Here, for instance, are the answers she gives to the question "Do men like being in love?"

> "Some men, when they fell deeply in love, felt it was not good."
> "Many mentioned that they did not like feeling out of control."
> "Others said they preferred a more daily, loving relationship to being 'in love.'"
> "A few said love was not that important."
> "But others liked being in love."

The point of such a question, obviously, is to differentiate quantitatively among the responses, which is exactly what Hite fails to do, both here and elsewhere.

THUS AS A SOURCE of information—comparable to the Kinsey or Masters and Johnson studies—*The Hite Report on Male Sexuality* is virtually useless. But it is, as I've suggested, not really a sex study at all but rather a sex book. A sex book has quite different purposes from a sex study. I take those purposes to be: amusement, titillation, diversion, and (in small doses) instruction by example.

The form of the *Hite Report* is ideally suited to these ends. In fact, to tell the truth, it's not so much a book as a string of quotations. The material written by Hite herself makes up less than 10 percent of the text, and it consists mainly of questions and single-sentence responses such as those I've cited above. The rest is given over to excerpts of varying length taken directly from the questionnaires. In the final chapter ("Thirty Men Speak about Their Lives") even the rudimentary question-and-answer format is dispensed with, and we are treated to over 100 pages of uninterrupted sexual autobiography. The book is in a time-honored tradition, stretching back to Richard von Krafft-Ebing's *Psychopathia Sexualis* and Havelock Ellis's *Studies in the Psychology of Sex*.

Ellis actually wrote his books (as opposed to putting them together with scissors and paste), but he always rewarded his readers with long appendices of case studies reported verbatim from his correspondents. One might describe the tradition as a form of genteel pornography, where the stimulating material is encased within polite and boring generalizations so as to disarm an otherwise troublesome conscience.

In terms of amusement value, Hite has managed to obtain some impressive one-liners from her respondents. Her men are especially witty about their penises. I was charmed, for instance, by the man who reported that his was "about five and three-quarters inches long and about four and a half inches in circumference." Clearly only a rough estimate. Another respondent sounds like the Franz Kafka of the penis: "I find it rather bizarre to have something that just hangs around most of the time and occasionally gets excited enough to stick out several inches in front of me." "A woman's clitoris is the greatest thing since the mop" will appeal only to unregenerate sexists. The same probably holds for the brazen fellow who wrote, "I could make a pork chop come."

Titillation and diversion are such personal matters that I'm reluctant to make recommendations. But in this huge compilation of sexual gossip (nearly 1,200 pages) there's something for everyone. If you have a weakness for freak shows, you will be intrigued by the man who can insert his penis into his own anus (he also claims to be able to ejaculate under these trying circumstances). There is also a splendid tale (which Hite in fact tells twice) about two boys, one ten, the other fifteen, who masturbate on a park bench. They are discovered by "two old ladies" who exclaim, "My word!" The older boy tells the women to mind their own business and promptly ejaculates at their feet, thereby exciting the ten-year-old to his first orgasm and dispatching the harridans in a state of apoplexy.

I found two sorts of accounts instructive. The first were from men who had come to terms with the sexual needs of women, learning, often slowly and painfully, that what was satisfying to themselves wasn't necessarily satisfying to their lovers. Some of their accounts achieve genuine pathos, especially when the men in question continue to inhabit a social world where their deepest feelings must be kept hidden. The story of a twenty-seven-year-old construction worker who considered himself a great lover until disabused by his wife ends, almost hauntingly, "I wanted to tell somebody about this. I could never tell any of my group." The other instructive responses came from three men who said they had sexual relations on a regular basis with both men and women. All three revealed that they were deeply troubled by their ambivalent sexual identity, and the heterosexual experiences of two of the three had been confined to a single woman, namely, their wives. The report will offer little comfort to the purveyors of bisexual chic.

I SHOULD NOT leave the impression that Hite's book is without ideas. On the contrary, it is full of them. They fall into three categories: those that are self-evident or banal; those that are interesting but unsubstantiated; and those that are wrong.

In the first group belong the propositions that gay men enjoy kissing other men more than straight men do; that unfaithful husbands blame their affairs on unsatisfactory sex lives at home; and that sexual relations in marriage have a tendency to become less exciting over the years. Nor will many readers be surprised to learn that "in masturbation . . . it is the hand that moves and rarely the body," though some may resist Hite's deduction that "it would therefore seem likely that thrusting during intercourse is due to the desire to cause an up-and-down motion on the penis."

The book's few interesting ideas are largely speculative. She suggests, for example, that men grow alienated from marriage because they begin to see their wives as mothers. She also contends that the emphasis on intercourse in sexual relations is a creation of patriarchy: intercourse is geared to the male orgasm, whereas women achieve orgasm more readily from manual or oral stimulation of the clitoris. This difference, Hite argues, explains why women aren't as interested in intercourse as men would like them to be. Both of these ideas are plausible enough, but neither is based on evidence in the report. They float freely above it as disembodied reflections of Hite's feminism.

Other contentions, however, are more than speculative. They are either irresponsible or simply incorrect. Thus the assertions that rape is a relative novelty in human history and that sexual intercourse was formerly practiced not for gratification but for reproduction are sufficiently controversial—and improbable—to require some sort of documentation. Yet none is forthcoming. Likewise, Hite's statement that "perhaps the cruelest stereotype about men is the idea that they are at their sexual peak when they are nineteen or twenty" demands to be supported by evidence. The statement presumably refers to Alfred Kinsey's finding that male sexuality, measured in terms of orgasms per year, reaches its apex in the late teens. Why does Hite label this a cruel stereotype? On the ground that "there was hardly a man in the entire study who did not report that his sex life was better than it had ever been before." Kinsey will not be put to rout by anything so flimsy and transparently self-deluding as that.

Hite's most spectacular exercise in wishful thinking is her contention that impotence is related to the aging process only accidentally: "Loss of erective ability has to do with certain degenerative physical conditions, which can occur at any age but which often accompany the decline in health many older people experience." She concedes, grudgingly, that getting an erection in one's seventies "can be more difficult." Fortunately, however, "Sexuality has little or nothing to do with erections."

In sum, this is not a book to be taken seriously, although it's sure to make a lot of money. As of October 1980 its forerunner had entered a fifteenth paperback printing. The only surprise is that a great publishing house like Alfred A. Knopf should have stooped to issue it. Material of this sort usually finds a less prestigious outlet. I take it as a sign that publishing has truly fallen on hard times.

2. Linda Wolfe, *The Cosmo Report* (1981)

Who could have guessed that "report" would become a dirty word, the sort of titillating substantive that, on the cover of a book, virtually guarantees sales? A less prepossessing candidate is hard to imagine. Reports used to be filed by coroners or wildlife commissions. Today, however, the word promises lascivious first-person narratives, as in *The Hite Report, The Spada Report, The Kahn Report,* and now *The Cosmo Report.*

Alfred Kinsey will doubtless be blamed for this lexicographic revolution. But the charge is doubly unjust. In the first place, Kinsey never published a book called "The Kinsey Report." His two studies bore the self-effacing titles of *Sexual Behavior in the Human Male* (1948) and *Sexual Behavior in the Human Female* (1953). More important, the Kinsey studies were products of enormous industry and powerful analysis, neither of which can be said to afflict the sex reports of more recent vintage.

Sex reports are composed according to formula, the chief ingredients of which are the following:

1. *A magazine questionnaire.* Ideally—as in the present instance—one has a magazine of one's own. But failing that, one can always borrow somebody else's. Shere Hite borrowed *Oui* for her first report and *Penthouse* for her second. James Spada borrowed the *Advocate* and *Christopher Street*. The questionnaires themselves should be brief, ethically loaded, and inanely specific. Cosmo asked only 79 questions—nearly all of them multiple choice—ranging from "Do you believe good sex is possible without love?" to "Have you made love on your lunch hour?"

2. *A countinghouse.* These are called "public opinion research companies." In the case of *The Cosmo Report,* this service was performed by the Simmons Market Research Bureau. (Such firms, I've noticed, are usually designated by a parade of nouns. Adjectives would seem to be anathema to them.) The countinghouse transforms questionnaire responses into simple percentages. This process lends the report an aura of statistical respectability, even though all sex reports share a blatant contempt for the logic of statistical analysis. *The Cosmo Report,* which is based on 106,000 questionnaires, makes patronizing remarks about the "mere" 6,000 women who provided the information for *Sexual Behavior in the Human Female*. But even a statistical dunce can tell that Kinsey's sample is reliable, while that of *The Cosmo Report* is hopelessly biased. Kinsey controlled his research population for such variables as age, marital status, education, and social class, thereby avoiding the distortions that might result from the overrepresentation of particular groups. By way of contrast, nearly 90 percent of the *Cosmo* replies come from women between 18 and 34; two-thirds of the respondents are unmarried; an even larger number—70 percent—have college degrees; only 7.2 percent call themselves "homemakers"; and almost a third claim family incomes over $25,000 a year. In short, these women are young, single, educated, employed, and, relatively speaking, rich. They are also readers of *Cos-*

mopolitan, and thus the bearers of a with-it philistinism that one dearly hopes has not yet established its national hegemony.

3. *An Author.* In sex reports, the author is generally an afterthought. He or she comes into the picture only when the work of the questionnaire and the countinghouse is finished. Ostensibly the author is chosen for reasons of style. Thus Helen Gurley Brown in her Foreword to *The Cosmo Report:* "More than 106,000 Cosmo readers had filled in and mailed their sex-survey questionnaires to us. Then came the task of interpreting the findings. Linda Wolfe, author, behavior and science writer and a fine writer *generally,* was engaged to study the results Simmons had compiled for us." One might be tempted to fault Linda Wolfe for writing sentences like, "Letters blizzarded the magazine." But that would be unfair. She is on the whole quite a decent stylist, and after Shere Hite her prose reads like Lionel Trilling. Indeed, her very articulateness will be a source of frustration to old-hand sex report aficionados.

4. *First-person narratives.* The author's primary responsibility is to select and edit the first-person narratives that constitute the heart of every sex report. In a masterpiece of the genre—such as Shere Hite's latest book—these stories occupy about 90 percent of the text. The author strings them together with a line or two of comment or a random generalization, which might be compared to the recitative between the arias of an opera. Linda Wolfe shows her inexperience when she allows her own prose to hog nearly half the pages of *The Cosmo Report.* She also squanders 88 pages on a statistical appendix, which will fool no one familiar with statistics and takes up valuable space that Shere Hite put to much more gratifying use when she capped her book with thirty uninterrupted autobiographies. Nevertheless, the publishers of *The Cosmo Report* have seen to it that the first-person narratives are set off typographically for quick identification. These stories, incidentally, don't come from the questionnaire but from 2,500 letters that the author solicited when she published a preliminary version of her findings in *Cosmopolitan* the preceding year.

5. *An upbeat tone.* Sex reports always bring good news, telling us how far we've come from the bad old days of Victorianism. At the same time, they strive for a proper balance between restraint and abandon. Linda Wolfe captures just the right mood in her observations about a woman

who had her first orgasm at 69: "Of all the letters received for *The Cosmo Report*, this one—which was written on lime-green stationery in a spidery, old-fashioned handwriting—was my favorite. I was touched by the simplicity with which the Minnesota woman made perhaps the most important statement that can be made about orgasm: that it can be learned." In her more vulgar way, Helen Gurley Brown achieves the same effect in the book's Foreward: "It's somehow reassuring to know that a whopping 92 percent said they prefer sex with commitment (even though 55 percent have made love on their lunch hour)." Sex reports invariably combine moral uplift with self-indulgence.

6. *A judicious blend of the banal and the quaint.* The primary function of a sex report is to arouse (see number 4 above). But it has the secondary task of reassuring and amusing. "Teen-age girls everywhere and in every era have always thought sexual thoughts," followed by a passage from *Romeo and Juliet*, answers to the first of these, while amusement is supplied by entries like, "Once I worked in a fast-food place, and every time the refrigerator turned on, I'd get a sexual rush. It was the sound that did it." Again, however, Linda Wolfe is no match for the veteran Shere Hite, whose book offers sexier narratives and zingier one-liners. None of the quotations in *The Cosmo Report* can compare with that from the fellow who wrote Hite, "My only sexual areas are my back and genitals. My breasts and asshole could disintegrate for all I care."

What, then, does this book tell us? Strictly speaking, nothing. That is, it contains no general conclusions that one can retail with any confidence in their accuracy. Moreover, even as a report on the sexual lives of Cosmo girls, it offers few surprises. The findings are very close to those uncovered by earlier studies with similarly biased samples, notably *The Redbook Report*, Hite's first book, and *The Kahn Report*. Cosmo girls have lots of sex, enjoy it, and want more. At the same time, they sometimes resent the pressure to perform—half of them think that the sexual revolution has gone too far. They find it easier to achieve orgasm through oral or manual stimulation than through intercourse. They prefer to have sex in the dark. They masturbate a great deal. They've had several different lovers, and they've been unfaithful. All of which is tiresomely familiar. It merely confirms our prejudices without adding to our knowledge.

The one thing the report documents unambiguously is a decline in the intellectual quality of sexual discussion over the past three decades. The Kinsey reports were much criticized at the time of their publication for various moral and conceptual shortcomings. But seen from the perspective of today's sexual discourse, they look like monuments to intellectual and ethical seriousness. That tradition in sexual research is not altogether defunct. Just this year Alan Bell, Martin Weinberg, and Sue Kiefer Hammersmith published a superb study of sexual preference, which exhibits all the empirical conscientiousness of Kinsey at his best. But where the Kinsey volumes, when they appeared, gained the sort of popular attention that is now reserved for pseudo-studies like *The Cosmo Report*, *Sexual Preference* (despite a notice in *Newsweek*) seems destined for academic oblivion. I don't relish sounding like the Oswald Spengler of sexology, but the trend, I think, is both clear and disheartening.

3. Alan P. Bell, Martin S. Weinberg, and Sue Kiefer Hammersmith, *Sexual Preference* (1981)

Sexual Preference asks why some people become homosexuals while others become heterosexuals, and it answers that question more satisfactorily than any previous study. The authors don't pretend to have the final word on the subject, but they succeed brilliantly in disqualifying most of the answers that have been offered in the past. The reason for their remarkable success lies in their method, which is so manifestly superior to all earlier efforts that one almost wonders why researchers have taken so long to fall upon it. But what seems perfectly obvious in theory often turns out to require enormous effort in practice. Thus, while a host of "experts" have been generalizing off the top of their heads or on the basis of ludicrously inadequate data, Professors Bell, Weinberg, and Hammersmith have devoted more than a decade to the hard, slow, empirical labor that alone permits one to address this sort of issue in a scientific fashion.

Their study begins from the premise that generalizations about sexual identity are just so much hot air unless based on an adequate sample. Therefore, in place of the isolated case study so beloved of the Freudians, or the handful of neurotics that figure in many of the clinical studies (such as that of Irving Bieber), they have assembled a sizable research population: 979 homosexuals, all of whom were interviewed in 1969–70. These men and women, living in the San Francisco Bay Area, constitute the largest empirical base ever gathered for an in-depth study of sexual preference.

By themselves, of course, sheer numbers don't guarantee accurate results. The sample must also be representative, thus reflecting the homosexual population of the country as a whole. One might fear that by locating the project in San Francisco the authors have defeated this purpose in advance. But they give excellent reasons for their conviction that San Francisco offered the best cross-section of American homosexuals they could hope to obtain. The interview population was controlled in terms of such nonsexual variables as age, educational level, occupation, sex, and race. Hence the study's findings are not disfigured by the presence of too many (or too few) young people, college graduates, wealthy white males, or whomever.

The authors also recognized that a large and representative sample would be meaningless unless the information garnered from homosexuals could be compared with similar information from heterosexuals. In other words, they needed a control group if they hoped to make useful generalizations. Accordingly, they also conducted interviews with 477 straight men and women. (For statistical reasons the heterosexual sample did not need to be as large as the homosexual sample.) This population was likewise controlled for the nonsexual variables of age, education, occupation, sex, and race. The members of both groups were individually interviewed for three to five hours, and all were asked identical questions about their childhood and adolescence. The authors were thus able to establish, virtually for the first time, how the early experiences of homosexuals and heterosexuals diverge.

Finally, Bell, Weinberg, and Hammersmith brought a sophisticated statistical technique to the analysis of the data retrieved from the interviews, which allowed them to distinguish true causal differences from merely reflective ones. The method they employ is called "path analysis" or "regression analysis." I can't hope to replicate their lucid explanation of this procedure, but in essence it involves taking all possible causes into consideration when trying to measure the significance of one of those causes. For example, if homosexuals turn out to have been closer to their mothers than heterosexuals, the precise importance of that fact is tested by ascertaining whether it by itself leads directly to a homosexual preference or whether it must occur in combination with other experiences. To the extent that a particular variable appears in homosexual histories only in association with other variables, its autonomous significance—and hence its predictive value—is diminished. In terms of my example, most young boys who are closely attached to their mothers grow up to be heterosexuals (not homosexuals, as Freudian theory supposes); they are likely to become homosexuals only if several other things also happen to them on their way to adulthood. In total, the authors identify fifteen areas of childhood and adolescent experience in which homosexuals differ from heterosexuals, and they attach a precise etiological value to each. In a separately published Statistical Appendix they present a detailed technical analysis of their evidence.

I HAVE DEVOTED considerable space to method because the book's massive empirical foundation and fine-tuned statistical procedure lend its findings unprecedented trustworthiness. Those findings are less remarkable for what they prove than for what they disprove. The authors obviously view themselves as demystifiers, and their book's greatest virtue is that it permanently retires many cherished ideas about the causes of homosexuality. It does so by the breathtakingly simple technique of showing that those ideas aren't supported by the facts.

Chief among the candidates for retirement are all the Freudian assumptions about the role of family relationships in the emergence of homosexuality. Psychoanalysts have tended to attribute male homosexuality to an overpowering, seductive mother along with a weak or detached father (with whom the boy fails to identify). Female homosexuality has been explained in terms of an equally overpowering but unpleasant mother who dominates her feckless husband, thus tainting all possible male object choices for the girl. The authors show that these (and related) family traits are barely more prominent in homosexual histories than in heterosexual ones, and when they do appear their effect depends heavily on their occurring in conjunction with a number of other experiences. As predictors of future sexual identity they are by themselves useless. I have little doubt that the shopworn psychoanalytic etiologies will continue to be marketed for years to come, since therapists have both a theoretical and an economic investment in them. But Bell, Weinberg, and Hammersmith document the intellectual poverty of the psychoanalytic hypothesis.

Another cliché they lay to rest is the notion that lesbians turn to members of their own sex because of disappointing or traumatic experiences with men. The interviews reveal that the early heterosexual histories of lesbians are practically identical with those of straight women. If anything, lesbians seem to have a slight advantage, finding their way into men's beds nearly two years earlier than straights and enjoying the experience just as much (or as little) as women who end up full-time heterosexuals. In other words, heterosexual failure turns out to be a nonstarter in any effort to account for lesbianism.

The most prominent feature in the early life of gay men and women —and the feature to which the authors attach the greatest importance— is what they call "gender nonconformity." This boils down to little boys who don't like supposedly masculine activities (like playing baseball) and little girls who feel something like the opposite. When one reads these findings, one is likely to worry that the authors may have confused cause and effect. After all, isn't gender confusion already the reflection of an evolving homosexual identity? Put another way, one wants to know why some children become gender nonconformists while most obviously don't.

The authors freely admit that they do not know the cause of gender nonconformity. But whatever its ultimate cause, they show that it bears little statistical relation to any of the family traits to which homosexuality has so often been attributed. The vast majority of boys who dislike sports have enjoyed no special attachment to their mothers, while, conversely, most boys with intense maternal ties develop the usual masculine tastes in childhood. But once gender nonconformity has been established, the chances of a person's becoming a homosexual are dramatically increased.

Although they can't prove it, the authors strongly suspect that the root cause of homosexuality is biological, or, more precisely, hormonal. Such a hypothesis, they point out, is entirely consistent with their findings. They speculate that a biological cause, if determined, will also explain the childhood gender nonconformity with which adult homosexuality is so strongly correlated. To the extent that the homosexual child's relations with its parents appear disturbed, that disturbance, they believe, is a reflection, not a source, of the child's biological inability to conform to parental expectations.

One finishes this book with the firm sense that much of the confusion about sexual identity has now been set right. Parents can safely rid themselves of the fear that their actions will somehow determine the sexual preference of their children, and psychotherapists can relax their fierce campaign to change adult sexual behavior by probing into early familial experience. Sexual identity, it appears, is so deeply ingrained that it remains impervious even to such powerful influences as mothers, fathers, and doctors. Under these circumstances, our authors say, the only reasonable attitude is to accept homosexuality as an inevitable sexual orientation for a certain percentage of the population. This counsel is offered without even a hint of despair, since their earlier work (notably, *Homosexualities: A Study in Diversity among Men and Women,* written before Bell and Weinberg teamed up with Hammersmith) has shown that, outside the sexual realm, homosexuals are remarkably similar to their fellow men and women of the heterosexual persuasion. In the best tradition of the late Alfred Kinsey (whose Sex Research Institute in Indiana sponsored this project), Bell, Weinberg, and Hammersmith seek to minimize the human significance of sexual differences and urge us to accept those differences with grace. We may as well, because apparently there's very little we can do about them even if we were so minded.

4. Edward O. Laumann, John H. Gagnon,
Robert T. Michael, and Stuart Michaels,
The Social Organization of Sexuality (1994)

The Social Organization of Sexuality is the most important study of American sexual behavior since the Kinsey volumes of 1948 and 1953. In one crucial respect this survey is in fact superior to the Kinsey reports: it is based on a fully representative sample of the American population. Kinsey believed that a statistically random study of sexual behavior was impossible, because many of the chosen respondents would refuse to cooperate or would give willfully inaccurate answers. In the more puritanical atmosphere of a half-century ago his pessimism was probably justified. Hence his sexual interviews were conducted with volunteers, leading to the suspicion that the more libidinous members of the population were overrepresented and that the incidence of homosexuality in particular was exaggerated.

The great strength of the new study is that its participants were selected according to the most sophisticated techniques of probability sampling, the same techniques used in modern political polling and marketing. Its findings can thus be generalized to the population at large with a high degree of confidence. Over a period of eight months in 1992, the staff of the National Opinion Research Center at the University of Chicago conducted 90-minute interviews with 3,432 individuals between ages 18 and 59. The subjects were randomly chosen from a cross section of American households. (The "institutionalized" population—those living in prisons, Army barracks, or college dormitories—was excluded.)

The 3,432 people interviewed represented an impressively high response rate of nearly 80 percent: four out of every five randomly selected individuals actually agreed to be interviewed. The authors of *The Social Organization of Sexuality*—two sociologists (Edward O. Laumann and John H. Gagnon), an economist (Robert T. Michael), and a researcher (Stuart Michaels)—then submitted the results to elaborate statistical analysis, measuring sexual behavior against other characteristics like age, sex, marital status, race, religion, and education (which serves as a kind of code for class). Their book is the most comprehensive and trustworthy portrait of sexuality in America yet achieved.

IN ONE REGARD, however, the study falls short of current scientific standards: its sample of 3,432 is less than a fifth of the 20,000 that the authors themselves felt they needed. The Kinsey volumes, for example, were based on nearly 18,000 interviews, while two very recent high-quality studies in Britain and France had samples of 18,876 and 20,055, respectively. A story of political malfeasance lies behind this shortcoming. Originally the study was to be supported by the federal government, but it encountered intense hostility from the political right, led by Senator Jesse Helms and former Representative William Dannemeyer (a Republican from California), who, the authors assert, feared that it would confirm Kinsey's findings about homosexuality. There were also demands that all questions concerning masturbation be eliminated, ostensibly on the ground that it was irrelevant to controlling the spread of AIDS (the reason for the government's initial interest in the survey).

The authors tried to allay these anxieties by modifying their questionnaire, but to no avail. The Bush administration ultimately caved in to conservative pressure and withdrew the project's financing. Support then had to be sought from private foundations, and the much-reduced budget limited the number of interviews that could be conducted. Thus was the precision of the survey's findings compromised, especially regarding the behavior of small subpopulations. The authors estimate, for example, that they should have had a sample of about 400 homosexuals to achieve an appropriately refined account of gay sexual behavior, but in the end they had to settle for fewer than 100.

Perhaps still stinging from their political mauling, the researchers seem eager to confound the dire expectations of their critics. The finding they stress more than any other is the essential sexual conservatism of Americans, who, they maintain, are remarkably faithful to their partners and modest in their indulgences. More than 80 percent of Americans, for example, had only one sexual partner (or no partners at all) in the preceding year, and that number rises to 96 percent among the married. Half of the population has had no more than three different partners (the median for men is six, and the median for women is two) in an entire lifetime. The authors also judge unfaithfulness to be surprisingly rare: 90 percent of the women and over 75 percent of the men claim never to have had extramarital sex. Likewise, one-night stands happen much more often on television or in the movies than they do in real life, where they count for only a tiny fraction of the encounters among even those sexually most active.

In short, we have sex mainly with people we know, indeed with people we know very well, and for the most part with people very much like ourselves. Moreover, we don't have it as often as is generally thought: couples are more apt to have sex a few times a month rather than two or three times a week. One final piece of good news for the family-values crowd: Americans report that sex is most satisfying, not only emotionally but also physically, in a sustained relationship. Extracurricular sex tends to be guilty and awkward, surpassing its faithful counterpart in only one measure (no surprise here): it is more thrilling.

NONETHELESS, THERE HAVE BEEN some striking changes in sexual behavior over the past half-century, changes the authors chart by dividing their sample into 10-year cohorts, the oldest coming of age in the 1950s, the youngest in the 1980s. Here we get a more licentious picture, one that lends some credence to the fears of conservatives. Like all recent studies, this one confirms the extent to which marriage has given way to cohabitation. Among the youngest cohort only 5 percent of the women and 2 percent of the men had intercourse for the first time on their wedding night, in contrast to 45 percent and 17 percent in the oldest cohort.

A similar pattern of generational change can be seen in two other significant measures of sexual behavior: oral sex and the number of partners. In both cases there are dramatic increases among those who came of age in the 1960s or later, confirming, as the authors warily admit, the reality of the sexual revolution. Indeed, they conclude that cunnilingus and fellatio represent the most important additions to the sexual repertory of the typical American couple, marking the triumph of the foreplay ethic over the unceremonious and single-minded focus on intercourse in earlier generations. Anal sex, however, is not nearly so popular, though the authors express surprise that 9 percent of the sexually active heterosexuals reported trying it at least once in the preceding year. Finally, they turn up some evidence of a sexual counterrevolution in the 1980s, reflecting the fear of AIDS and the new puritanism of the Reagan-Bush era: 10 percent of the youngest men reported still being virgins at age 20, while the figure was a mere 1 percent for the older men.

Also serving to disturb the reassuring marital image the authors generally convey are their findings about the difference between the sexual experiences of men and women. Here they echo Kinsey, who discovered that men and women have radically different patterns of sexual aging. Men, he showed, quickly reach their peak of activity in the late teens, after which they tail off over the rest of their lives. Women, by contrast, experience a very gradual increase into their late 20s, remain on a plateau over the next two decades or so, and then enter a slow decline. Sexually speaking, Kinsey concluded, men and women were like ships passing in the night.

The authors of the new study are suspicious of the essentialist biological assumptions informing Kinsey's portrait, preferring to think that sexual behavior is socially constructed—or, as they say, "scripted." Nonetheless, their findings repeatedly show women to be far less sexually expressive than men. Men, for example, are distinctly more devoted masturbators: more than three times as many men as women report masturbating at least once a week, though more men also report feeling guilty afterwards. Oral sex, whether giving it or receiving it, appeals to about twice as many men as women. Men are also much more likely to have multiple partners (and to have more of them), and they are vastly more excited by sexual fantasies, visual materials, and the prospect of group sex. Perhaps most striking, three-quarters of the men report always reaching orgasm in intercourse, while the fraction for women is nearer one-quarter. In these and many other respects men and women appear to be races apart, creating, the authors glumly note, a major source of tension in relationships. Happily, the discrepancy is less pronounced among the youngest cohort, a trend that holds out the possibility of a rapprochement between the sexes.

THE AUTHORS EXPECT their findings about homosexuality to be the most controversial in the report, mainly because of recent public squabbles about the 10 percent figure associated with the first Kinsey report. As they rightly note, Kinsey never said that 10 percent of the population was homosexual. He was in fact a radical nominalist in sexual matters, insisting that there were no homosexual persons only homosexual acts. His 10 percent figure referred to the number of men who had had more or less exclusively homosexual relations for a three-year period. More important were two other figures: 37 percent, for the number of men reporting at least one homosexual experience (leading to orgasm) in their life, and 4 percent, for the number claiming to have had exclusively homosexual relations.

Several of the findings in the new report lend themselves to direct comparison with Kinsey's figures, and in all cases they suggest lower incidences of homosexuality, often dramatically so. In contrast to Kinsey's 37 percent, only 9 percent of the men in the present sample say that they have had at least one homosexual encounter in their lives. But nearly 8 percent of them confess to experiencing homosexual desire, and nearly 3 percent actually had sex with another man in the preceding year. Nearly 3 percent of men also identified themselves as homosexuals (or bisexuals), a number that, at a stretch, might be compared with Kinsey's 4 percent for men with exclusively homosexual experience. The percentages for women were about half those for men, except in the case of desire, which was roughly equal.

How do we account for the considerable discrepancies between Kinsey's findings and those of the new study? Undoubtedly part of the answer lies in the overrepresentation of homosexuals among Kinsey's volunteers, quite a few of whom came from prisons and reform schools (where situational homosexuality is high) or from the homosexual networks that Kinsey cultivated. But there are at least two reasons to believe that the new study underreports homosexuality. First, its sampling technique does not satisfactorily address the intense geographical concentration of homosexuals not only in particular cities (New York, Los Angeles, San Francisco) but in particular neighborhoods within those cities. Indeed, Kinsey's 10 percent figure probably "feels right" to many gay people because, as the new study reports, in America's 12 largest central cities self-identifying homosexuals or bisexuals in fact constitute 9 percent of the population. But I'm inclined to think that a more important reason lies in Kinsey's distinctive skills as an interviewer. He conducted some 8,000 of the interviews himself, and by all accounts he was a charismatic, even seductive, interlocutor. Typically he broached this issue by asking his subjects when they had their first homosexual experience, thereby creating the expectation that everybody did it and forcing the individual into either passive assent or active denial.

The present authors repeatedly confess that, because homosexuality continues to be stigmatized, their findings probably understate its prevalence. They themselves call their numbers "lower-bound estimates." Even so, those numbers are higher than the ones in the recent British and French surveys, which found a lifetime figure not of 9 percent, as in America, but of 6 percent in Britain and 4 percent in France. The debate, one can safely predict, is far from over, especially given the widespread sense that sexual identity is becoming ever more unstable.

LET ME FINISH by mentioning just three other findings to which the authors attach particular importance. The first is that, as Kinsey also found, sex in America is very much class-coded. Put broadly (but not inaccurately), the poorer segments of American society incline toward an unadorned, no-nonsense, silent approach to sex, like that found among the older cohorts, while those better off practice a more self-conscious, elaborate, even mannered sexuality, especially when it comes to masturbation and foreplay. The second is the disturbing discovery that more than a fifth of the women report having been forced to do something sexual against their will at least once, while 12 percent of the men and 17 percent of the women say they were touched sexually before puberty. For girls the experience was usually with an adult friend of the family or a relative (though rarely—pace Jeffrey Masson—the father), while for boys it was more apt to be with an adolescent girl and to be pleasurable. Lastly, in their extensive discussion of sexually transmitted diseases, the authors demonstrate that with every additional sexual partner the chances of infection increase not arithmetically but geometrically, because one's partners are themselves likely to have multiple partners, thus linking the couple to a rapidly expanding germ pool. The authors offer no advice, but this finding nicely complements the marital ethos that is perhaps the study's most salient feature.

Judged simply as a piece of writing, *The Social Organization of Sexuality* is unfailingly lucid. Even for the most technical matters it gives explanations that any educated reader can comprehend. It is, finally, a major achievement, which may well prompt as vigorous a public and scholarly debate as did the Kinsey studies half a century ago.

CHAPTER TWELVE

For the Love of Big Brother:
The Sexual Politics of *Nineteen Eighty-Four*

Written for a collection on Orwell's novel edited by Peter Stansky and published by the Stanford Alumni Association in 1983, this essay explores the sexual argument (explicit and implied) of Nineteen Eighty-Four. *It stresses Orwell's association of totalitarianism with sexual repression and his insinuation that the authoritarian leader is ultimately a homoerotic love object, very much as does Thomas Mann in his novella* Mario and the Magician *and as does Freud in* Group Psychology and the Analysis of the Ego.

In *Nineteen Eighty-Four* George Orwell presents a distinct theory about the relation between sex and society under totalitarianism. Put very simply, he argues that sexual fulfillment and political authoritarianism are incompatible.

"The aim of the Party," Orwell writes, "was not merely to prevent men and women from forming loyalties which it might not be able to control. Its real, undeclared purpose was to remove all pleasure from the sexual act." Significantly, the Ministry of Repression in Orwell's fictional country Oceania (i.e., the police) is called the Ministry of Love. The Party also disapproves of erotic talk, and Party members are expected to avoid profanity. In Orwell's famous dystopian language "Newspeak," sexual life is entirely encompassed by two words, *sexcrime* (sexual immorality) and *goodsex* (chastity): "Sexcrime covered all sexual misdeeds whatever. It covered fornication, adultery, homosexuality, and other perversions, and, in addition, normal intercourse practiced for its own sake.

There was no need to enumerate them separately, since they were all equally culpable, and in principle, all punishable by death." In his final peroration, the malevolent apparatchik O'Brien reveals that the Party seeks not just to curtail sex or diminish its pleasure but to do away with it entirely. "The sex instinct will be eradicated," he announces. "Procreation will be an annual formality like the renewal of a ration card. We shall abolish the orgasm." Moreover, the regime's puritanism is no mere ideological fluke but essential to its survival. As the Party theoretician Emmanuel Goldstein explains, "All the beliefs, habits, tastes, emotions, mental attitudes that characterize our time are really designed to sustain the mystique of the Party and prevent the true nature of present-day society from being perceived."

The government of Oceania has already made remarkable strides toward its goal of desexualization. The people we meet in *Nineteen Eighty-Four* are among the most unprepossessing, the least sexy, in all literature. "Nearly everyone was ugly," observes Winston Smith, looking around the canteen in the Ministry of Truth. The men are described variously as beetlelike, frog-faced, chinless, and dumpy. The women are grayish, dusty, and wispy-haired. To be sure, Winston's wife, Katherine, is "a tall, fair-haired girl, very straight, with splendid movements," but she is also the most complete realization (to date) of the regime's antisexual ideal: she detests intercourse, her body stiffening the moment Winston touches her. Even more horrible, she insists on a weekly enactment of this "frigid little ceremony," which she refers to as "our duty to the Party."

Although desexualization is the ultimate fate of Winston and his lover Julia (at their final meeting the thought of intercourse is detestable to both of them), their political rebellion, appropriately, is linked to sexual liberation. Indeed, in an important sense their revolt and their adultery are one and the same, as Winston repeatedly explains. He had hoped, for example, to arouse his wife from her erotic numbness not for his own pleasure but because of its political implications:

> What he wanted more even than to be loved, was to break down that wall of virtue, even if it were only once in his whole life. The sexual act, successfully performed, was rebellion. Desire was thoughtcrime. Even to have

awakened Katherine, if he could have achieved it, would have been like a seduction, although she was his wife.

He is thrilled to hear that Julia has slept with Party members scores of times, wishing only that it had been hundreds or even thousands. "Anything that hinted at corruption always filled him with wild hope." Similarly, her bawdy talk registers with him as an act of political opposition. And after they make love for the first time he gives succinct expression to its revolutionary significance: "Their embrace had been a battle, the climax a victory. It was a blow struck against the Party. It was a political act."

Orwell carefully insists it is sex, not love, that contains the promise of revolt. He was by temperament, one feels, too tough-minded, too antiromantic, to propose that love might be the answer. "Not merely the love of one person," reflects Winston, "but the animal instinct, the simple undifferentiated desire: that was the force that would tear the Party to pieces."

Winston's formulation is overstated and doesn't represent Orwell's considered opinion. In an earlier discussion of the Party's attitude toward prostitution he had written, "Tacitly the Party was even inclined to encourage prostitution, as an outlet for instincts which could not be altogether suppressed. Mere debauchery did not matter very much, so long as it was furtive and joyless." Presumably, therefore, the revolutionary sexuality Orwell has in mind is something less than love but more than a mechanical discharge of sexual tensions. It might best be called "humanized" sexuality: sexual pleasure, not just sexual relief—the latter being what the members of the working class, the "proles" get and what Winston himself got (much to his dissatisfaction) when he visited a prostitute.

Oceania presents certain sexual anomalies that don't fit the pattern of repression. The most glaring of these would seem to be the proles, who are explicitly exempted from the regime's antisexual policies. Indeed, the proles are positively incited to libertinage. A whole bureau in the Ministry of Truth is devoted to creating pornographic novels and films for them. The explanation for this anomaly, of course, is that the Party considers the proles less than human. The encouragement of a kind of animal sexuality among them (they are repeatedly compared to animals in the novel) prevents them from developing the political consciousness that might pose a threat to the regime. They are victims of what Herbert Marcuse called "repressive desublimation."

A more intriguing anomaly is the Junior Anti-Sex League, to which the lusty Julia belongs. This is one of Orwell's better jokes, but I wonder if he has caught its full irony. The first hint of the regime's puritanism comes when Julia is introduced in her Anti-Sex League costume: "She was a bold-looking girl of about twenty-seven, with thick dark hair, a freckled face, and swift, athletic movements. A narrow scarlet sash, emblem of the Junior Anti-Sex League, was wound several times around the waist of her overalls, just tightly enough to bring out the shapeliness of her hips." Freud would call this "the return of the repressed." Not only does the Anti-Sex League's emblem highlight the wearer's sexuality, but its scarlet color is heavily freighted with biological and literary associations of an unmistakably erotic nature. The repressed also makes a return in the Party's idealized physical type: "tall muscular youths and deep bosomed maidens, blond-haired, vital, sunburnt, carefree." Here Orwell takes an obvious swipe at the prurience of the Nazis.

In spite of such complications, both the Party and its enemies (that is, Winston and Julia) agree that authoritarianism is intimately connected with sexual repression. What seems a good deal less clear is the nature of that connection. Why, we must ask, does the regime's survival depend on its imposition of a puritanical sexual code?

Two possible answers immediately suggest themselves but must be dismissed as illogical or inadequately supported by the text. The first is the idea that sex threatens the regime because it is natural; as an unmediated biological instinct, it necessarily stands in opposition to the artificialities of Oceanic society. The notion of the subversive naturalness of sex is associated with Freud's *Civilization and Its Discontents*, which maintains that culture is based on sexual repression and hence that sex in the raw, so to speak, undermines social order. Whether or not Orwell held such a view, it is obviously too general to distinguish the peculiar society of Oceania—that is, a totalitarian one—from all other societies.

A second inadequate hypothesis argues that sex is subversive because of its privateness—because it creates a realm beyond the Party's control. But in Oceania sex is not in fact private. There are telescreens and hidden microphones everywhere (including bedrooms), and the microphones are sensitive enough to detect even a heartbeat. Under such circumstances only sex that is completely silent and conducted in absolute darkness can remain secret. Winston and Julia think that they go undetected when they have intercourse above Mr. Charrington's antique shop, but the Thought Police have eavesdropped on them from behind a picture. Even their seemingly isolated lovemaking in the woods has been observed (though Orwell does not explain how), and Winston eventually recognizes that "no physical act, no word spoken aloud" had been undetected by the police. "They had played sound tracks to him, shown him photographs. Some of them were photographs of Julia and himself. Yes, even . . . " The theory that sex is subversive because of its privateness fails on empirical grounds.

Two characters in *Nineteen Eighty-Four*, O'Brien and Julia, articulate their own explanations for the regime's puritanism. Neither theory is entirely satisfactory—neither adequately accounts for the sexual information contained in the novel—but they bring us closer to understanding Orwell's meaning.

O'Brien's explanation might be called the theory of competing pleasures. It advances in three steps. First, the goal of the Party, he says, is to seek power "entirely for its own sake." Second, one asserts power over another human being "by making him suffer." Finally, since the sole object of the Party is power, and since power reduces itself to inflicting pain, the Party must create a world in which "there will be no emotions except fear, rage, triumph, and self-abasement. . . . All competing pleasures will be destroyed." Hence his conclusion: "We shall abolish the orgasm." Even for doublethink, O'Brien's argument is unusually tortuous, and one worries that there has been some logical slippage. The same line of reasoning would appear to rule out eating, defecating, scratching, and any number of other "competing pleasures" with which the regime seems prepared to make its peace. Orwell nowhere elaborates the theory or addresses its obvious difficulties, and we sense that it is intended mainly to convey O'Brien's talent for extravagant casuistry.

Julia's theory is more promising. It is down-to-earth (like Julia herself) and finds greater resonance in the novel as a whole. A Freudian would call it an "economic theory," because it is based on a notion of displaced libido:

> Unlike Winston, Julia had grasped the inner meaning of the Party's sexual puritanism. It was not merely that the sex instinct created a world of its own which was outside the Party's control and which therefore had to be destroyed if possible. What was more important was that sexual privation induced hysteria, which was desirable because it could be transformed into war fever and leader worship. The way she put it was:
>
> "When you make love you're using up energy; and afterward you feel happy and don't give a damn for anything. They can't bear you to feel like that. They want you to be bursting with energy all the time. All this marching up and down and cheering and waving flags is simply sex gone sour. If you're happy inside yourself, why should you get excited about Big Brother and the Three-Year Plans and the Two Minutes Hate and all the rest of their bloody rot?"

The same logic—"bottling down some powerful instinct and using it as a driving force"—leads Orwell to describe Hate Week as a "great orgasm . . . quivering to its climax." We have come to associate the economic metaphor—the notion of a closed economy of psychic energy—with psychoanalysis, but it was in fact the common property of Western sexual thought well into the twentieth century. Thus no direct indebtedness need be assumed.

The trouble with the economic theory, like the naturalness theory, is that it's too general. It serves to explain the libidinal dynamics of all societies, and nothing about it points to the uniquely authoritarian character of Oceania. Much more apposite is another idea associated with Freud: the proposition, set forth in *Group Psychology and the Analysis of the Ego,* that societies hold together because their members fall in love with the leader—or, to use Freud's own language, are attached to the leader by "aim-inhibited libidinal ties." The idea was taken up by Thomas Mann in his novella *Mario and the Magician,* a parody of Italian Fascism, in which the erotic bond between leader and led is made quite explicit. Like Freud and Mann, Orwell, I would suggest, argues that the totalitarian society of Oceania requires that all its members be in love with the society's leader,

Big Brother. And since Big Brother's power is absolute, the love his subjects bear him must also be absolute. Unlike an ordinary society, Oceania demands that its subjects' sublimation be complete. Hence the regime's goal of abolishing sex altogether.

Whether or not Big Brother exists is, of course, irrelevant. Indeed, all the better if he is merely a fabrication of the Party, because then he can be fashioned precisely to fulfill his essential role as love object. O'Brien explains, "Big Brother is the guise in which the Party chooses to exhibit itself to the world. His function is to act as a focusing point for love, fear, and reverence, emotions which are more easily felt toward an individual than toward an organization." The projected image of Big Brother, moreover, is strikingly erotic. He is "a man of about forty-five, with a heavy black mustache and ruggedly handsome features." Burt Reynolds might be our contemporary equivalent. No other male in the novel is described as handsome, and indeed the vast majority of them are positively hideous. Big Brother is always spoken of as potent: he is "full of power and mysterious calm," "all-powerful," "omnipotent," a potency enhanced by his invisibility and unknown whereabouts. His voice is "enveloping." His "hypnotic eyes" are like "some huge force . . . pressing down upon you." Only once is more than his face mentioned, and on that occasion we learn that his statue has displaced Admiral Nelson's as the corona of London's most prominent phallic symbol.

Orwell makes entirely explicit that Oceanic society depends for its survival on its members being in love with Big Brother. The final line of the novel, marking Winston Smith's complete capitulation, states simply, "He loved Big Brother." Before Winston's, the "conversions" of the traitors Jones, Aaronson, and Rutherford were complete when they, too, loved Big Brother. "It was touching," says O'Brien, "to see how they loved him." O'Brien interrupts his own paean to hatred and torture (in which he abolishes the orgasm) to remark, "There will be no love, except the love of Big Brother." The exclusiveness of that love is essential: to rule absolutely, the leader must monopolize all aim-inhibited affection.

Orwell indicates in numerous ways that sex lies at the root of this affection. Although Big Brother is loved equally by men and women, we learn several times that women in particular are drawn to the Party's zealous puritanism. The Junior Anti-Sex League advocates complete chastity for both sexes, but its membership seems to consist entirely of women. During the Two Minutes Hate a characteristically drab and repressed female Party member erupts into orgasmic ecstasy at the leader's appearance on the telescreen:

> The face of Big Brother seemed to persist for several seconds on the screen, as though the impact that it had made on everyone's eyeballs were too vivid to wear off immediately. The little sandy-haired woman had flung herself forward over the back of the chair in front of her. With a tremendous murmur that sounded like "My Savior!" she extended her arms toward the screen.

The Hate induces a thinly disguised sexual response in all the participants:

> At this moment the entire group of people broke into a deep, slow, rhythmical chant of "B-B! . . . B-B!" . . . It was a refrain that was often heard in moments of overwhelming emotion. Partly it was a sort of hymn to the wisdom and majesty to Big Brother, but still more it was an act of self-hypnosis, a deliberate drowning of consciousness by means of rhythmic noise.

Not only during this "general delirium" but even in casual moments, the loved one is addressed in familiar, even intimate, terms. He is not Big Brother but "B.B." We may safely conclude, then, that Oceania's puritanism results from the logic of libidinal displacement. The sexual attachment of citizens to one another must give way to a uniform, sublimated attachment to the leader.

THE DISPLACEMENT THEORY, I believe, does fullest justice to the novel's explicit arguments and evidence. But it fails to come to terms with a more subtle level of erotic persuasion in the book. There is surely a profound paradox in the fact that George Orwell, who is among the least sensuous of writers, should have argued so vehemently for the revolutionary potential of sexuality. And, indeed, *Nineteen Eighty-Four* exhibits an alarming discrepancy between its strenuously prosexual doctrines and its unfailingly anemic representation of sexual passion.

The affair between Winston and Julia is both a literary and a sexual dud, its erotic scenes flat and cliché-ridden. Orwell places the lovers' first encounter in a pseudo-Laurentian wood full of bluebells and singing thrushes. But the language remains resolutely earthbound ("He pulled her round so that they were breast to breast; her body seemed to melt into his"). They next have intercourse in an abandoned church tower (a setting that brings to mind the comic seduction scene in *Madame Bovary*), and Orwell's account is as mechanical as before. Mercifully, he then permits them to retire to the room above Mr. Charrington's, where, perhaps knowing his weakness, he restricts himself to short, general descriptions —mere indications, actually—of their lovemaking.

He also seems relieved to allow the process of sexual routinization to set in as quickly as possible. Winston is happy to have found a place "where they could be alone together without feeling the obligation to make love every time they met," and where, in fact, they spend most of their time lying on the bed or sleeping. Julia remains the more erotic of the two ("a rebel from the waist downwards"), while Winston clearly prefers reading Emmanuel Goldstein's book to fulfilling his sexual responsibilities.

Inevitably one feels that were it not for his abstract conviction that sex is revolutionary Orwell would be perfectly comfortable with the regime's puritanical ideals. Measured by any literary standard, his dionysian protest is a failure.

Nineteen Eighty-Four does, however, contain scenes of genuine erotic power. They occur not between Winston and Julia but between Winston and O'Brien, and (as I will suggest in a moment) they are intimately related to Orwell's explicit theory about the political significance of libidinal displacement. Winston's relationship with O'Brien takes the literary form of an illicit courtship. Perhaps this is simply because illicit sex and political conspiracy share a similar experiential structure. But the erotic flavor of the relationship is nonetheless remarkable. Let us briefly follow the stages of their romance.

It begins with "an equivocal glance," but a glance so meaningful that it inspires Winston to his first act of revolt, the writing of his diary:

Momentarily he caught O'Brien's eye. O'Brien had stood up. He had taken off his spectacles and was in the act of resetting them on his nose with his characteristic gesture. But there was a fraction of a second when their eyes met, and for as long as it took to happen Winston knew—yes, he knew!— that O'Brien was thinking the same thing as himself. An unmistakable message had passed.

The scene is a not-so-distant relative of the "dumb charade" between Baron Charlus and Jupien in Proust's *Cities of the Plain*. Winston becomes convinced that O'Brien belongs to a secret organization with the significant name of "the Brotherhood," which is also described in remarkably suggestive language:

Some days he believed in it, some days not. There was no evidence, only fleeting glimpses that might mean anything or nothing; snatches of overheard conversation, faint scribbles on lavatory walls—once, even, when two strangers met, a small movement of hands which had looked as though it might be a signal of recognition.

Later Winston wonders whether Julia might not belong to "the fabulous Brotherhood," and Orwell's language, in a nice unconscious touch, effectively denies that the organization contains women: "Perhaps the Brotherhood existed after all! Perhaps the girl was part of it! No doubt the idea was absurd. . . . "

Even before that equivocal first glance, Winston felt himself "deeply drawn" to O'Brien. The glance creates a "strange intimacy" between them, and Winston comes to feel that he is writing his diary both for and to O'Brien, as if it were a kind of love letter. The furtive glance is followed by a furtive encounter. "Laying a friendly hand for a moment on Winston's arm," O'Brien invites him to his flat to look at a new edition of the Newspeak dictionary. This "equivocal remark" excites "secret imaginings" in Winston. And when they finally meet at the flat, "a wave of admiration, almost of worship, flowed out from Winston toward O'Brien."

It would, of course, be ludicrous to suppose that *Nineteen Eighty-Four* is a homosexual roman à clef. But the suggestion of a libidinal tie between Winston and O'Brien contributes significantly to the erotic argument of the novel. For in every sexual sense (and several nonsexual ones as well) O'Brien is transparently the same person as Big Brother. O'Brien has a "prize-fighter's physique," with a "powerful chest," and his grip is so ferocious that it "crushed the bones of Winston's palm." We are repeatedly reminded how he towers over the scrawny, maladroit, and fragile Winston, who with his "pale and meager body" and his horror of odors, exercise, and rats is made to seem distinctly womanish.

The psychological identification of O'Brien and Big Brother is more than a matter of similar anatomy. Orwell several times permits O'Brien and Big Brother to coalesce in Winston's imagination. When Winston examines a portrait of Big Brother on the frontispiece of a children's history book, "the face of O'Brien, not called up by any obvious association . . . , floated into his mind." Again later, "the face of Big Brother swam into his mind, displacing that of O'Brien." Thus the infatuation with O'Brien, which starts out on such a bright revolutionary note, culminates logically in Winston's love affair with Big Brother. O'Brien is not merely the agent of this transformation—the matchmaker, as it were. Psychologically speaking, he and the ultimate love object are interchangeable.

There is one final level of erotic argument that I would like to draw attention to, and it also plays upon the theme of displaced homosexual attachment in the totalitarian polity. In one sense, as I've suggested, O'Brien is Big Brother. But in another (and entirely compatible) sense he is also identified with Winston's mother. *Nineteen Eighty-Four* is replete with potent maternal images, massive females who dwarf and absorb their children. These mothers are the only figures in the novel, outside of O'Brien, of course, to whom Orwell attributes physical substantiality and robustness. The most important of them, naturally, is Winston's own mother, whose "large shapely body" recurs several times in his dreams and fantasies, and for whose murder he feels himself responsible. She is replicated in a number of other real or fanciful matriarchs: a "middle-aged woman" in a movie who holds a three-year-old boy between her breasts, trying to protect him from bullets, as both are about to drown; a fifty-year-old proletarian grandmother, "her thick arms reaching up for the line, her powerful marelike buttocks protruded," whom Winston finds distinctly "beautiful"; and a foul-mouthed drunk—"an enormous wreck of a woman, aged about sixty"—who is dumped on Winston's lap in jail and who, on learning that both of them are named Smith, says, sentimentally, "I might be your mother!"

Orwell's preoccupation with maternal fantasies, and with the child that has somehow murdered his mother, has an almost Wagnerian obsessiveness about it. Indeed, the powerful mother who inspires both awe and guilt seems to represent the psychological bedrock of the novel, although I won't pretend to understand the full logic of Orwell's conception (any more than I do Wagner's). But that O'Brien's relationship with Winston is at some level maternal is made repeatedly and abundantly clear. Throughout the final scenes of Winston's torture, O'Brien looms over his recumbent victim as over a child in a crib. Orwell is quite explicit about the matter: Winston, he writes, "clung to O'Brien like a baby, curiously comforted by the heavy arm around his shoulders." In his growing attachment to his maternal tormentor one detects Winston's effort to atone for his guilt, and we may be reminded of Freud's contention that guilt—or aggression directed against the self—is the fundamental psychological cement holding society together. Apparently the roots of desexualization reside not merely in a libidinal bond between ruler and ruled but, at the deepest, in the mysteriously ambivalent ties between mother and child.

Doubtless one must resist the temptation to make too much of the sexual argument in *Nineteen Eighty-Four*—either the explicit one or the subterranean one that I have sought to excavate. In general, Orwell interested himself more in the intellectual apparatus of totalitarianism than in its instinctual dynamics. He was, above all, a novelist of ideas, and the most memorable aspects of his book are its exposition of such intellectual phenomena as doublethink and Newspeak. Nor does he appear to have worked out the book's sexual argument with the same thoroughness that he brings to the conceptual issues. There is, for example, no appendix on sexual doctrines to complement that on Newspeak.

Nonetheless, Orwell comes back again and again to his libidinal theme, giving it pride of place in the novel's wrenching final moments. Moreover, his treatment of it exhibits a characteristically Orwellian twist. *Nineteen Eighty-Four* is, of course, a book much loved by conservatives. But I doubt that they can be entirely pleased that it embraces such frankly libertine sexual doctrines. They would be even less pleased, I suspect, with my suggestion that its sexual politics have a good deal in common with certain of Freud's ideas. Least of all would they care to hear that, at its deepest, it plunges into the psychologically murky waters of sublimated homoeroticism, maternal identification, and masochistic guilt. But in fact Orwell's vision in *Nineteen Eighty-Four* is as quirky and ideologically heterogeneous as that of such earlier works as *The Road to Wigan Pier* and *Homage to Catalonia,* which leftists have generally found more congenial. The book manages to preach both anti-Stalinism and sexual liberation, just as it unites rationalistic common sense with an uncanny sensitivity to life's erotic and emotional undercurrents.

CHAPTER THIRTEEN

"Dear Paul":
An Exchange between Student and Teacher

This correspondence between me and a Stanford undergraduate took place at the end of the 1970s. With the student's enthusiastic permission the correspondence was published in an issue of the journal Salmagundi *(Fall–Winter 1982–83) devoted to homosexuality. It is a coming-out story, based on a hilarious misunderstanding, and it documents a historical moment in the emergence of modern gay consciousness. The fact that the exchange of letters occurred on the eve of the AIDS epidemic gives it, in retrospect, a decidedly poignant flavor.*

I

San Francisco
June 18, 1979

Dear Paul,

I'm returning the final essay you wrote for my course. Although I haven't had a chance to talk with you since we had lunch in the middle of the quarter, I've often had you on my mind, especially this past week. Let me put what I have to say in schematic form: first your essay, then yourself, and last how they're related.

The prevailing mood of your paper might be described as cynical. Or, if that's too strong, then we can call it irreverent. Moreover the tone is perfectly in keeping with the personal impression you leave. You make your points quickly and move on, which means you occasionally risk sounding superficial, but you're never dull. Just beneath the surface of the paper, however, I detect a sense of uncertainty, a pervasive doubt, a fear on your part to feel or commit yourself strongly, which the tone you've adopted serves to disguise.

Now for Part Two. Let me risk a large indiscretion. If I've got this all fucked up, I'll trust you not to betray me. But I think you're gay. I'm not pretending to tell you something you're unaware of. Perhaps I should say, more precisely, I think you know you're gay. If you're interested in why I think so (and I'm not so crazy as to have dreamed this up out of whole cloth), come see me when you get back to school and I'll tell you a good story. It's a good story even if you're not gay, so don't forget to ask. But I should reassure you that nothing about the way you look, act, or speak makes me think that you're gay, although I don't consider it any particular virtue among homosexuals to be able to pass.

The reason I tell you of my suspicion is because I feel it is intimately tied up with your efforts to find yourself intellectually. It relates to your paper, to the rest of your work as a student, and ultimately to your career.

If my premise is wrong, you can forget about what follows (you can also forget about most of what precedes as well)—save, perhaps, as a particularly fine instance of intellectual extravagance. But I cherish the notion that the question of your sexual identity has got deeply enmeshed with that of your broader identity. When we had lunch together you talked, somewhat despairingly, about how your new interests, which pointed in the direction of an academic career, were alienating you from your parents, who had fairly practical notions about what you should become. But I now think that your "identity crisis" is much more thoroughgoing. It is one thing to tell your pragmatic parents that you're not going to become a doctor or a lawyer. It becomes altogether more awesome when the full message is not only will you not become a doctor or a lawyer but you're not going to become a husband and father either, because you love men.

The challenge you face, I think, is keeping these two things separate and under control. They are connected, to be sure, but the connection is not automatic. You need to sort out the elements of your alienation, and not allow your sexual inclinations to play an unjustifiably large role in determining your life. Sex is important, God knows. But it shouldn't tyrannize us. There are other things that deserve a certain autonomy. For example, there's friendship. The question of career falls into the same category, as do recreation, aesthetic sensibility, and political opinion. Each has its legitimate claims.

I make it all sound much too much like a trial. In fact, I feel just the opposite. Under the right circumstances and with the right qualities of character, being gay is an enjoyable experience. I'm almost embarrassed to confess how happy my own life is, and I frequently tell students who are coming out (and thus in a state of high anxiety) that there will come a time when they will think, "Thank God I'm gay." It's a life whose pleasures are many and varied, although it has its own special trials as well—and I say this as a man who was married for several years, with a child, and who spent his entire high-school and college years chasing after women (but not in my heart).

The most academic hypothesis I want to advance here (Part Three) is that your being gay also explains the tone of your paper. For one thing, there is the pervasive undercurrent of despair that I spoke about earlier. The paper's brittleness seems to echo your general feeling of discontent. More speculatively, I've come to associate a certain tone of "serious unseriousness" with what might be called a homosexual sensibility. Speaking very broadly, it seems to me that the distinctive contribution of homosexuals to literary culture is their wit, their intolerance for abstraction and ponderousness, and their love of quick, lucid movement and distaste for murky profundities (Heidegger is surely the straightest writer ever). The quality is wonderfully captured in Andrew Holleran's novel *Dancer from the Dance*, and your paper, too, has something of the same flavor.

Now, if I'm not totally out to lunch (in which case I'll sell this as a short story), please come around for the anecdote. In any event, drop me a line. This is the most indiscreet letter I've ever written, and you could be put in prison for mental cruelty if you fail to enlighten me. Cheers!

Paul

P.S. It occurs to me that what I've written here is characteristically professorial. That's because we've dealt with each other only on this basis. But right now you may be much more interested in fairly practical matters, and, believe me, I'm full of opinions about even the most mundane details of gay life. Of late, it seems, most students who come to see me—both gay and straight—mainly want to talk about how to get laid, which is one of my favorite topics. Our bodies are overwhelmingly real and demanding, and only intellectual snobs pretend that such talk is beneath their dignity.

II

Iowa
June 22, 1979

Dear Paul,

I received your letter today with my final, and it left me absolutely thunderstruck. I simply cannot imagine (and for once I mean it) how you managed such an insight. I read it while driving back to work, nearly crashing several times. No one has EVER read me like that before. I have to admit it frightens me a little. Although I don't try to act straight anymore, neither did I think I was readily identifiable as gay. I guess you picked up the general nature of my personality, the lightly shielded despair, the ambivalence about a lot of things, and so forth. Frankly, it seems obvious to me that I'm gay and show it, but evidently most straight people are blind to the signs. I'm not entirely convinced, though, that you would write such a detailed letter solely on the basis of your analysis of my character. For instance, I'm very curious about this anecdote, and I'm wondering if it doesn't have something to do with Jim Cady, who was also a student in your course. I certainly won't forget to ask.

Your letter arrived at an odd moment. I, too, had been planning to write you (this evening, in fact) to explain some things about myself that I felt you should know. You've already guessed a good deal of it, which spares me the trouble of making a roundabout confession draped with qualifications. This has been a landmark year for me, a year in which I finally had to begin dealing with a truth I had already acknowledged long ago. I've known I was gay since I was twelve. Never a doubt. Fortunately, there was no real sexual pressure on me in high school, which meant I never thought about my future in terms of being homosexual. Freshman year, also, was easy: everyone was too busy trying to survive and make friends to worry about sex.

But by last spring I recognized a very significant thing: I was in love with my best friend, the guy I roomed with this year. You can probably imagine the ensuing disaster. He was straight and got involved with a girl, and the whole thing fell apart. I was torn between my jealousy and my desire to preserve the best elements of our friendship—the intellectual dialogue, the almost instinctual understanding, the laughs. I failed. This winter was hell. I told him I was gay, and he took it well enough, though deep down I always got the feeling that he looked on me as something of an alien. I was pretty unhappy and got depressed a lot, which showed up in my grades.

My first paragraph sounds a little cold. I want you to know how much I appreciate your taking the time to write a letter that has already had a profound impact on my state of mind. It's just that the absolute accuracy of everything you said really stunned me. You answered questions that I've been asking myself for months or years.

Do you have any more sage counsel and advice to offer? That's what I was going to ask for in the first place. Nobody needs it more than I: I really don't know how to order my life, what to do. And I've never really talked about being gay with another, let alone wiser, gay before. Which explains why this is such a disjointed letter: I don't know where to begin. Once again, thank you for your time, interest, and intellection: you can't know how much good you did for me today. If you have the ambition, please write. I will keep you posted on my plans for the fall.

Paul

III

San Francisco
June 25, 1979

Dear Paul,

Well, that's a relief. You have no reason to apologize for your letter, which was really very generous. As to the anecdote, you're sort of on the right track, but if you figure the whole story out I'll award you my private Pulitzer Prize for fiction. I'm embarrassed to confess, however, that I missed all those signs you were posting. Like your straight friends, I left our luncheon together without it ever having crossed my mind that you might be gay. Honest to God. I may be unobservant, but I think you're too subtle. Too subtle for me anyway.

I have a kind of standard lecture, which you apparently are in need of. So here goes.

First, the facts. You are a good looking, intelligent man, with enough distinctive qualities of character to make you interesting and enjoyable company. All of which means that there are many men who will be attracted to you, and presumably you'll find some of them attractive also. But you have to put yourself into an appropriate situation. That is, you have to think rationally—which to a considerable extent means thinking statistically—about your circumstances and find your way to places where the right things will happen. Trying to make it with a roommate is wonderfully romantic but altogether impracticable. The chances of it working are probably less than 1 in 25. To begin with, there's only 1 chance in 10 that your roommate will be gay (accepting the most "optimistic" Kinsey statistics), and even if he is it doesn't necessarily follow that he will be in love with you. I know several gay men whose hearts have been broken, and their lives nearly ruined, because they fell in love with an impossible object—usually their best friend—to whom, eventually, they confessed their love, with results very similar to those you experienced.

People fall in love with roommates mainly because they're not around authentic possibilities. You can improve your chances in any number of ways. For example, there is the Gay Students Union, which has various functions, the majority of which are social, because their real purpose is to allow students to find one another. There are also all sorts of places to go in the city, a number of which don't serve liquor and are thus accessible to people under age.

By now you must have figured out that the structure of gay sexual life is rather the reverse of straight life. That is (to put it as baldly as possible), sex comes before love. Or, more positively, love grows out of sex. Thus in order to find your way, you have to give up (or at least mod-

ify) the notions of courtship that you got from your heterosexual upbringing. I'm not passing judgment on this difference, just taking note of
it. There's no question that gays begin having sex at a much lower level
of emotional commitment. I suspect this is because we are a minority: we
have to test the waters before we can even think of diving in, whereas
straights can take it for granted that the objects of their affection, speaking categorically, also desire them. That's exactly the way you conducted
your romance with your roommate: like a straight romance, which
would have been perfectly sensible, with a good chance of success, if
only your roommate had been a woman.

So we are beating our heads against the wall when we fail to take our
minority circumstances into account. That's why bars and discos and gay
student unions exist. They make it possible for us to have a reasonable sex
life.

Needless to say, I don't know what your experiences, your desires, or
your fears might be. Everybody's different—but not that different.
Much of gay life, like any kind of life, has to do with the simple mechan-
ics of how do we get together, how do we get to bed, how do you come,
and endless other interesting trivia. These are things that you find out by
trial and error, that you bungle, that you talk about. You have to be prepared for some dead ends, screw-ups, and disasters, if also a good deal of
fun, an occasional laugh, and—with a reasonable amount of luck—a
little ecstasy as well.

I'm being willfully hardhearted, because so many people refuse to
bring simple intelligence to bear on their erotic lives, even though sex,
like everything else, benefits from the application of reason. But I'll confess that it can also be very emotional. You have already had an invaluable experience, which, in retrospect, you will probably see as having
enriched you. But it's not the sort of experience you want to repeat end-
lessly. Being disappointed in love is the greatest agony there is. It is ex-
quisitely painful, as you know. People who haven't suffered over love are
lesser.

But sometimes it works, or at least it works long enough for you to
remember more than the disappointment. You are transparently a romantic. Only romantics have the emotional energy to sustain impossible
relationships over the period of time you sustained yours with your

roommate. That's most fortunate for you. Many gay men have a totally shattered psychology, which means that they never have a relationship in which they can make much of an investment. Your problem, I suspect, will be to avoid being victimized by your romanticism, because, as I've said, the structure of gay life demands a suspension of that proclivity so that things can get started. One might say you need to have love in reserve, to be dispensed when the right object has been found.

One thing in your letter was absolutely on the money: the way straight people feel when they find out you're gay. When you say you had the feeling that your roommate came to think of you as somehow alien, you've identified a response that straights, even the most enlightened, simply can't escape. I believe that every straight person, at some level of his being, is happy he's not gay. I also believe that every man at some level feels the same thing about not being a woman, and that every white person feels something comparable about not being black. We have a responsibility to reduce those feelings as much as possible, and never to act on them, but that won't make them go away. Maybe there will be a time when these prejudices are truly overcome, but I doubt that it will be during our lives. Meanwhile I think one has to be satisfied that straights manage as well as they do, given the emotional equipment they've been born to. Still, you have to be prepared for a lifetime of disapproval, even if it is of the most reasonable variety.

I'm sending you a copy of a book I like a lot, John Reid's *The Best Little Boy in the World*.

My best,
Paul

IV

Iowa
July 16, 1979

Dear Paul,

Thanks for the book. Actually I read it for the first time several years ago, while I was still in high school, but yours was a revised version so I read it again. I think it's a marvelous book, and I've asked some of my friends to read it. I've wondered off and on since springtime if maybe you hadn't written it, but you more or less implied in your letter that you hadn't.

I've read a fair amount of homosexual fiction. Vidal's *The City and the Pillar*, Gordon Merrick's *The Lord Won't Mind* and *One for the Gods*, part of John Rechy's *City of Night*, Christopher Isherwood's *A Single Man*, and (my favorite) James Baldwin's *Giovanni's Room*. I also went down to the library to look for Holleran's *Dancer from the Dance*: it's card-catalogued but not on the shelves, which probably means that someone swiped it. It's not easy to buy or check out such books here without attracting attention.

I wish I could give you a clear picture of what's on my mind. I've told my closest friends here, with mixed results. I told my best high-school friend several years ago. He took it well then and has been fantastic ever since. In spite of what you write, I honestly don't think he feels any differently about me. The other people, though, aren't quite sure what to say. This is, after all, fag-hating country, and all of them, no matter now liberal they want to seem, are a little flustered by this particular revelation. "Are you sure?" "Would a girlfriend help?"—questions that tell me they really have no grasp whatsoever of the issue. I try to be perfectly frank and open and willing to answer questions, but by and large they prefer to ignore it (or so I get the feeling). I guess I really don't blame them.

Another big question is my parents. I am extremely reluctant to say anything at all to them. I think my mom could handle it, but my dad . . . my dad really hates queers. He says so at every opportunity. I've thought a lot lately about why he's so hostile; I guess it's just the way people around here think. My parents may suspect (mom, for instance, has often praised San Francisco for its tolerance and cosmopolitanism), but I doubt they'd mention anything. For the time being, I'm not going to, either.

One part of your letter bothered me—the part about sex before love. Being, as you said, a romantic, I find that prospect (or that reality) profoundly depressing. It's not that I never recognized it, or never thought about it. But I think it throws the balance between mind and body out of kilter. Maybe I'm taking this too seriously. I certainly don't believe it's necessary to be in love with someone to have sex with him. But the impersonality of what you suggest chills me. Don't you have to like some-one, to know him a little, to feel that you care, even if just a bit? I don't find the idea of gay bars, gay discos, and gay wing dings alluring in the slightest, not because they're gay, but because I just don't like them. I can't stand bars of any sort, and I've never felt comfortable at big parties. You're going to say that I will have to suppress my distaste for such things, and maybe that's true. I don't know how much peace of mind I'm willing to give up, though, in order to make a bunch of pickups. I may eventually force myself into it, but basically I'm pretty quiet.

Another thing that worries me is the unattractiveness of homosexu-als, physically and otherwise. So many gays look gay—not effeminate, just recognizably gay. And most of the gay people I've seen (not all that many, I admit) are not terribly good looking. Are there many "cowboy" students like me, who just look regular? I suppose there must be. Looking at the men at school can be a depressing experience, however: all that physical beauty, yet I can't imagine any of them being gay. Or willing to admit it. I know a lot of people (well, several) who exhibit what strike me as telltale psychological signs—bitter humor, sporadic depression, seeming insecurity about women, and the like. I see all those things in myself, and I recognize their principal source. Mightn't it be the same for others? (The answer, I recognize, is—yes, possibly—but, then, there could be countless other reasons that I can't see because I'm obsessed with my own.)

You said I was "sort of" on the right track about Jim Cady and that you would give me a Pulitzer if I figured it out. Here goes:

Last May I sent Jim a little note that basically amounted to a proposi-tion. It seemed like a fairly safe way to approach him, although in retro-spect I did so on flimsy grounds. I signed only my first name. Maybe he thought you had sent it, so you two went out and had a blast. Then later he says, "Gee, Paul, it's a lucky thing you sent me that note so that you and I could get together," to which you say, "But Jim, I sent no note!" Then you go over the course list and find my name—the only Paul en-rolled—and I'm convicted.

Or maybe he just brought you the note and said, "What kind of idiot would do such a thing?" (This can't be it—it wouldn't make a good story at all.)

I guess he must be straight, and he asked your advice on how to handle a gay issue like this. Then again, I've seen enticing tidbits that suggest he may be gay, which is why I think my first speculation is closest to the truth. Obviously all this shows that I have no idea what the fuck is going on and that I'm dying to know. So any broad hints or outright revelations you're willing to provide would be appreciated.

Thanks again. I hope to hear from you.

Paul

V

San Francisco
July 19, 1979

Dear Paul,

I like your letters so much they make me want to respond immediately. I apologize if that's oppressive. I also apologize for being coy about Jim Cady. Your splendid fictions definitely earn you the prize. I like the first one best, since I get to have such a good time. I guess the only reason I haven't told you the story—besides my being a tease—is that I have a vague feeling it might be somehow disloyal to Jim.

In fact your first rendition is the closest, only the ending is wonderfully wrong. This was about the wildest thing that has happened to me as a teacher, and it goes as follows:

After I had handed back the mid-term exams, Jim came to see me about the corrections and comments I had written on his. Or at least that was his ostensible purpose. Just as it was time to leave, he launched a sensational piece of dialogue:

J.: "I got your letter."

P.: "What letter?"

J.: "The one you sent me from San Francisco."

P.: "And just what did I say in this letter?"

J.: "You said, 'Seeing how it is Gay Awareness Week, I thought I would give it a try.

Paul.'

And you're the only Paul I know."

P.: "O no, I'm not!"

I first thought this whole story was an attempt to get one foot out of the closet, so I asked him directly if he was gay. He said no. It took some time before I fully convinced him that the letter wasn't from me. Apparently you wrote in the same kind of ink I use to correct exams, and apparently the post-office sent the letter through San Francisco, as they often do.

He was completely nice about all of this, just as you would expect. He had come primarily to disabuse me gently; it was almost as if he were ashamed that he wasn't interested! I told him I admired his courage and good will, and then I sent him off to do "research." I was sure the "Paul" in question must be someone in his dormitory, so I suggested he begin there.

A few days later he returned to inform me that there were two Pauls in his dorm, and both had every appearance of being heterosexual (girl-friends, etc.). But he also reported that he had received a call that morning from a Paul in my class who wanted to borrow his notes. It didn't take long before we had identified you with some confidence. I was truly surprised, as I said in my first letter.

So, you see, I wasn't that smart, after all. Now, let me see if I can turn this episode to good pedagogical use.

The fact is, the whole incident is of a piece with your falling in love with your roommate: if you send ten such notes, one of the recipients might be a homosexual. But then there are further contingencies: Does he accept the fact that he's homosexual? Is he interested in you? And even if he is homosexual, self-accepting, and interested, does he know how to proceed? So what are your chances? Shitty. That is what I meant by being victimized by your romanticism. I believe that I'm as romantic as anyone this side of Keats. But I'm enough of a realist to know that things don't always happen as they seem to in novels. In fact it occurs to me that you've probably read too many, not too few, gay novels, because they will keep you from devoting some hard thought to the less glamorous aspects of your situation. The important thing here is not to despise intelligence. Thinking is a crucial part of loving, and falling in love demands an exercise of the mind, paradoxical as that may sound. Naturally the experience is essentially emotional and physical, but you have to bring your intelligence to bear on its contingencies.

I expressed myself perhaps too unqualifiedly when I said that for gays sex comes before love. In a strict sense that's true. But I didn't mean to imply that the sexual relations in question were entirely without emotional content. I don't believe such things exist. Sex is too much a mental thing. Something happens; some element of affection is nearly always present; the "body" is, in some degree, a "person." So you're right: yes, you have to like someone to have sex with him, or at least you have to think that you like him.

I feel you need to get your ideas about the general issue of relationships straight before you become bogged down in the particulars of bars, parties, and the like. You can meet other gay men in a more intimate context as well, although the process is slower. But even when you meet a man through friends, the basic structure of courtship is not that dramatically altered. Naturally you'll know him somewhat better than you would a guy you met in a bar or at a party, but in most instances you'll be expected to get in the sack long before you are willing to say that you're in love. What I sense in your letters is an excessively rigid set of distinctions about sex and love, which reflect a profoundly romantic (and largely heterosexual) intellectual tradition. Somehow, I think, you've got to lower your guard. Love is not austere or pristine. It's sort of a ragged thing, not even a thing for that matter, and the circumstances under which it emerges are generally messy, slightly ambiguous, and sometimes even tawdry. You obviously can't go against your nature, and I have no interest in trying to persuade you that bars and the like are fun (I don't enjoy them myself). But, as I've said, the issue goes deeper: you have to develop a more tractable attitude toward your emotional and physical needs.

How have you formed your impression that gay men aren't attractive? I would have said just the opposite: gay men, it seems to me, are on the whole better looking than straight men, in part because homosexuality is based on a certain degree of narcissism, in part because they take better care of themselves, and in part because they do not, like heterosexual men, tend to drop out of the race at marriage. But maybe it is precisely the attractiveness that you find unattractive. What I read between the lines of your letter is the same message one gets in *The Best Little Boy in the World:* lack of sexual interest in anyone who seems obviously gay, and not much tolerance for even nonsexual relations with such folks. We can't do much about what appeals to us sexually (obviously—otherwise we could go in for women). I do, however, think we have an obligation to associate with the noncowboys. You can't expect straight people to approve of you if you disapprove of other homosexuals. By that I don't mean you have to like every homosexual. That would be ridiculous. But "obvious gayness" shouldn't be a categorical justification for dissociating yourself from someone.

I think you are instinctively doing the right thing about your parents. It's nice, of course, to be able to tell one's parents. But often it is pointless and even cruel to do so. From what you write, it sounds to me as though both your parents, at some level of their minds, know what's up. Parents have a funny way of knowing and not knowing at the same time, and I think one has to respect their limitations. It's a measure of your love for them that you don't punish them with your homosexuality. I doubt that your father's remarks have the general cultural inspiration that you attribute to them. They sound very much like a form of aggression, though doubtless unconscious. And your mother sounds as if she were asking to be taken into your confidence. But I would exercise restraint. The confessional mode is seductive: we get a nice righteous feeling of being honest. But, as far as I'm concerned, telling the truth is no virtue when it mainly serves to hurt somebody. After all, your parents also have to struggle with existence.

Maybe I have an entirely erroneous picture of you, but I imagine you as someone who's thought a lot but done very little. And I have the quite oppressive sense that you are cheating yourself. Perhaps I think that because I spent my undergraduate years in a state of total abstinence, and I've always regretted what I imagine to be the many opportunities I missed. You write as if there were a great desert out there, whereas I know for a fact that there are vast numbers of attractive and willing men, and instead of suffering you should be enjoying. But then you wouldn't be you, I suppose, and I firmly believe that suffering (or at least delayed gratification) builds character.

How charming of you to think that I might have written *The Best Little Boy in the World*.

Paul

VI

Iowa
August 28, 1979

Dear Paul,

After checking the date on your last letter and discovering it to be July 19, I calculate that I have generously allotted myself a full six weeks to respond. That's not very courteous, but I've been busy boring myself to death at my job.

Some clarification on what I think homosexuals look like and why I find them unattractive. When I said many of them looked "obviously gay," I didn't mean effeminate. Rather I had in mind the guys with short hair, granny glasses, and ESPECIALLY those ghastly short-clipped beards. Most of the guys who I think look gay could probably have a pleasant conversation with my father without getting their faces punched in. But they just don't turn me on.

The Jim Cady debacle has left me trembling sporadically from humiliation. Christ, Christ, Christ, what a dumb thing to do! Actually, I was almost certain (for a number of reasons) that he was gay. Which gives you some idea of my perspicacity in such matters. He sent me a very gracious note a few weeks ago, which made me feel a little better. At least I think I can face him now.

Your speculation that my life as a homosexual has been more thought than deed is essentially correct. Back in 9th and 10th grade I got into some rather intense sexual bouts with a couple of guys (mutual jerking off, a few attempts at headers). That's supposed to be normal with young boys, but in my case I knew I was gay and that I was getting exactly what I wanted. After that I became involved with a couple of girls—the first, a slut whom I dropped after a few weeks because I could see it was hopeless; the second, one of the most remarkable people I've ever met. I think I may have been in love with her. Anyway, that went all to hell in late 10th grade, and for the rest of high school I just froze up. By the end of high school, guys began to become definitely "heterosexual," which I could not manage. So I learned how to put interested women off pleasantly and to protect myself from possible derision. Hence my humorous pessimism. My personality bristles with defense mechanisms.

I'm not as romantic as I've led you to believe. In fact I'm always torn between romantic and cynical impulses, between idealism and realism. I guess I've taken a devil's advocate stance in response to what I sensed might be your firmly antiromantic posture. You know: you say, "Well, sex comes before love," and I say (like a prim and proper damsel), "No, you must love someone before screwing them." Which actually I don't much believe; it's just that I'm not going to let sex rule me, as I sense it rules so many people. A lot of other things matter—like good humor or sitting and watching the rain, or just thinking (I truly love to think)— and the prospect of becoming a "Dancer" character, of living for sucking cocks, is one-dimensional and unappealing. I'm afraid I could get carried away, and I don't want that to happen. I would like to enjoy it while keeping it in perspective.

I hope to be back in the Bay Area before September 22. I'll call or send a post card when I arrive.

Thanks for everything.
Paul

VII

San Francisco
August 30, 1979

Dear Paul,

Just a note in anticipation of your return.

I very much like what you say about love and sex in your letter. I suppose you can't help feeling mortified by the Jim Cady business. But I wish you wouldn't. From my perspective what you did looks altogether different. It was, as I have said, impracticable but also wonderfully bold, even imaginative. The net effect is not to make you look silly but intrepid. Before the Revolution (when it was permitted), we would have said, "Now, there's someone with balls."

Let's arrange some ornate reunion. In the meantime I'll get a haircut, buy a new pair of granny glasses, and trim my beard.

Yours in the faith,
Paul

Postscript 1982

The correspondence you have just read is now more than two years old, and you may be wondering how Paul's life has progressed in the meantime. Our exchange of letters found him wrestling with the second great crisis in the life of a homosexual: locating a sexual partner, or, more generally, finding one's way into a world where sex becomes a reasonable possibility. He had already passed, seemingly without much difficulty, the crisis of identity in which some homosexuals remain permanently mired: the simple recognition of what one is. Ahead of him—and already implicit in the way he had addressed the sexual issue—lay the question of romance. For many gays the exigencies of sexual life make falling successfully in love even more precarious than it is for straights. The observation is familiar: the emotional facility that helps in finding sexual partners tends to be romantically corrosive.

Paul hasn't escaped the pattern, but he has distinguished himself by the equanimity of his response to it. When he returned to school in the fall of 1979 he rather quickly made a number of sensible adjustments in his life, which brought him a degree of sexual satisfaction, a new group of friends, and the expected romantic discontents. But I should let him speak for himself:

> It now appears that virtually every stand I adopted over the course of the correspondence was wrong. It seems to me in retrospect that most of my "romanticism"—i.e., what I said about the interdependence of love and sex, the moral squalor of bars, and so forth—was simply fear, espe-

cially fear of sex, dressed out as something more abstract, inscrutable, and consonant with my heterosexual upbringing. Bars are really not all that bad and can even be fun. And of course there is a lot that can be said for sex, although it's been neither as ecstatic nor as demanding (i.e., as enslaving) as I anticipated.

My main problem is that I don't get emotionally involved with people. I'm beginning to think that the experience with my roommate scarred me more deeply than I originally recognized. I don't have a lover and I don't want one in any more than a purely hypothetical way. So I suppose the long-term prognosis is not good if that doesn't change. In the absence of a love relationship, however, I've found that I appreciate friends much more.

On the whole I've been much happier. I don't have sex that often, but that's due more to my own fussiness and maladroitness than to lack of opportunities. My parents still do not know: that is the only area in which there has not been substantial change. And I don't foresee any. But who knows? Two years ago I could never have foreseen where I am today.

I take it as the chief accomplishment of the correspondence to have set the stage for Paul's less rigid attitude toward his sexual circumstances. The letters seem to have helped diffuse a good deal of pointless anxiety. All of this is in the spirit of liberation championed by such historical figures as Havelock Ellis and Alfred Kinsey. Nowadays we are inclined to undervalue this process, or to stress its liabilities. We know that putting one's sexual house in order doesn't necessarily lead to happiness. But the agony of sexual repression is perhaps too easily dismissed by those who have risen to the higher miseries. Paul's letters convey a vivid sense of just how much it hurts when one's erotic needs seem not merely unacceptable but unmentionable, and his simple assertion that he's now much happier commemorates a modest triumph of light over darkness.

There is a final observation I would like to make pertaining not to homosexuality but to relations between student and teacher. Some readers may be uncomfortable with my vigorous intrusion into the private life of one of my students, sensing in it a certain indecorousness, even a hint of self-deception. And I must admit that, to a degree, I have come to share their misgivings. A straightforward reading of the letters casts me in an altogether favorable light: I appear here as a teacher who cares enough about his students to write them concerning their personal problems, and who does so without exploiting that intimacy for his own ends. I'm still prepared to defend such a reading, but I will confess that I found my correspondence with Paul suspiciously pleasurable. As a result I'm now more conscious that a teacher seldom interests himself in his students from the Olympian, affectless ground of a noncombatant. One's passions are engaged, if only vicariously, and a failure to monitor one's own needs can transform what should be a valuable experience into something faintly unhealthy.

The potential dangers here range from the innocent (if sad) plight of a teacher who lives his erotic life through his students, to the actual sexual bullying of students by their teacher. But as a sometime Freudian, I would argue that this sort of emotional involvement is inherent in all teaching, if one takes the job seriously. The process of enlightenment is also a process of seduction—which is simply another way of saying that teaching is a form of sublimation. Socrates was the teacher par excellence, and he was also, of course, a lover of young men. The matter is especially delicate when the teacher goes beyond his usual intellectual responsibilities, as I did in this correspondence. Then the need to exercise self-criticism becomes even more urgent: one must keep an eye on one's own feelings and, to the extent that one can, subject them to discipline. There are moments in this correspondence that now make me wince because I see that discipline slipping (the "P.S." to the first letter is especially shy-making). Thus if, on the whole, I am pleased with my role in the story, I have grown more wary of the possible abuses of that role. There is a fine line separating pedagogic virtue from private vice.

OTHER VITAL MATTERS

CHAPTER FOURTEEN

Three Essays on Freud

Appearing respectively in the journals Halcyon *(1985),* Raritan *(Spring 1987), and* Constellations *(March 1999), these essays represent my most important writing on Freud outside the two books I've published on him. The first assesses the anti-Freudian turn of the recent past and provides a broadly conceived historical defense of Freud's achievement. The second offers a corrective to the familiar feminist critique of Freud by drawing attention to the more sympathetic appropriations of him by three important feminist theorists,* Juliet Mitchell, Nancy Chodorow, and Jane Gallop. *The last takes issue with attempts to pin the origin of modern homophobia on Freud. All three essays began as talks and retain the style of the podium.*

Freud under Siege

The subject of my ruminations here is the place of Sigmund Freud in the history of our culture, with particular attention to the recent criticisms to which Freud and his ideas have been subjected. There is, of course, a long tradition of anti-Freudian writings, going back to the very early 1900s. But I think it fair to say that by the 1960s—when Freud had been dead more than two decades and when his main ideas had been before the public for over half a century—he appeared on the verge of settling comfortably into the role of a classic. He had become a figure on whom the mantle of history had begun to descend, a process significantly aided by the publication during the mid-1950s of Ernest Jones's three-volume authorized biography.

But apparently this enshrinement was premature, because Freud has again come under severe and wide-ranging attack, and his attackers treat him not as a historical eminence but more as a contemporary whose ideas are to be challenged and, so they hope, routed. My object in what follows is to characterize this recent body of criticism, to pass at least provisional judgment on it, and to offer some observations about its significance for the way we think of Freud. In the course of doing so, I wish to address myself to three related, albeit distinguishable, questions: (1) What does the already existing evidence allow us to conclude about Freud's place in the intellectual history of the twentieth century? (2) How are the recent criticisms likely to alter our estimate of him or to affect his influence in the future? (3) And, most important, can we say with any confidence that Freud is not merely an influential thinker but also one who has told us something valuable about ourselves? Does he, in other words, belong among the epochal figures of our heritage, a man who can rightfully claim his place in that grand intellectual succession that reaches back to the Greeks and whose major representatives (whether Plato, Augustine, Dante, Newton, or Marx) form the core of what we call Western civilization? From the way I have framed the question (and from the litany of names I have just invoked) I hope to suggest that what one means by "true" and "valuable" when speaking of the major thinkers of our past is a decidedly complex matter. In particular, the truth or value we continue to find in thinkers like Plato or Dante or Marx is not at all incompatible with our rejection of many of their specific ideas, even many of their fundamental assumptions.

By way of final introductory remark, I should note that I am confining myself to the question of *Freud's* reputation, not the reputation (or estate) of contemporary psychoanalysis. The two are, of course, related, if only because Freud saw himself as launching not simply an intellectual movement but a therapeutic profession as well, and in his writings he frequently linked the one to the other. But contemporary psychoanalysis, I believe, has grown estranged from its conceptual roots, and its vicissitudes are increasingly irrelevant to our understanding of Freud himself.

I WOULD LIKE to begin by conveying some impression of just how wildly disparate present-day estimates of Freud's stature actually are. As I have sought to take the temperature of current thinking about Freud, I have had the sense of attending to two utterly separate communities of opinion. For one group—and it includes not merely practicing psycho-analysts but also literary critics, social theorists, and philosophers—Freud's place as one of the greats is so unambiguously established that they pay no attention to the voices of dissent. We look in vain in their footnotes and bibliographies for the merest acknowledgment that the nay-sayers exist. On the other side, the critics, if not quite so insouciant about the actual existence of Freud's admirers, typically adopt a tone of incredulity and moral exasperation, the effect of which is to leave the reader feeling that Freud's continued sway is rather like (if you'll forgive me) a bad dream. We find ourselves, then, confronted with radically an-tithetical points of view: one camp tells us that Freud belongs among the giants of the Western tradition; the other camp tells us, no less vehe-mently, that he is little better than a fraud who will soon be sent to the well-deserved oblivion reserved for intellectual charlatans.

The tone of these contrary evaluations is perhaps even more striking than their substance. Writing in the *New York Review of Books* in 1975, the Nobel laureate in medicine P. B. Medawar volunteered this implaca-ble judgment: "Doctrinaire psychoanalytic theory is the most stupen-dous intellectual confidence trick of the 20th century: and a terminal product as well—something akin to a dinosaur or a zeppelin in the his-tory of ideas, a vast structure of radically unsound design and with no posterity." Medawar's judgment is cited approvingly by the literary critic Frederick Crews in an article published in *Commentary* magazine in 1980, and Crews goes on to offer his own verdict on Freudianism: "Psycho-analysis, I would expect, will fade away just as mesmerism and phrenol-ogy did"—in other words, just as did earlier intellectual fads whose claims were equally suspect. By way of contrast—to put it mildly—Crews's fellow literary critic Steven Marcus issues the following pro-nouncement in a collection of essays, *Freud and the Culture of Psycho-analysis* (1984): "[Freud's] reputation and place in the history of the modern world have never stood higher or enjoyed a firmer security than they do today"; "nothing," he continues, "has come along in seventy years that remotely resembles [Freudian theory] in explanatory power, coherence, and integrity."

Tributes and, as it were, antitributes of this sort could be multiplied almost indefinitely. Hardly an issue of the *New York Times Book Review,* the *Times Literary Supplement,* or any of the journals read by the broader intellectual public appears without some sort of allusion to Freud, and more often than not they fall into the dichotomous pattern I have just identified: either he gets the back of the hand, or, alternatively, the writer, stopping as before a votary altar, doffs his hat, and genuflects.

Before we examine the recent criticisms and what they might augur for Freud's intellectual fate, we might take comfort in noting that his critics and detractors do seem to agree on at least one thing. They are virtually obliged to do so, because their agreement reflects a plain reality that can no longer be disputed: to wit, that Freud has by now clearly established his right to be considered the most influential thinker of the twentieth century. Indeed, he has no serious challenger in this role, unless it be Albert Einstein (whose influence, though perhaps deeper, is also narrower). Thus E. M. Thornton, a British historian of medicine and the author of a book entitled *The Freudian Fallacy* (1984)—which seeks to explain Freud's ideas in terms of his supposed addiction to cocaine—concedes that "probably no single individual has had a more profound effect on twentieth-century thought than Sigmund Freud." A less critical (but hardly orthodox) observer, Janet Malcolm, writing in the *New Yorker,* makes an even bolder claim: "Psychoanalysis," she asserts, "has detonated throughout the intellectual, social, artistic, and ordinary life of our century as no cultural force has (it may not be off the mark to say) since Christianity." I'm not sure about the two millennia since Christianity made its entrance onto the historical stage (Freud would come up against some pretty stiff competition in those 2000 years), but the fact remains, in the twentieth century he is without peer.

To chart the breadth and depth of Freud's influence would require the full-time efforts of a veritable army of scholars. We see only its more visible peaks when we note the extraordinary impact he has had on modern art and literature, on the social sciences, and on formal philosophy. In recent decades, just as his influence in this country seemed on the wane, he has become a central figure in the great eruptions within French intellectual life known variously as structuralism, post-structuralism, and deconstruction. Moreover, as everyone knows, Freud's influence extends well beyond the realm of thought, finding its way into psychiatry, child rearing, educational practice, social work, and many other domains of practical life as well. Still, I continue to be persuaded that Freud's deepest influence remains intellectual, at least if we use that term in its most inclusive sense. I am thinking, above all, of the way he has altered what might be called the intellectual manners of nearly every one of us. Here I would point to our inclination to look for meanings beneath the surface of behavior—to be constantly on the alert for the "real" and (presumably hidden) significance of our actions. I would also point to our inclination to seek explanations of behavior in terms of earlier experience—to assume that the mysteries of the present will become more transparent if we can trace them to their origins in the past, perhaps even in the very earliest past we can remember (or, more likely, not remember). And I would point, finally, to our heightened sensitivity to the sexual, above all to its presence in arenas (such as the family) where earlier generations had been disinclined to look for it. W. H. Auden surely had just this sort of pervasive, if unsystematic, influence in mind when, in a poem commemorating Freud's death in 1939, he wrote:

> To us he is no more a person
> Now but a whole climate of opinion

As Auden correctly sensed, the world is a different place because of Freud. Or, to paraphrase the nineteenth-century Liberal chancellor of the Exchequer Sir William Harcourt (who was accused of being a socialist), "We are all Freudians now."

As an intellectual historian, therefore, I find answering the question about Freud's stature in the twentieth century relatively easy. It is simply too late to wish him away. For better or worse, he has left a massive and indelible imprint on our times. I would also observe that one of the main shortcomings of the recent criticism of Freud is its failure to offer a satisfactory explanation for the powerful hold that he has had on modern thought. In fact most of the critics don't even address this question, or if they do they are content with feeble observations about Freud's skill as a writer or the perennial need people supposedly feel for an intellectual system that will explain everything to them. In other words, they imply that psychoanalysis has enjoyed its success because it is a kind of ersatz religion that has been handsomely packaged. What such explanations ignore is that Freud has appealed to the very best (and, presumably, most discerning) modern intellectuals—to many of our finest novelists, poets, and critics, to our most incisive and original philosophers and social theorists—and not to marginal figures or persons given to uncritical enthusiasms. Precisely here, it seems to me, the comparison with mesmerism and phrenology breaks down, because, in marked contrast to psychoanalysis, those older intellectual movements notably failed to win the respect or adherence of the major thinkers and artists of their day. After all, Freud was celebrated as "a great scientist" not by some literary hack but by Thomas Mann, the preeminent German writer of the century. A fully persuasive critique of Freud, I am suggesting, must also offer an explanation of his appeal. Otherwise it leaves unanswered the question of why so many brilliant, sophisticated, and creative minds have been deeply affected by him.

Of course, it does not follow because we ourselves are Freudians—whether strict ones or, as I think is more often the case, relatively diluted and unselfconscious ones—that our descendants will be Freudians. And clearly Freud's recent critics hope to get the Freudian monkey, if not off *our* backs, at least off the backs of our children. I would like now to turn to those critics and to begin by proposing that they can be usefully divided into three schools, according to the particular aspect of Freud's thought they criticize. Two of them are visible to the general intellectual public, while the third has been confined to the world of scholars, particularly philosophers of science. Let me, if I may, take these schools of criticism up for individual examination.

THE OLDEST of the "new" attacks on psychoanalysis actually dates from the early 1970s, but it has remained very much a fixture in anti-Freudian writings ever since. It can be labeled the feminist critique, and its *locus classicus* is Kate Millett's influential book of 1970, *Sexual Politics*. The critique was not without precedent, but it emerged as part of a wider revival of feminism in this country and, as such, was pursued with unexpected vigor. One of the minor ironies of this story is that Kate Millett wrote *Sexual Politics* as a doctoral dissertation at Columbia University, where her mentor was none other than Professor Steven Marcus, whom she thanks warmly in her acknowledgments and from whose book on Freud I have already quoted an encomium to the Master.

Millett's case against Freud is concerned less with how his ideas are wrong than with how they are pernicious. Naturally, she thinks him mistaken, but she does not dwell on his errors of logic or the inadequacy of his evidence. In fact she is distinctly respectful, calling Freud "a great pioneer, whose theories of the unconscious and of infant sexuality were major contributions to human understanding." It is thus more in sorrow than in wrath that she records how Freud betrayed his progressive instincts when he fashioned a female psychology that confounds the efforts of women to achieve their full humanity.

The feminist critique aims its fire, above all, at two Freudian ideas: first, the notion that penis envy is the primary motor of female psychological development, and, second, the notion that the so-called vaginal orgasm (as opposed to the clitoral orgasm) is the true test of sexual maturity in a woman—the significance of this distinction being that clitoral orgasms can be achieved through masturbation while a vaginal orgasm (in theory) requires sexual intercourse. If one steps back from these particulars and assesses the feminist critique in more general terms, one can say that it finds Freud guilty of treating women as something of an afterthought, of defining their psychological experience not on its own terms but in terms of how it fails to measure up to the experience of men. Psychoanalytic theory, the feminists charge, portrays women as maimed or incomplete males: males without penises, males without fully developed superegos (and therefore not truly fit for the moral life), males incapable of assuming the burdens of civilization.

The upshot of what Millett calls the "habitual masculine bias of Freud's . . . terms and diction" is to justify women's subservience to men, because it affirms that their inferiority is rooted in biology. One might be inclined to defend Freud against this complaint by noting that, after all, he grew up within the confines of the nineteenth century, and it can hardly be surprising that his thought should have perpetuated the patriarchal values of Victorian culture. But such an exculpation simply will not do if we also wish to argue that Freud's work marks a revolutionary break with the psychological assumptions of the past—that he is the first great modern. There is, in other words, a discrepancy between his advanced ideas about human psychology in general and his retrograde ideas about women. More to the point, Freud didn't simply *perpetuate* the old stereotypes, he dressed them out in smart new language—the dispassionate language of sexual frankness—thereby giving them renewed vogue just as they were beginning to appear rather shopworn in their familiar Victorian garb. Altogether the question of women in psychoanalytic thought, and the response it has elicited from feminists, remains the most vexed aspect of his legacy, and although I don't feel comfortable with the by-now ritualistic dismissal of Freud as a misogynist, neither do I think that he can be readily excused from the charge.

THE FEMINIST COMPLAINT has resurfaced in somewhat different guise, as we shall see, in the second school of Freud criticism, to which I now wish to turn. This more recent school is distinguished by its focus on the early years of Freud's career—the years before the publication in 1900 of *The Interpretation of Dreams*, the book generally taken to mark the full-fledged emergence of psychoanalysis proper. The most severe of these attacks is Jeffrey Masson's book *The Assault on Truth: Freud's Suppression of the Seduction Theory* (1984). Masson himself was the subject of a brilliant *New Yorker* profile by Janet Malcolm (later published in book form as *In the Freud Archives*), and he has been the source of much disgruntled talk about Freud and of a growing sense that his reputation may be in danger.

Masson, however, is just one of several critics who have turned their attention to Freud's early career. Alongside him one should also mention Frank Sulloway, Marianne Krüll, Marie Balmary, and E. M. Thornton. These writers have raised a variety of embarrassing questions about the young Freud, but their indictment has centered on two issues. In both instances they pretend to identify a habit of thought that also infected Freud's mature work, if not in so blatant a form.

First, these critics raise doubts about Freud's therapeutic commitment, suggesting that his claim to be a great healer was largely bogus. Their contention is not simply that psychoanalysis doesn't work but, more radically, that Freud wasn't really interested in curing mental disorders and was only using his patients as a kind of laboratory for his theories. The critique has focused particularly on Freud's attitude toward his female patients (most of his early patients were women), whom he is accused of treating in a prosecutorial fashion, blaming them for their own sufferings when in fact they were often the victims of male aggression, sexual and otherwise. By extension, these critics have found Freud no less insensitive to the wrongs inflicted on children, whom he made the villains in a sexual drama—the Oedipus story—whose true malefactors, they insist, are in fact adults. Jeffrey Masson even accuses Freud of legitimizing the sexual abuse of children. I hardly need add that these criticisms have been warmly received by feminists (since they confirm the older charge of patriarchalism), and they have come to the fore at precisely a moment in our own history when the public is growing increasingly exercised about incest and child abuse.

I will say immediately that I find much less merit in these criticisms than I do in those of Kate Millett and other feminist writers. Indeed, I am confident that Freud will weather the assault on his therapeutic impulses, because it is based on a shallow and ultimately sentimental notion of what it means to be a healer. In many instances it amounts to little more than saying that Freud wasn't always nice to his patients, and it refuses to take seriously the idea—integral to Freudian therapy—that mental illness will not relent in the face of simple human kindness but requires a disciplined and above all theoretically informed attitude on the part of the doctor. Even the reproach that Freud used his patients largely to gather information reveals a considerable shortsightedness about the healer's calling, in that it implicitly denies that a research scientist can be motivated by the same hope of improving the human lot as a clinician or a surgeon. The austerity or even hostility that Freud exhibited in dealing with his patients must be judged according to a more sophisticated set of criteria than that employed by his recent critics. He may well be found wanting, but he should not be convicted by an appeal to the gallery.

The charge that he aggressed against the innocence of childhood is not merely sentimental but, in a way, historically incoherent. Confronted with it, one is tempted to say, "Indeed! That's just the point!" Freud's principal claim to mark a watershed in the history of thought lies precisely in his having subjected received notions about childhood to a systematic and, I believe, lasting critique. The fact that children, like women, are often the objects of abuse is hardly incompatible with the proposition that they entertain sexual and aggressive instincts of their own. If there is one idea in the Freudian corpus that l would expect to remain a permanent component of our intellectual heritage—Freud's ticket to immortality, if you will—it is his insistence on the continuity of experience from childhood to maturity and his rejection of the notion that we live the first blissful years of our lives under one psychic dispensation followed by a disabused adulthood under an entirely different dispensation. The particulars of his theory of infantile sexuality may be modified or even discarded, but he added profound resonance to Wordsworth's affirmation that "The Child is father of the Man."

The other issue raised by the recent literature on the young Freud is that of intellectual extremeness. His critics have detected a lamentable pattern of reckless and one-sided theorizing in his early career: an insistence on seeing things from only a single point of view, of ignoring inconveniently contradictory facts, and of stating claims in an absolute fashion rarely justified by the thin evidential base on which those claims rest. Moreover, they suggest, he was so desperate to hit upon an all-encompassing explanation of human behavior that he rushed from one irresponsible idea to the next, looking first to cocaine, then to hypnotism, and finally (before coming up with his own distinctive concoction) to the patently crackpot ideas of his friend Wilhelm Fliess. Fliess was the author of a bizarre numerological theory that explained all biological phenomena through permutations of the numbers 23 and 28 (the former representing the male principle, the latter the female principle), and for a decade Freud warmly supported this crazed notion. Freud's mature psychological system, the critics argue, suffers from the same intellectual extravagance on display in these various enthusiasms of his early years.

There is much truth in this representation of Freud's intellectual style. To be sure, mature psychoanalytic theory is more nuanced and disciplined than the ideas with which he toyed in the 1880s and 1890s. But it remains undeniably singleminded and, one might say, imperialistic.

Freud typically insisted that things were one way rather than another (he had little tolerance for compromise), and he was very much inclined to express his ideas in the most inclusive, universalizing terms. He was not satisfied, for instance, to assert merely that some dreams are wish-fulfillments; rather, he insisted that *all* dreams are wish-fulfillments. Likewise, he would not settle for saying that some slips have a meaning; rather, he said that they *all* have a meaning. In short, his thought was eminently injudicious.

But his recent critics, I would argue, have not asked the right questions about this undeniable intellectual propensity. Or, better, they have not established the proper frame of reference within which to judge it. And here I will simply propose—without trying to document it in this context—that a tendency to extreme and inflexible statement is characteristic of many, perhaps even most, important innovators in the history of thought. One makes intellectual revolutions not through the even-handed, modest elaboration or correction of earlier ideas but by the ruthless, sometimes foolhardy, pursuit of a single point of view. To complain of Freud that he lacked the scientific restraint of his sometime collaborator Josef Breuer (a complaint registered by Frank Sulloway) may be just, but it is also naïve. Instead, I suggest, we should compare his intellectual manners with those of a Galileo, a Newton, a Darwin, or a Marx. When judged in this company his proclivity for extreme and inflexible statement turns out to be anything but unusual. There are, apparently, certain virtues of mind that the great innovators must forgo, and, no matter how much we admire those virtues in ordinary mortals, they are dysfunctional in persons of genius. Arguably, Freud may have exceeded the bounds of extravagance we tolerate in our intellectual revolutionaries, but it is against those bounds, not the narrower limits we set for scientific journeymen, that his work ought to be measured.

I NOTED THAT there was yet a third recent school of Freud criticism, one that differs from those I have mentioned thus far in being largely confined to the academic world. Nonetheless, it pursues themes already present in both the feminist critique and the critique directed at the young Freud, but it does so in a much more rigorous fashion. Essentially it is an attack on the methodological foundations of psychoanalysis, and it argues that Freud's ideas simply lack adequate empirical grounding. Those ideas may be interesting, it allows, but they are unproven. The central figure in this story is the philosopher of science Adolf Grünbaum, who developed his arguments in a series of erudite scholarly papers before publishing them in a book entitled *The Foundations of Psychoanalysis* (1984). The title is unwittingly ironic, because Grünbaum's main contention is that psychoanalysis lacks foundations.

The critique mounted by Grünbaum is extremely impressive, and it is also conducted in a dense, highly technical philosophical language light years removed from the slashing, polemical style of the criticisms I have discussed up to this point. It is in fact far too recondite for me even to attempt recreating it in this brief survey [although I do so in my 1993 book *Freud and His Critics*]. At its heart stands the assertion that Freud's ideas do not meet the austere standards of induction that the scientific community demands before embracing the sort of broad empirical generalizations—such as those about dreams, slips, and neuroses—that psychoanalysis advances.

Although I won't rehearse Grünbaum's arguments, I do want to draw attention to something quite striking about their manner. And that is, despite taking psychoanalysis severely to task for its methodological failings, Grünbaum also pays Freud innumerable compliments, both implicit and direct, the overall effect of which is to leave us with an enhanced appreciation for Freud's powers of mind. For one thing, the very fact that Grünbaum subjects Freud's ideas to such intricate, detailed examination inevitably serves to lend those ideas greater weight and dignity. Nobody as smart as Adolf Grünbaum, we are inclined to feel, would waste a decade of his life on an unworthy opponent. Even more remarkable, much of Grünbaum's energy goes into showing how Freud is vastly more intelligent than nearly all his critics. Grünbaum's sharpest barbs are reserved for Freud's wrong-headed opponents or his patronizing defenders, while Freud himself, even when in error, remains "brilliant," "daring," "admirably rich and lucid," as well as "sophisticated," "meticulous," and "careful." Not surprisingly, Grünbaum counts many psychoanalysts among his admirers and scholarly correspondents, and—in marked contrast to the other schools of criticism I have mentioned—he has elicited a series of judicious responses from within the analytic community. For all its power and incisiveness, then, Grünbaum's critique may ultimately redound to Freud's credit. At the very least, it undermines the notion that psychoanalysis is to be classed with the likes of mesmerism and phrenology, as Frederick Crews would have it.

WHAT, THEN, IS the balance sheet with regard to these recent criticisms, and how are they apt to affect Freud's image? I don't wish to preempt the debate or to settle matters with undue haste, but I am not yet persuaded that the critics have ushered in a moment of genuine crisis in the history of his reputation. Still, the situation is undeniably more volatile than it was in the 1950s and 1960s. As must be evident by now, I am least impressed by the recent attacks on the young Freud, both by their tone, which seems to me excessive, and by their substance, which is often alarmingly thin. On the other hand, I find it difficult to predict the long-range effects of the respectful but thoroughgoing criticism of an Adolf Grünbaum. In its present form it is virtually inaccessible to the public at large, and it defines the issues rather too narrowly. But modest scribes content to work within the academy and through the musty agencies of scholarly journals and professional conferences have been known to set off time-bombs. Surely, however, most unsettling of all, and with the greatest potential for doing permanent damage, are the moral (as opposed to methodological) flaws exposed by the feminists. I am far from certain how this challenge will or should be met, although, obviously, one possible defense would be to argue that Freud's ideas about women belong to the periphery of psychoanalytic theory and that at its deepest structural level his thought is not inherently misogynous. Such is the position taken by the three intellectuals I examine in my essay "Freud and the Feminists."

Imbedded in what I have had to say is my own conception of which elements in Freud's achievement will prove lasting, and which are merely ephemeral. I would like to conclude by highlighting that conception, and to do so by way of a distinction between what I will call "hard Freudianism" and "soft Freudianism." It's the sort of distinction one could draw for any of the major figures in the history of thought (we do it all the time, for instance, in the case of Marx), and I think it is a useful and legitimate exercise.

By "hard Freudianism" I mean adherence to the explicit doctrines of psychoanalytic theory more or less as they appear in the canonical writings—in Freud's own writings, of course, but also in those of his orthodox followers. A hard Freudian is committed to a precise body of ideas about the function of dreams and slips, the etiology of the neuroses, the stages of psychosexual growth, and many other matters as well; he is also committed to a particular therapeutic program, with its distinct procedures and expectations. "Soft Freudianism," by way of contrast, steps back from these explicit, often rebarbative formulations in order to find Freud's value in a more broadly conceived set of assumptions about human experience. From the perspective of the soft Freudian, Freud is important and revelatory because he introduced a dramatically new way of thinking about ourselves.

I have already alluded to the main components of this new way of thinking. They include, first, a complex and, if you will, layered conception of the self as divided between motives we are conscious of and those we are not. They include, further, an expanded awareness of the role of sexuality in our lives. And they include, finally, a profound sense of the continuity of human experience over time. If Freud's idea of the unconscious mind fractures the unity of the self, his developmental notion of character restores that unity in a transfigured guise: at any given moment our actions may lack wholeness (they may reflect conflicting motives), but over the long haul of a complete lifetime we remain very much the same person. I like to say that Freud is the great critic of conversion—of the notion that human beings can shed their old, unsatisfactory selves and step forth as something new and better. The weight of the past, Freud insists, will not tolerate such trifling with the self's integrity.

This conception is deeply conservative and, to many, dispiriting. Moreover, it might seem at variance with the psychoanalytic commitment to curing people of their neuroses—which certainly implies some sort of change. But the contradiction is only apparent, for when we examine Freud's therapeutic ideal more closely it turns out to be remarkably modest. Freud promises not a transformation of personality—not a conversion, as I have called it—but merely the palliation of certain carefully circumscribed, discrete mental disturbances. The larger psychological construct we call the self remains fundamentally intact: we endure with the burdens of our history. As Freud expressed it, in a sentence that I admire perhaps more than any other in his writings: psychoanalysis aims at "transforming . . . hysterical misery into common unhappiness."

This I take to be the characteristic Freudian ethos, and, perhaps even more, the characteristic Freudian tone: sober, disabused, ironic, and utterly alien from the uninflected therapeutic optimism and intellectual excess that his critics so often ascribe to him. We hear that tone once again in a wonderful remark of 1914 when he observed: "Anyone who promises to mankind liberation from the hardship of sex will be hailed as a hero, let him talk whatever nonsense he chooses." In such dark, stoic, unsparing pronouncements—and his mature writings are filled with their like—I discern echoes of a profound and tragic sensibility that will, I believe, ensure Freud a lasting place among the great figures of our heritage. It is in this sensibility, I would maintain, that his truth and value are to be located.

Freud and the Feminists

The larger issue behind the observations I want to make about Freud and feminism is very much related to my own—and my generation's—response to Freud over the past three decades. Surely the first thing that comes to mind these days when one speaks of Freud's reputation is that it is under attack—that he has been the object of a sustained onslaught of criticism impugning his motives, questioning his intelligence, and generally regretting his influence. Moreover, the embattled situation in which he currently finds himself stands in marked contrast to the intellectual ascendancy that he had attained in the 1950s and 1960s.

By 1960 much of the American intellectual community seemed to agree that Freud was not only the most influential thinker of the twentieth century but one of those epoch-making figures, like Marx or Darwin, who had profoundly altered our basic assumptions about the human condition. Freud, so went the prevailing wisdom, had effected a transformation in Western man's understanding of himself and his world. Yet in

the past quarter century we have witnessed a remarkable effort to qualify—and in some quarters completely to revise—this estimate. I think
the moment has arrived to take the measure of this recent questioning of
Freud's intellectual stature, to sort out its elements, judge their respective
merits, and, in the end, reach some conclusions about Freud himself—to
arrive, in other words, at a more considered sense of his place in the
Western intellectual tradition. By coming to grips with his recent critics
we can hope to clarify our views as to what is valuable and lasting in his
achievement, in contrast to what is merely ephemeral and unfortunate.

My own assessment begins with the preliminary judgment that the
recent criticism of Freud can be said to fall into three categories. The first
of these, the feminist response to Freud, is the one I wish to address in
this essay. But in order to place the feminist critics in perspective, and to
delimit the territory I want to cover, let me briefly mention the two other
bodies of criticism that must be reckoned with.

One is the revisionist literature on Freud's early career, particularly
in the 1890s. The focus of the revision, broadly speaking, is Ernest
Jones's three-volume authorized biography of Freud, which appeared in
the mid-1950s, and above all Jones's account of the sequence of events
that led Freud to his revolutionary hypotheses about the human psyche
—his ideas of the unconscious mind and infantile sexuality. The past two
decades have seen the publication of a series of writings that challenge
both the accuracy and persuasiveness of Jones's version of the story. At
stake in this literature, among other things, is whether Freud was genuinely concerned with curing his patients or only using them as psychological guinea pigs; whether his deepest intellectual convictions were
those of a scientist or those of a romantic adventurer; whether his famous self-analysis was in fact the conceptual breakthrough that he (and
after him Jones) portrayed it to be; whether the traditional account of his
adoption and later rejection of the seduction theory—the proposition
that neuroses originate in childhood seductions—will hold up; and even
whether his supposed insights into the psyche may not have originated in
a cocaine addiction previously thought to have been confined to the
1880s.

The other category of criticism that needs to be examined is more
easily encompassed than the revisionist literature on the early Freud: this

is the attack on the empirical foundations of psychoanalysis launched by the philosopher of science Adolf Grünbaum. In a series of articles and then a book, Grünbaum has argued that the basic tenets of Freudian theory are epistemologically flawed—"fatally" flawed, he likes to say— and thus cannot be considered scientific. In contrast to the revisionist writings on Freud's early career, the focus of Grünbaum's critique has not been Freud's character—his therapeutic commitment, his intellectual honesty—but rather the conceptual integrity of psychoanalytic theory in its mature formulations. In particular Grünbaum raises doubts about such fundamental analytic ideas as the theory of repression and the doctrine of parapraxes (or Freudian slips), and he also questions the effectiveness of psychoanalysis as therapy. His pursuit of Freud's intellectual shortcomings has been ruthless and systematic, if not always lucid.

I want to begin with the feminist critics for the good historical reason that they were the first: it is in the writings of feminist intellectuals some three decades ago that we find the beginnings of the current reversal of Freud's fortunes. But, having said that, I must immediately add that I really have two stories to tell: the story I expected to find, that of the pronounced reaction against Freud among what are generally referred to as "the new feminists" of the late 1960s and early 1970s, and the very different, indeed contradictory, story of a developing love affair between certain feminist intellectuals and Freud, a love affair that, if anything, has grown more intense just as he has come under attack from different quarters. In fact, odd as it may seem, some of the most interesting recent defenses (or implicit defenses) of Freud have issued from thinkers who consider themselves proponents of the feminist cause.

Let me begin, however, with the more familiar story. Of the many neofeminist critiques of Freud to appear in and around 1970, I take Kate Millett's *Sexual Politics* to be the most important. Millett's discussion of Freud is both longer and more incisive than those in other feminist manifestos of the day, and I can report from my own reading of it at the time that it effected a significant dampening of Freudian enthusiasms among those of us who considered ourselves intellectually and politically progressive. Freud emerged from *Sexual Politics* as one of the architects of modern sexism, and in the atmosphere of the early 1970s that was a substantially greater liability than it might seem today.

Still, it's important to recall that Kate Millett was but one voice in a larger chorus of detractors, all of whom reached a quite remarkable consensus about Freud. Her most important intellectual predecessor was Simone de Beauvoir, whose critique of psychoanalysis in *The Second Sex* predated *Sexual Politics* by more than two decades, and she had also been anticipated, if in a somewhat slapdash manner, by Betty Friedan in *The Feminine Mystique* (1963). Among her immediate contemporaries, very similar attacks were launched by Germaine Greer in *The Female Eunuch*, Eva Figes in *Patriarchal Attitudes,* and Shulamith Firestone in *The Dialectic of Sex*. Like Millett's *Sexual Politics,* the books of Greer, Figes, and Firestone all appeared in 1970, further suggesting that that year marked a watershed in the history of Freud's reputation—the beginning, as it were, of his fall from grace. Above all else, the neofeminists wished to show that Freud's ideas about women were ideologically loaded: they emphasized the way his theories lent scientific respectability to some very old prejudices. As Millett saw it, Freudian psychology was part of the counterrevolution against modern feminism.

By now we are all familiar with the aspects of Freud's thought that the neofeminists found most objectionable. Without doubt pride of place belongs to the theory of penis envy, the notion that women's psychology is based on a sense of genital inadequacy, from which follows, according to the theory, their greater passivity, narcissism, and masochism. Millett in particular admitted that the sense of inferiority was real enough, but she insisted that Freud had erred in attributing it to the little girl's envious perception of her brother's genitals, when in fact female inferiority was a social and historical creation, fully explicable in terms of very concrete arrangements that have kept women in a position of dependency. The unfortunate element in Freud's theory, Millett argued, was that it anchored that sense of inferiority in the immutable facts of anatomy. It made women's lesser station into a biological inevitability, since—as the infamous phrase goes—"anatomy is destiny."

At a more fundamental level, I believe, Millett and her colleagues objected to Freud's theory because, regardless of its political implications, it struck them as offensive to the dignity and humanity of women. It had the effect of representing women as incomplete males—more precisely, as castrated males or, in Germaine Greer's phrase, "female eunuchs." Women were men without penises, whose psychic lives seemed to be dominated by attempts to compensate for that fundamental defect. Freud drew the cultural consequences of this insinuation when he argued that women, because of the less traumatic (and hence less thorough) resolution of their Oedipus complex, did not develop the powerful superegos that might make them the bearers of civilization. That is, according to Freud, women never learned to sublimate as completely as men did, and as a result they remained intellectually inferior and ethically more pliant. And because civilization was for him essentially a work of sublimation, their contribution to the civilizing process remained unequal to men's.

The Freudian corpus, of course, contains other ideas that the new feminists criticized, such as the theory of the vaginal orgasm and the notion that women desire children at least in part so as to obtain substitute phalluses. But most of these other ideas can readily be seen as corollaries of the theory of penis envy and the underdeveloped female superego.

In the years since Kate Millett and her contemporaries first made these complaints they have become in effect a fixture of the American intellectual landscape, reiterated and echoed in countless books, articles, and reviews. Moreover, anyone who has tried to teach Freud to American students will know that dealing with the feminist criticism of his ideas has become a regular part of one's pedagogical duties, just as anyone who lectures on Freud will have come to expect a good deal of enthusiastic head-nodding during those passages that treat the inadequacies of his female psychology.

By saying that the neofeminist critique has become an intellectual fixture, I mean quite deliberately to suggest that not much has been added to the strictures that Millett and others articulated three decades ago. If there has been any change, it has been a shift of attention away from the abstract doctrines of Freud's psychology of women toward an emphasis on his sometimes high-handed treatment of his female patients. The famous case of Dora has proved an especially rich hunting ground in this regard. In it we find Freud browbeating an eighteen-year-old girl for her failure to respond to the advances of one of her father's middle-aged friends. The case virtually cries out for somebody to come to Dora's defense and put Freud and his male cronies in their place. At the same time, the neofeminist critique has allied itself with the growing body of writings on child abuse, incest, and rape. Because the most prevalent forms of child abuse and incest involve adult males and young girls (archetypally, fathers and daughters), Freud's theory of infantile sexuality, which locates desire as much in the child as in the adult, has been attacked as serving to rationalize these often violent and damaging practices. Hence, for example, Freud comes in for some pretty rough treatment in Judith Lewis Herman's book *Father-Daughter Incest* (1981).

My second story, that of Freud's feminist admirers, is intrinsically more interesting, if only because it frustrates our expectations. But I don't want to pass on to it without noting that, whatever the inadequacies of the neofeminist reading of Freud, it should not simply be dismissed. To ignore the hostility that Freud arouses in women would be profoundly un-Freudian, just as it would be self-confirming and circular to label it another manifestation of penis envy. So while I'm inclined to sympathize with those feminist thinkers who have tried to get beneath the misogynistic rhetoric of Freudian theory, I'm uncomfortable about making the task too easy. The fact that many women find Freud insulting—and that it requires great effort on their part to get beyond this immediate response—is itself a significant intellectual datum (not merely a psychological datum), one whose weight and import need to be justly assessed.

I WOULD LIKE to introduce Freud's feminist advocates by examining three important books written by feminist thinkers who offer an impression of Freud, and of his relation to feminism, very different from the one we've come to consider orthodox: Juliet Mitchell's *Psychoanalysis and Feminism*, Nancy Chodorow's *The Reproduction of Mothering*, and Jane Gallop's *The Daughter's Seduction*. Juliet Mitchell's book appeared in 1974, Nancy Chodorow's in 1978, and Jane Gallop's in 1982. By themselves, of course, Mitchell, Chodorow, and Gallop can't be said to chart the full trajectory of recent feminist opinion on Freud, but I think it is fair to treat them collectively as a major subversive tradition that ought to be better known.

These works command attention first of all because they are, to my knowledge, the most substantial and detailed feminist discussions of psychoanalysis to have been written in English. I find it convenient to speak of them as constituting a "tradition" because, although they reflect very different loyalties and concerns, they all suggest that, far from being the enemy of women, Freud in fact provides the sole intellectual basis from which women can hope to throw off the shackles of patriarchy. They suggest, in other words, that feminists dismiss Freud at their peril. The books are further united in that they take the debate out of the narrowly American context to which their neofeminist predecessors tended to confine it and locate it on a wider intellectual stage. Juliet Mitchell is herself English, and she writes with considerable awareness of Continental developments. Nancy Chodorow, though an American, achieves a similar broadening of intellectual horizons by basing her work on developments in British psychoanalysis, notably on the object relations school (which stresses the child's internal relationship to mental representations of its mother and father). And Jane Gallop, another American, is perhaps the most European of all, intellectually, since she translates the entire debate over Freud into the categories of French psychoanalytic thought. In her book we are made to think about Freud from the perspective of Jacques Lacan and his various feminist disciples and critics.

JULIET MITCHELL, the first of my protagonists, is a practicing psychoanalyst in London. She wrote *Psychoanalysis and Feminism* in direct response to the neofeminist critics of the early 1970s. So far as I know, she is the first person to diagnose feminist hostility to Freud as a peculiarly American phenomenon, to be explained, she argues, by the biological and determinist emphasis in popular American Freudianism. In contrast, she notes that in France, where Freud has been interpreted in linguistic and symbolic terms, psychoanalysis and feminism characteristically go hand in hand. One of the most prominent French feminist organizations, for instance, calls itself Psychoanalysis and Politics.

Mitchell accuses all the American neofeminists of the same error: without exception, she says, they operate from outside the basic assumptions of psychoanalysis, and, above all, outside the assumption of an unconscious mind. Hence their criticisms of Freud's psychology of women are in her view essentially preanalytic, pre-Freudian. Of course, by today's standards this complaint might not seem especially weighty, since anti-Freudians like Frederick Crews or Jeffrey Masson are quite ready to dispense with the unconscious. But it catches Kate Millett and most of the other neofeminists in a contradiction, because they in fact profess to accept Freud's fundamental insights, especially his discovery of unconscious mental processes. Mitchell argues that the neofeminists reject not just Freud's psychology of women—the theory of penis envy and so forth—but his entire conception of mental life. "Desire, phantasy, the laws of the unconscious or even unconsciousness," she writes, "are absent from the social realism of the feminist critiques. With Millett's, as with the other feminists' studies, empiricism run riot denies more than the unconscious; it denies any attribute of the mind other than rationality." I think this judgment is correct. Kate Millett does indeed regard women's psychology as adequately explained by their conscious reaction to the political and social realities (including the organization of the family) that constantly remind them of their inferiority. Any appeal to the unconscious is thus gratuitous.

In her own account of psychoanalytic theory Mitchell insists on a purely psychological point of view, a point of view that locates the unconscious at the center of mental life. But I think the most important feature of her reinterpretation is that it directs attention away from the Oedipus complex and back to the pre-Oedipal period, that is, back to the first couple of years of childhood. This shift allows her to stress the moment in psychological development when boys and girls have virtually identical emotional experiences: for both sexes the pre-Oedipal phase is dominated by an attachment to the mother. This movement away from the Oedipal years (when the troublesome issue of penis envy emerges) thus gives her account a distinctively egalitarian tone. Preceding and underlying the later developments that will launch men and women on different psychological courses, she suggests, is a more basic maternal romance that they share: "In all the passions of the first mother-attachment the little boy and little girl are alike."

Eventually, of course, Mitchell must attend to the crucial years of sexual differentiation, to the Oedipal years. Yet even here she continues to stress the homologous structure of male and female experience. She effectively defangs the notion of penis envy by making it simply the little girl's version of a more general psychological process, the "castration complex," through which children of both sexes must pass, and which carries no invidious connotation for Freud. There is nothing to prefer, she insists, between worrying about losing the penis one actually has— the little boy's version of the complex—and envying the penis one has already lost (in fantasy)—the little girl's version. Even more important, both of these are entirely unconscious responses whose anatomic basis (that is, whether or not one happens to have a penis) is made to seem almost incidental. Mitchell's infants are always distanced from immediate bodily sensations or perceptions; their experience is resolutely psychological. Again her stress is on the unconscious, on the structural similarities between male and female experience, and on the irrelevance of any prescriptive motive in Freud's account. (She notes, in this context, that no woman writer before Karen Horney seemed to take Freud's theory as a reproach.) Her great theme, one might say, is Freud's discovery of the profound common elements in the psychic life of both men and women. It is only against the notion of shared unconscious and infantile experiences that his ideas about sexual differentiation make any sense.

She also contends that the differentiation brought about by the castration complex is not between men and women, as a hasty reading of Freud might lead one to conclude, but between masculinity and femininity—in other words, between two psychological patterns, neither of which can be flatly identified with gendered individuals of one sex or the other. This is an important but, as one might imagine, extremely elusive part of her argument, and it is a distinction that I find difficult to sustain in my own mind. Repeatedly, however, Mitchell insists that Freud was talking about the development not of two sexes but of two psychological constructs, and that we misunderstand him if we assign those constructs without further ado to gendered individuals: "Freud . . . was arguing for a theory in which there is an important gap between, on the one hand, biological femaleness and maleness and, on the other, psychological femininity and masculinity." This tactic is perfectly sensible as a way of rescuing Freud from his biological and reductionist interpreters. But it rather improbably makes the categories "masculine" and "feminine" seem sexually neutral, and it considerably underplays Freud's conviction that psychic maturity entails the closest possible fit between men and masculinity and women and femininity.

Mitchell's way of dealing with the misogynistic elements in Freud's thought—the "anatomy is destiny" motif—is to shove them as much as possible to the periphery. She treats them either as offhand remarks reflecting Freud's personal prejudices or as biological backslidings, residues of his older intellectual commitments, that are marginal to the psychological point of view he adopts in his mature works. This eagerness to "de-biologize" Freud she shares with all of his recent feminist defenders, and it offers a useful corrective to Frank Sulloway's influential reading of Freud as a crypto-biologist (although one could object, of course, that it also represses the authentically biological component in Freud's thought). Here she complains that the neofeminists have ignored how his thinking about women grew more complex and nuanced from his first pronouncements in the *Three Essays on Sexuality* of 1905 to his final position in the chapter on "Femininity" in the *New Introductory Lectures* of 1933. It's in the later writings that the focus shifts from the Oedipal to the pre-Oedipal phase and where masculinity and femininity are most completely loosed from their anatomic moorings. She also makes the rather effective observation that the neofeminists, for all their talk of history and social circumstances, fail to treat Freud's own misogyny in an appropriately historical fashion. As it turns out, Freud belonged on the feminist left within the Viennese intellectual context of the early twentieth century, where the tone was set by the rabid woman hater Otto Weininger.

Finally, and most strikingly, Mitchell argues that psychoanalysis stands in the service of women's liberation. Unfortunately, she is not very good at explaining just how this connection works. If I understand her correctly, the importance of Freud for women is that he alone has given an accurate account of their interior life, and thus no program of liberation can hope to succeed if it ignores his findings. Without Freud women are doomed to misconceive the problem, to remain external to its fundamental logic. "In violently rejecting a Freud who is not Freud," she concludes, "I would argue that the only important possibilities for understanding the psychology of women that we have to date have been lost, and that in misconceiving and repudiating psychoanalysis a crucial science for understanding ideological and psychological aspects of oppression has been thrown away."

Her own solution to women's oppression is a socialist revolution, which will also mean, she believes, a cultural transformation. But she can't satisfactorily explain how such a revolution will alter the unconscious processes or structures that have been the main object of attention in her book. Even more telling, she doesn't really identify just what needs to be changed in the psychic realm (presuming now that a socialist revolution could effect such a change). Her discussion of this entire issue is highly truncated and abstract. She writes, for example, "When the potentialities of the complexities of capitalism—both economic and ideological—are released by its overthrow, new structures will gradually come to be represented in the unconscious." But she doesn't get any more specific. So her political solution sits rather arbitrarily, even mysteriously, atop the psychological analysis she has produced.

From my perspective (that is, from the perspective of someone trying to take the measure of feminist reactions to Freud), the inadequacy of her "way out" is less important than her unqualified conviction that Freud holds the key to women's psychology and hence to their liberation. Reading *Psychoanalysis and Feminism,* one can doubt neither the authenticity of Mitchell's feminist politics nor the depth of her intellectual commitment to Freud. Her book's historical significance, I'm inclined to argue, rests in its eloquent advocacy of a union between two causes that, in the early 1970s, seemed destined to oppose one another.

NANCY CHODOROW'S *The Reproduction of Mothering* is a very different kind of book from *Psychoanalysis and Feminism.* Where Mitchell is primarily a literary scholar, Chodorow is a sociologist (she describes her book as a work of "psychoanalytic sociology"). Similarly, where Mitchell is concerned with defending Freud against the neofeminists, Chodorow writes in a much more confident—if you will, much less defensive—manner from within the analytic community. She takes Freud's discoveries more or less for granted, and she also feels no embarrassment about disagreeing with him on particular issues. In fact, her various demurrers, some of them quite sharp, imply a secure confidence in the essential harmony of Freudian and feminist causes. Also unlike Mitchell, whose advocacy is pretty much confined to Freud, Chodorow draws on the full spectrum of psychoanalytic authorities. She thus conveys the impression of a rich and ongoing intellectual tradition, which harbors considerable room for disagreement, including disagreement on the question of female psychology, where, as she notes, Freud's ideas were challenged as early as 1927 by no less an authority than Ernest Jones.

The aim of *The Reproduction of Mothering* is to explain how men and women develop distinctive psychological identities that incline women to become childrearers while men pursue careers in the marketplace. In other words, she wants to account for the basic characterological differences between the sexes, as well as the division of labor that seems to follow from those differences. The explanation she offers is, of course, Freudian. She holds that the differences between men and women can be accounted for neither as instinctual predispositions (the notion, for example, that women have an instinct for mothering) nor as conscious adoptings of different traits and roles. Like any good Freudian, she believes that profound psychological qualities must originate during childhood and in processes that are sustained, pervasive, and above all unconscious. It is precisely because such qualities are deeply imbedded psychologically that they are so difficult to change.

The heart of Chodorow's book consists of a rigorous, clinically based account of the origin of these temperamental differences. Like Juliet Mitchell, she focuses on the pre-Oedipal ties between mother and child. But unlike Mitchell, she emphasizes the ways that the mother's relationship with her daughter differs from that with her son. Mothers, she says, treat their daughters as extensions of their own egos (because they view them as projections of their earlier selves), while they treat their sons much more as external objects, indeed, as partial replacements for their frequently absent husbands. The effect of this differential psychic economy—in which the daughter becomes an appendage of the mother, the son a kind of eroticized other—is that girls develop a psychology based, as Chodorow puts it, on "fusion, . . . narcissistic extension, and denial of separateness," whereas the psychology of boys emphasizes otherness, boundedness, and independence. Girls acquire the nurturing and incorporative traits that suit them to becoming mothers in their own right; boys acquire the sharp ego boundaries and the sense of autonomy that will prove serviceable in the world of work.

This construction modifies the classical Freudian portrait in at least two ways. First, it subordinates sexual motives to a more broadly conceived notion of relationships. (Here, in particular, one sees Chodorow's debt to the object relations school.) Attraction and hostility between parent and child no longer express themselves primarily in sexual terms, even though sexuality still plays a role. Second, Chodorow locates the initiative in these relations almost entirely on the side of the parent. It is the mother who perceives her child as belonging to one sex rather than the other and treats it accordingly. For their part, children know nothing of sexual differentiation. Although they remain sexual creatures for Chodorow, their sexuality is largely reactive. Freud, by way of contrast, makes the child the erotic protagonist in the family drama, even if only in imagination.

One might consider these modifications already radical enough to disqualify Chodorow as a true Freudian. I myself would have been inclined to deal rather severely with her earlier in my life, when any departure from Freud's instinctual theory seemed to me an abandonment of the very thing that was most distinctive in his thought. But under today's more trying circumstances this deviation appears less consequential than her continued emphasis on the unconscious and on childhood, even if there is a lingering worry that she may have rather sanitized the classical analytic teachings.

Chodorow deals briskly, indeed summarily, with the familiar embarrassments in Freud's female psychology. Certain of the notorious formulations—all those, for example, deriving from the theory of woman's weaker superego—she dismisses as obiter dicta without any clinical basis. She makes the ingenious (and I think just) assertion that these notions are essentially un-Freudian, because they lack support from the one kind of evidence Freud himself considered definitive, that is, clinical evidence. As for the theory of penis envy, which *is* clinically based, it gets reinterpreted along object relations lines—that is, in terms of its significance for the general tenor of relations between the girl and her parents.

Little girls in the Oedipal phase do envy the penis, according to Chodorow, but they envy it as a symbol of power. In Lacanian terms, it is not a penis but a Phallus. Penis envy is a manifestation of their attempt to win independence from the mother during these years. You could say that penis envy, in Chodorow's account, is subjected to a kind of cosmetic surgery, and Freudian purists might be inclined to suspect that the patient has died under the knife.

The most important feature of Chodorow's reinterpretation, in my view, is that it points unambiguously to feminist conclusions. Much more clearly than Juliet Mitchell, Chodorow can argue that *her* psychoanalytic explanation of male-female difference affords a way out of our current situation. It does so by showing that the association of women with mothering is purely conventional. There is nothing inherent in women's anatomical or instinctual constitution—nothing turned up by psychoanalysis at least—that destines them for the role of primary caretaker. Thus when the task of mothering is shared by women and men (or when it is taken over in part by day-care centers) children presumably will no longer be subjected to the differential treatment that has produced the temperamental split between the sexes. This will be a revolutionary change in and of itself, but, even more important, it will deprive patriarchy of its deepest psychological anchor. Women will cease to be uniquely nurturant, men to be uniquely self-contained and purposive. Chodorow makes good, one might say, on Juliet Mitchell's promise that psychoanalysis holds the key to women's liberation.

TO MOVE FROM Nancy Chodorow and Juliet Mitchell to Jane Gallop is to enter an utterly transfigured, even unrecognizable, intellectual landscape. Her book, *The Daughter's Seduction,* introduces not only a whole new cast of characters but a radically different way of thinking about the entire issue of Freud and women. Indeed, one might even wonder whether the filiation isn't so tenuous as to have become meaningless. Yet at its very start Gallop describes her book as "the continual working of a dialectical tension between 'psychoanalysis' and 'feminism.'" "Psychoanalysis," she continues, "can unsettle feminism's tendency to accept a traditional, unified, rational, puritanical self—a self supposedly free

from the violence of desire. In its turn, feminism can shake up psychoanalysis's tendency to think itself apolitcal but in fact be conservative by
encouraging people to adapt to an unjust social structure."

I need to spend a little time describing just what kind of book Gallop
has written. It is very much a product of the recent French intellectual
invasion, and it reflects state-of-the-art literary manners as they are practiced in Paris and New Haven. It is, in other words, a book about books,
or, to use its own language, a text about texts. Nearly all the texts in question come from the world of Parisian psychoanalysis, at whose center
stands the enigmatic figure of Jacques Lacan. In fact, her book, along
with Sherry Turckle's *Psychoanalytic Politics,* provides an admirable introduction to the Lacanian dispensation—its personalities, its squabbles,
and its habits of mind and expression. In particular, it introduces us to the
work of Lacan's main feminist disciple and critic, Luce Irigaray, whose
two best-known writings are *Speculum of the Other Woman* (1974) and
This Sex Which Isn't One (1977).

This is not the place—and I am not the person—to expound the
ideas of Jacques Lacan. But to make sense of Gallop one does need to
know certain things about him. First, one needs to know that he is exceptionally obscure (a matter, as we shall see, of some importance for Gallop's feminist reading of Freud). Second, his work involves a linguistic
transformation of psychoanalysis, in which the self is constituted not
through desire and its repression (the libidinal economy that Freud talks
about) but rather in, with, and through language; the self, in fact, is an ar-
tifact of language for Lacan. And, third, the emergence of this linguistically fashioned self is associated with what Lacan calls "the symbol of
the phallus." I won't pretend to understand Lacan's reasoning here, or to
explain how Freud's essentially preverbal infant can be reconciled with
Lacan's linguistic fabrication, but one needs to recognize that within the
world of Lacanian psychoanalysis the self is a symbolic creation, and the
privileged symbol or "signifier" (to use his own terminology) is the phallus. So selfhood, language, and phallic consciousness all belong to the
same order of things, to the same intellectual register.

Each of the figures in Jane Gallop's book, including Gallop herself,
accepts these Lacanian assumptions. Hence the confrontations she
arranges in her individual chapters, which pit one text against another,

take place within a framework of basic intellectual agreement. In these dialogues Gallop assigns different roles to her various players. Lacan, for instance, becomes the archetypal father, Irigaray the daughter; or, alternatively, Lacan speaks for psychoanalysis, Irigaray for feminism, and so forth. The seduction in the book's title alludes to the incestuous seductions that Freud thought he had discovered among his female patients in the 1890s, although what worries Gallop is not physical seduction (which she in fact looks rather indulgently on) but intellectual seduction—the way daughters are persuaded to take on the values and mental habits of the paternal regime.

The most striking thing about Gallop's book, however, is not its substance but its manner. She deliberately adopts incongruous and irreverent language, and just as deliberately violates the accepted canons of exposition and argument. The style of the book is playful, self-referential, and often disorderly. As one catches onto it, one recognizes its similarity to the method that Freud devised for interpreting dreams and neurotic symptoms, that is, the method of free association and evenly hovering attention. Thus, instead of reporting someone's ideas or reasoning (which might be compared to the manifest content of dreams), she focuses on odd and seemingly insignificant details, which, like symptoms, are taken to reveal the deeper (the latent) content of the text under analysis. Whole paragraphs, for example, are devoted to discussing an incorrect definite article, or a missing letter in someone's name, or a preposition that shows up three times in the title of a book. There is an almost Joycean infatuation with puns, conceits, double entendres, and dirty jokes. (She repeatedly, and gleefully, calls Lacan himself a prick, which in the book's curious rhetorical system turns out to be something of a compliment.) Much of the writing is quite funny, which contrasts sharply with the sociological solemnity of Nancy Chodorow's *Reproduction of Mothering*.

The reader might be wondering what all this has to do with feminism, or with the relations between feminism and psychoanalysis. To which I would answer, a very great deal. In fact, when you understand the logic (or illogic) of Gallop's style, you are, I believe, well on your way to understanding perhaps the most important connection in her view between Freud and feminism. For Gallop, Freud is the architect of a new

intellectual manner, a revolutionary habit of mind that subverts the established intellectual regime, and, along with it, the patriarchal society
that it both reflects and supports. In the intellectual realm, patriarchy expresses itself through the rule of language, that is, through the domination of mental life by discursive rationality. It is a world of theory,
argument, evidence, deduction, proof, and clarity, and it allows virtually
no conceptual room for play, for variety, for multiplicity, or, to adopt one
of the master terms of Lacanian psychoanalysis, for "difference." And,
of course, this is exactly the world that Gallop's book assaults—assaults
not so much in its assertions as in its style.

Now, to the extent that Freud himself propounded a theory—just to
the degree that his prose aspired to lucidity—his work also belongs to
the repressive intellectual order that knows only one truth, one standard
of judgment, one modus operandi. Indeed, in Freud's female psychology
the repression of plurality, of difference, achieves perhaps its greatest triumph, because Freud holds that little girls, in the unconscious, actually
think of themselves as little boys: there is only one sex, just as there is
only one mode of thought and speech. But insofar as Freud discovered
a novel method of inquiry that violates the rules of discursive rationality—one employing free association and attending to the primary processes—he is rightly thought of as an intellectual liberator, and a
liberator of women in particular. From this perspective, Jacques Lacan,
in his turn, brings Freud's revolution to completion, because he not only
rescues psychoanalysis from its outworn biological assumptions but also
replaces Freud's misguided lucidity with his own uncompromising opacity. And if Lacan himself sometimes falls back into the old patriarchal
ways (advancing theories, pressing arguments, writing polemics, even
giving into occasional bouts of clarity), his successors, like Irigaray or
Gallop herself, step forward to make amends for his lapses.

So psychoanalysis and feminism, in this reading, meet in their shared
subversion of the discursive order. What this alliance implies from a tac-
tical point of view, I gather, is a commitment to writing books like Gallop's own or like those of Luce Irigaray, books in which psychoanalytic
themes are playfully rehearsed and the expectations of linear rationality
constantly frustrated. As you can imagine, it is a difficult, perhaps impossible, stance to maintain, because any sequence of words that is not en-

tirely random has a way of slipping into coherence and thereby restoring
the hated discursive regime. Put another way, if repression originates in
language, then even the most playful text must ultimately be compromised. And Gallop's own work is notably flawed in this respect, since it is
a good deal more readable than those of most of her French counterparts.

Still, even if the project is utopian, I think Jane Gallop has identified
an important moment of congruence between psychoanalysis and feminism. Discursive rationality does in fact supply the intellectual glue of
the modern social and political order (this is a point made repeatedly by
the critical theorists of the Frankfurt School, notably by Horkheimer and
Adorno in *The Dialectic of Enlightenment*), and, needless to say, the oppression of women is an integral part of that order. It is also true that psychoanalysis—viewed as a method rather than as a theory—serves to
destabilize our familiar intellectual manners. So Gallop is onto something credible when she implies that Freud, despite his misogyny, is a
significant ally. In this connection, we should perhaps recall the extraordinary role played by women in the history of psychoanalysis. I can
think of no other major intellectual movements, unless it be feminism itself, in which so many women have achieved such eminence. In this respect, Freud's misogynistic science stands in dramatic contrast to the
ostensibly more progressive heritage of Marx and Engels.

WHEN I BEGAN this inquiry I rather assumed that Freud's reputation
was most endangered by the criticism emanating from feminists. But after reading Juliet Mitchell, Nancy Chodorow, and Jane Gallop, I am now
inclined to consider this the quarter from which he has least to fear and
indeed most to hope. The objectionable elements in psychoanalysis remain, and they will doubtless continue to rankle. But these writers persuade me that the affinities run deeper than the antagonisms. Their work
suggests that the psychic processes explored by Freud are as relevant to
the lives of women as of men. It also suggests that understanding those
processes is essential to diagnosing women's oppression and to devising
a strategy to overcome it. Finally, it hints at a deeper alliance—a secret

alliance—between psychoanalysis and feminism in opposition to the reigning intellectual assumptions of our culture.

Freud and Homosexuality

My topic here, to state it in a necessarily crude and abbreviated fashion, is the question, "Has Freud been good or bad for homosexuals?" The question is worth asking because a number of recent scholarly writings have represented Freud as among the foremost inventors of modern homophobia—just as, a quarter of a century ago, Kate Millett represented him as the forefather of modern misogyny. I am thinking of books like Jonathan Ned Katz's *The Invention of Heterosexuality* (1995) or Daniel Boyarin's *Unheroic Conduct* (1997), in which Freud appears as a chief architect of the modern medical category of the homosexual (as well as that of the heterosexual). These categories—so the argument goes—created the tendentious notion that humanity is divided between those (presumably a small minority) devoted exclusively to sexual relations with their own sex and those (the vast majority) no less exclusively devoted to relations with the opposite sex.

I think this conception is fundamentally wrong. But it contains an element of truth, especially if we expand our view to include not just Freud himself but the psychoanalytic tradition as a whole, especially its American variant in the middle years of the twentieth century.

I don't want to get into the broader argument about whether in fact "the homosexual" was invented—or merely codified—by the turn-of-the-century sexologists (an argument that pits "essentialists" against "social constructionists"). The kernel of truth that links Freud to what can legitimately be considered a homophobic discourse is his famous developmental conception of identity formation, according to which heterosexual object choice is the ideal, or at least the "normal," outcome of the child's psychic evolution. As Jonathan Ned Katz points out, Freud repeatedly, almost compulsively, refers to heterosexuality as the "normal" result, and he uses "normal" not just in a statistical sense but evaluatively, equating it with psychic maturity. By way of contrast, homosexuality in this scheme is always construed as regressive; Freud invariably speaks of it as an atavism, in which the child gets stuck—fixated—at some more primitive stage of psychic development, whether it be narcissistic, oral, or anal. Freud's language, in other words, is "normalizing," although one needs to point out that Freud's feelings about "normality," like his feelings about "civilization," were ambivalent. One strain in his thought protested against the libidinal sacrifice that "normal" adult genitality entailed and, as thinkers like Herbert Marcuse and Norman O. Brown argued years ago, one can read Freud as, at least in part, a critic of normalization and a prophet of a liberated, "polymorphously perverse" sexuality. In *Civilization and Its Discontents*, for example, Freud gives a distinctly critical account of the sacrifices that so-called psychic maturity entails: "As regards the sexually mature individual," he writes there, "the choice of object is restricted to the opposite sex, and most extra-genital satisfactions are forbidden as perversions. The requirement, demonstrated in these prohibitions, that there shall be a single kind of sexual life for everyone disregards the dissimilarities, whether innate or acquired, in the sexual constitution of human beings; it cuts off a fair number of them from sexual enjoyment, and so becomes the source of serious injustice."

Although Freud's treatment of homosexuality was "normalizing," it was not "pathologizing." The distinction is important, because later on American psychoanalysts would argue, unambiguously, that homosexuality was a sickness. But Freud insisted that it was not a sickness. He did so most famously in his 1935 letter to the mother of an American homosexual, in which he wrote, "Homosexuality is assuredly no advantage, but it is nothing to be ashamed of, no vice, no degradation; it cannot be classified as an illness." In fact, one can argue that Freud conceived of homosexuality as the opposite of sickness. As he said, more than once, the neuroses were, in his view, the "negative" of the perversions, by which he meant that homosexual urges become pathogenic only when repressed. The person who acted on his or her homosexual impulses was in theory immune to neurosis, whereas those impulses became dangerous precisely when they were driven into the unconscious. Perhaps the best-known instance of the phenomenon is Freud's theory of paranoia, worked out in the Schreber case, where paranoia is said to be caused by repressed homosexual desire.

Even more fundamentally, however, the notion that Freud participated in the radical conceptual separating of homosexuals from heterosexuals gets the story exactly backwards. On the contrary, he opposed any notion that homosexuality can be so isolated, or that homosexuals constitute an essentially separate class of persons and that heterosexuals are thus safe from homosexual contamination. Freud expressly opposed the version of this idea advanced by such homophile theorists as Karl Heinrich Ulrichs and Magnus Hirschfeld, even though he supported the political goal that the conception was meant to advance—namely, the decriminalization of homosexuality—because, he contended, it ignored the evidence, turned up by psychoanalysis, that homosexuality is universally present in psychic development. As he says in *Three Essays on the Theory of Sexuality*, "All human beings are capable of making a homosexual object-choice and have in fact made one in their unconscious." To use the language invented by Eve Sedgwick, Freud's conception of homosexuality is unambiguously "universalizing," as opposed to the "minoritizing" ideas advanced not only by homosexuals like Ulrichs and Hirschfeld but by such influential straight thinkers of the period as Richard von Krafft-Ebing and Havelock Ellis. In Freud's psychic universe, homosexuality is everywhere, insinuating itself into the mental lives of the most impeccably "normal" and presentable individuals. Indeed, no one has done more to destabilize the notion of heterosexuality than Freud. In Freud's world there simply are no heterosexuals, at least not psychologically. Similarly, he insists that manifest heterosexuality, far from being a fact of nature, is a precarious psychic achievement, and one that must be accounted for. As he writes, again in the *Three Essays*, "The exclusive sexual interest felt by men for women is also a problem that needs elucidating and is not a self-evident fact based upon an attraction that is ultimately of a chemical nature." Nor did Freud exempt himself from this universalizing conception: he frequently diagnosed his own relationship with Wilhelm Fliess as a manifestation of a passive homosexual attachment on his part, most famously at the time of his fainting spell in Munich in 1912 when, speaking of his long connection with Fliess, he remarked in a letter to Ernest Jones, "There is some piece of unruly homosexual feeling at the root of the matter."

The universalizing conception is spectacularly on display in the

great case histories. The only one who appears to be innocent of homosexual desire is the Rat Man, and here we almost feel that Freud missed
the obvious homosexual implications of the Rat Man's rat fantasy. With
the exception of Leonardo, all the male protagonists in the case histories
(I'll come to the women in a moment) were manifest heterosexuals. Yet
homosexual urges are found in each of their psychic lives, most emphatically in the case of the Wolf Man and Schreber, where the repression of
the desire to be sodomized by the father, Freud argues, is the fundamental source of their illness. I would also suggest that Freud's attitude toward these men ranges from admiration (in the case of Leonardo, with
whom, in fact, Freud deeply identified) to at the very least dispassionate
interest and sympathy. Admittedly, he is most enthusiastic about a homosexual such as Leonardo who has sublimated his desires and thereby become a culture bearer, rather like the Jews in *Moses and Monotheism*. He
is made more nervous by passive anal sex than he is by fellatio, which, as
he notes in the Leonardo case, is "loathsome" in the eyes of "respectable
society" but, he goes on to say, "may be traced to an origin of the most
innocent kind," namely, the child's sucking at its mother's breast. I would
point out that, from a historian's point of view, perhaps the most remarkable thing about Freud's discussions of homosexuality is their astonishing rhetorical evenhandedness, which contrasts not only with the
habitual prejudice of his society but also with the more judgmental tone
of even such relatively enlightened figures as Krafft-Ebing and Ellis. As
he says when introducing the sexual aberrations in the *Introductory Lectures*, "What we have here is a field of phenomena like any other."

The story is very different when it comes to the two most famous lesbian case histories, Dora and the anonymous woman of 1920. These
cases are remarkably alike: both involve prepossessing young women in
their late teens who react to Freud with marked hostility and whom he
treats with a corresponding contempt, which, of course, invites the suspicion that the real problem is Freud's, not his patients'. Put another way,
I see in Freud's failure to extend to lesbians the same dispassion he lavishes on his male homosexuals a reflection of his larger difficulty with
women. Indeed, I think it is hard to separate lesbianism from femininity
in Freud's conceptual universe, because both are analyzed by him in
terms of women's psychic problems with the penis and their disappoint-

ment in men. It's also interesting that although Freud states that in men there is no necessary connection between homosexual object choice and "character inversion" (that is, effeminacy), he makes just the opposite assertion about lesbians: in his view they are nearly always mannish. In other words, I don't think Freud's hostile treatment of lesbianism—which contrasts both substantively and above all rhetorically with his treatment of male homosexuality—can be separated from his misogyny.

More important, finally, than any of the issues I've addressed so far—all of which might be said to belong to the "sticks and stones" category—is the question of therapy: the question of whether homosexuality can be treated or, more radically, cured. Although Freud often said that (manifest) homosexuality was probably grounded in some constitutional predisposition, the general thrust of his thinking was to insist that homosexuals are made rather than born, which seems to leave him open to the possibility that they might be "unmade"—that is, turned into heterosexuals. But in fact he took just the opposite position. Although his statements aren't absolutely categorical, he comes very close to saying that homosexuality is entirely beyond the range of not only analytic therapy but any therapy whatsoever: "In general," he writes, "to undertake to convert a fully developed homosexual into a heterosexual does not offer much more prospect of success than the reverse."

Freud's humane therapeutic pessimism must be contrasted with the profoundly homophobic and insanely utopian therapeutic optimism of his American acolytes, above all the evil trio of Edmund Bergler (a European transplant), Irving Bieber, and Charles Socarides—who, alas, is still among the quick and still issuing the same mad pronouncements. Not only do they call all homosexuals pathological, as well as manipulative liars, but they also insist that the homosexual's only hope is to convert to heterosexuality. Bergler went so far as to claim that such "cures" could be effected "in 99.9 percent of all cases of homosexuality." Here we are no longer dealing with sticks and stones but with a brutally oppressive therapeutic practice that profoundly damaged a generation of American gay men in the middle decades of the twentieth century. If you want to take the measure of that damage in an individual life, I recommend the autobiography of Martin Duberman, entitled *Cures,* which documents the horrific treatment that Duberman received at the hands of three American Freudians in the 1950s and 1960s. In effect, American psychoanalysts exactly reversed Freud's ideas as well as his therapeutic practice. They transformed homosexuality into a disease, and a curable one at that, and they categorically separated it from "normal" heterosexuality by rejecting Freud's universalizing notion of constitutional bisexuality. They even reversed Freud's prejudices on the subject, because in the mid-century American literature lesbianism is ignored, whereas male homosexuality, toward which Freud had a distinct softness, is thoroughly demonized. As the historian of this unhappy story, Kenneth Lewes, has said, in America the Freudian theory of homosexuality ceased to be a matter of the history of ideas and became instead a matter of the history of prejudice. And as Lewes further suggests, the transformation had much more to do with the Cold War and McCarthyism—and with the eagerness of foreign-born analysts to ingratiate themselves with their American hosts—than with anything that Freud ever wrote on the subject.

There is a sweet Freudian footnote to this lamentable history: Robert Socarides, the son of the last and arguably the most vulgar of the American psychoanalytic homophobes, Charles Socarides, is not only a gay man himself but an activist in the cause who served as Bill Clinton's main liaison with the gay community. I like to think of it as the return of the repressed.

CHAPTER FIFTEEN

H. Stuart Hughes and Intellectual History

I've here reprinted two pieces on my mentor H. Stuart Hughes. The first was delivered at a symposium, Approaches to European Intellectual History, held at the University of California, San Diego, in May 1986 to honor Hughes on his retirement. Three of his other students, Dominick LaCapra, Martin Jay, and John Toews—all important figures in the field—also spoke, and the keynote address was given by Peter Gay. My remarks, which were subsequently published in the Intellectual History Newsletter *(April 1987), chart the evolution of intellectual history from the "social history of ideas" of Robert Darnton through the "linguistic turn" (or deconstructive project) of Dominick LaCapra. Against both I urge a return to Hughes's practice, which focused on seminal thinkers and aimed at identifying the unifying intellectual assumptions of an era. Stuart Hughes died in the fall of 1999, and in the second piece, also originally published in the* Intellectual History Newsletter, *I offer a memorial tribute.*

I

As it happens, I am trying right now to fulfill the responsibilities of a job that Stuart Hughes held exactly thirty years ago, namely, the chairmanship of the Stanford History Department. I am certain that Stuart managed this task with more grace than I have, and I am even more certain that it did not mark for him, as it has for me, an unqualified caesura in the life of the mind. When Allan Mitchell invited me to participate in this celebration, he asked me what I was writing about, and I had to inform him that there could be no talk of writing, unless, of course, he meant the writing of memoranda. Indeed, it seemed to me ages since I had even *read* anything. By way of sorry and shameful contrast, during precisely those years when Stuart Hughes was head of the Stanford Department in 1955 and 1956, he was deeply involved in the reading and thinking that led to the publication in 1958 of his most important book, *Consciousness and Society.*

My purpose in drawing this unflattering contrast between Stuart and me is not merely to pay tribute to his extraordinary resourcefulness—his ability to do so much more than the rest of us ordinary mortals—but to provide an excuse for myself as well. I mean to apologize for the fact that I have not prepared a substantive paper that can stand comparison with those of Professors Jay, Toews, LaCapra, and Gay. Rather, what I want to offer is a series of brief and informal reflections, and I intend them quite simply as a gesture of thanksgiving to Stuart for what he has represented to me and to the discipline as a whole.

Unfortunately, this gesture must assume an ironic form. When I cast my mind over what intellectual historians have been up to during the past two decades, I'm most struck by the ways that they have deviated from the example set for them by Stuart Hughes, and deviated, in my opinion, largely to their disadvantage. I won't pretend to speak with anything approaching statistical accuracy, and I'll confess to an almost constitutional aversion to this sort of disciplinary self-examination, which in general seems to me a narcissistic waste of time. But let me indulge in it just long enough to suggest that in my professional lifetime two different projects have captured the fancy of intellectual historians, and both of them have diverted us from the sort of scholarship that Stuart Hughes pursued. During the 1970s it was the social history of ideas, epitomized in the work of Robert Darnton, that took center stage. In the 1980s it has been the so-called linguistic turn, as practiced by, among others, Hayden White and Dominick LaCapra, that has achieved a similar ascendancy. I want to talk a little about both of these tendencies, with a view to specifying how they differ from the intellectual history written by Stuart Hughes and how, as I've already intimated, I think we would be better off if we had remained more loyal to Hughes's example.

The social history of ideas emerged in the 1960s and 1970s as one manifestation of the larger shift toward social history that was probably the most salient characteristic of the historical profession as a whole in those decades. It was very much influenced by French historiography—that is, by the Annales school—and, appropriately enough, its most articulate spokesman, Robert Darnton, worked (and still works) in the field of eighteenth-century French history.

The fundamental assumption of the social history of ideas was that the subject matter of intellectual history ought to be determined by one criterion, and one criterion alone: consumption. The ideas with which historians concerned themselves should be the ideas that people actually held, and the larger the number of people holding a particular idea (or attitude, or value) the more deserving it was of the historian's attention. Even to speak of "ideas" or "ideas being held," as I have just now, rather distorts what the social history of ideas aimed to capture, because the mental processes in question generally lacked the self-consciousness or reflectiveness associated with ideas or intellectual opinions. Hence the preference for speaking of mentalities. Since, moreover, historians seldom can have direct access to people's minds (that is, the minds of people who don't set their ideas down on paper), the social history of ideas relied on reconstructing mental universes by means of inferences drawn from the production and purchase of books, pamphlets, and newspapers. Its primary documents—its evidential bases—were publication, sales, and circulation records.

One can see a classic confrontation between the social history of ideas and traditional intellectual history in a review Robert Darnton wrote, in 1971, of Peter Gay's second volume on the Enlightenment. In it Darnton compared Gay's work unfavorably to a number of French studies of eighteenth-century intellectual life, studies that examined not the writings of the well-known philosophes (who were Peter Gay's primary sources) but the popular literature—if you want, the junk literature—known to have circulated widely in France during the century. Darnton made his point—a simple one—over and over: you can't write the intellectual history of a period unless you know what people actually read. In eighteenth-century France they read not the *Social Contract* of Jean-Jacques Rousseau but the Bibliothèque bleue—cheap, popular books that retailed, as Darnton put it, "mumbo-jumbo" stories about "magic num-

bers, physiognomy, and primitive rituals." Darnton implied, not so subtly, that the traditional intellectual historian was an effete creature of the
library, whereas the social historian of ideas didn't fear getting his hands
dirty: he lived in the real world—the world of hard knocks—with his tie
loosened and his sleeves rolled up. "Digging downward in intellectual
history," Darnton wrote in 1971, "calls for new methods and new materials, for grubbing in the archives instead of contemplating philosophical
treatises." The metaphors pretty much speak for themselves.

Against the kind of scholarship advocated and practiced by Robert
Darnton, Stuart Hughes's work obviously stands for a very different
conception of the intellectual historian's calling. I think the best way to
specify that difference is to say that his work rests on a more complex notion of the criteria by which ideas, as it were, qualify for our attention.
"Consumption," or influence, is only one of the considerations that must
be reckoned with, and even consumption itself is no simple democratic
matter, because some instances of influence are more important than
others. Beyond the matter of influence lie the no less significant matters
of novelty and—for lack of a better word—complexity or profundity.
These considerations make us recognize that we can't ignore Rousseau's
Social Contract simply on the grounds that it went unread in Rousseau's
lifetime. In this respect, the intellectual historian resembles less the social
historian than the historian of music or the historian of art, neither of
whom construct the history of music or art solely—or even largely—in
terms of what pieces were played and what paintings were bought.

This point of view is so much an organic part of Stuart Hughes's
practice as an intellectual historian that, so far as I know, he has never felt
the need to articulate it explicitly. But let me cite just one example from
his writings where we can see this richer, more complex set of criteria at
work. I have in mind his decision, in *Consciousness and Society*, to make
Sigmund Freud and Max Weber, as it were, the co-centerpieces in his intellectual portrait of turn-of-the-century Europe. Had he relied solely on
the doctrine of consumption—of influence—the notion of giving Max
Weber equal billing with Freud would have been indefensible. In terms
of almost any measure one might use, Freud's influence simply dwarfs
Weber's. But Hughes recognized that when we also take into account
such other considerations as complexity, richness, and creative respon-

siveness to the broadly felt intellectual concerns of the day, Weber can very plausibly stand as one of the two giants of the era.

Needless to say, I think Stuart Hughes's scholarship represents the superior example in this regard. In fact, if the social historians of ideas had had their way—as it seemed they might in the 1970s—the result would have been a dramatic impoverishment of our work.

I DOUBT THAT ANYONE could have guessed, even ten years ago, that the 1980s would have brought such a dramatic reversal in the agenda of intellectual history. In retrospect, of course, it makes perfect sense. The antielitist, democratizing effort to make intellectual history simply a branch of social history inevitably called forth its opposite: a movement among certain practitioners to return to the text with a vengeance—and the more recondite, the more complex, or, if you will, the greater the text, the better. The only thing that the "linguistic turn" of the 1980s has in common with the social history of ideas of the 1970s is its shared French provenance. But where the earlier rebels found their inspiration in French historiography, the newer school has found it in recent French philosophy and literary theory, above all in deconstruction.

From the perspective of traditional intellectual history—the sort of intellectual history practiced by Stuart Hughes—the distinguishing feature of this latest development has been the fierce interpretive attention it devotes to individual texts, whose complexity, nuance, and capacity to disturb it hopes not so much to reveal as to protect. Indeed, I find it most useful to think of the linguistic turn of the 1980s above all as a defensive maneuver—a maneuver to defend great writings against certain real or perceived intellectual depredations. Those writings must be defended, first of all, against the crude, flat-footed consumptionism of the social history of ideas. But just as important, they must be protected from the abuse to which they were purportedly subjected by traditional intellectual history as well.

The advocates of the linguistic turn seem to be inspired by an utter horror of the simplification and reduction that great works of philosophy and literature sometimes suffer when they fall into the hands of old-fashioned historians of ideas. Traditional intellectual historians, in this view, rob the text of its inherent richness and ambiguity by seeking to paraphrase it (telling us in a page or two, for example, what Thomas Mann's *The Magic Mountain* is "about"). They pummel and distort the text so as to make it fit into the larger story of an "intellectual career"— that is, as one moment in a unified trajectory that constitutes the author's lifework. And perhaps worst of all, they reduce it to a mere instance of some banal generalization about the climate of opinion—an illustration (God forbid) of the Zeitgeist.

If the linguistic turn is best understood as a defense mechanism, how does that defense mechanism work? In a number of ways, obviously. The first of them is to stick very near to the text—to practice the kind of radically close reading that inhibits thoughts about the author or the era or other larger unities from entering the picture. The second is to read the work in a purposefully fragmented, partial, and even disorganized fashion so as to prevent any falsely unitary or coherent image of even the work itself from emerging. (This is the defense against paraphrase.) And the last is to cultivate a prose style that through its neologisms, opacity, and systematic confusions serves as a shield against the bright, clear interpretive reductions that are so intolerable. Intellectual history, thus construed, aims to protect great works of literature, philosophy, and social theory from the terrible simplifiers of the textbook tradition.

Moreover, as far as I am concerned, it is entirely successful in this objective. Naturally, I agree with LaCapra & Co that great writings sometimes need to be protected. But the price, in this instance, is exceedingly high. I am as annoyed as the next person by the textbook manner, where every sentence brings a new idea, every paragraph a new thinker, and where insights that once seemed either subtle or terrifying are ground into a kind of intellectual pablum. But I am not prepared to believe that the only alternative lies in artful obscurantism. It is precisely here that Stuart Hughes's example seems to me invaluable.

LET ME FINISH by calling attention to two important ways in which Stuart Hughes has managed to avoid the excesses into which the discipline now seems ready to plunge:

The first is that he succeeds in the subtle art of fashioning intellectual generalizations that don't abuse the writings upon which those generalizations are based but serve rather to illuminate them. This, in my view, is the highest accomplishment of any intellectual historian, because we know how easily generalizations degenerate into clichés and banalities. In part, Hughes's ability to manage this feat is a matter of fineness of touch and sensibility. But it is also a result of his commitment to the notion that all such generalizations have about them a certain fictional status: they are conceptual conveniences, to be embraced with delicacy, and to be released when they no longer fulfill their intellectual function. This habit of mind allows him, in *Consciousness and Society*, to sketch a general intellectual portrait of the early twentieth century that lends the period coherence (albeit only a tentative, "as-if" coherence) by setting its individual figures and works in a kind of mutually reflective, but never oppressive, light. One comes away from the book not with Freud, or Weber, or Sorel having been reduced to a paraphrase—or a mechanical instance of some numbing generality—but rendered more interesting, richer, and above all more comprehensible for having been located within a larger intellectual network. The individual texts have not been violated, but neither do they remain mysteriously inviolate.

The second thing I want to mention—and it is the quality of Hughes's work that I admire more than any other—is his prose style. Few of us can aspire to the elegance that is his trademark. But we can all aspire to the more fundamental virtues of his writing, namely, clarity and economy. He is the master of the plain style. It is here that I find the most lamentable discrepancy between his work that of the recent advocates of the linguistic turn. Of course, the discrepancy makes perfect sense if you believe, as I have suggested, that the primary impetus behind the linguistic turn is a defensive one—the desire to defend great writings from reduction and simplification. Clarity, under these circumstances, becomes a questionable virtue.

But again the price is exceedingly high. What's at stake here is the matter of the audience we address and expect to read our writings. For Stuart Hughes that audience is first of all the historical profession as a whole, reflecting the fact that he is a general historian before he is an intellectual historian. But it is also the intellectual community at large, the community that reads, say, the *New York Review of Books*. By way of contrast, the audience implicitly addressed by the practitioners of the linguistic turn is radically more specialized. It consists of other intellectual historians (and by no means all of them) and certain literary critics and philosophers. In my view, this stylistic choice will ultimately mean a great diminution in the importance of intellectual history. It threatens to lead to the kind of hermetic provincialism that has afflicted philosophy and, more recently, literary criticism.

Naturally, I would like to hope that we will come to our senses and remember the commitments and accomplishments of the previous generation not to imitate them but to preserve what is best in them. Nobody in that generation offers a more admirable example than Stuart Hughes. Above all, as I've tried to convey in these remarks, he provides a model of scholarship that is at once complex and intelligible, ambitious yet not imperialistic, and, most crucial, accessible to his fellow historians and to the intellectual community at large. We should not only honor his remarkable achievement but also strive to keep it alive and admonishing before our inner eye.

II

H. Stuart Hughes died October 21, 1999. He was arguably the most influential European intellectual historian of his generation, the generation that came of age during World War II and dominated the field in the second half of the twentieth century. In the years he taught at Harvard, from 1957 to 1975, Hughes trained more Ph.D.'s in the field than any other scholar. He told me he had been the advisor for almost seventy Harvard dissertations. To be sure, that extraordinary number reflects the fact that, during his tenure there, Harvard was still seen by many as the necessary place to go if you wanted to land a good job, and the university's wealth allowed it to admit a large number of applicants. (My own entering class of aspiring modern European historians in 1963 contained more than a dozen members.) Still, Hughes's remarkable record also testifies to his real attractions as a mentor: he was a brilliant teacher and a presence of undeniable glamour, and in Harvard's generally Darwinian universe he was also civil, even ingratiating. Several of his students became prominent intellectual historians of the next generation, among them John

Toews, Martin Jay, and Dominick LaCapra. Hughes's only rival in this regard was Carl Schorske, who during his years at Berkeley and Princeton trained some equally distinguished scholars, if not in the numbers Hughes did.

Although he became a (somewhat reluctant) member of the Harvard establishment in the 1960s and 1970s, Hughes's career was anything but orthodox. It contained moments of high drama, and it belonged almost as much to politics as to scholarship. His origins were prophetic: he was the grandson of Charles Evans Hughes, the Republican candidate for president in 1916 and later a powerful (and reactionary) chief justice of the Supreme Court. In his splendid autobiography, *Gentleman Rebel*, Hughes recalls his youthful admiration for his famous grandfather, as well as his later disillusionment. The decisive moment came at his graduation from Amherst, when the chief justice was persuaded to give an address (this after FDR had branded the members of the Supreme Court "nine old men"). Here is Hughes's own account of the episode: "As I listened to the speaker's old-fashioned oratorical periods roll on, an inner discomfort seized me. Little by little I began to understand why. What I was hearing was bullshit." (As a measure of his fundamental kindness, Hughes dined twice a week with his widowed grandfather during the last two years of the older man's life.) Hughes had "converted" to socialism in 1932, but by the time of his graduation he had become a supporter of Roosevelt's. Thereafter he generally allied himself with the left wing of the Democratic Party, although he sometimes found himself embracing figures and causes beyond the party's pale.

He completed his Ph.D. at Harvard in 1940. His thesis was on an unlikely subject: "The Crisis of the French Imperial Economy, 1810−1812," a topic he chose, he said, to curb his literary inclinations. Hitler's war interrupted his young scholarly career. He enlisted in the army as a private, but, like many intellectuals of his generation, he soon found his way to the Office of Strategic Services. Within three years he became chief of the OSS's Research and Analysis Branch in the Mediterranean Theatre, where he followed the Allied armies up the Italian peninsula. The experience, one likes to think, inspired the deep love of Italy that later led him to include Benedetto Croce, Vilfredo Pareto, and Gaetano Mosca in *Consciousness and Society* and to write his beautiful study of Italian Jewish writers, *Prisoners of Hope*. After the war he headed the State Department's Division of Research for Europe, where he struggled in vain to prevent the outbreak of the Cold War. In 1947 he left Washington in despair and returned to Harvard. Any hope of a career in government ended in 1948 when he supported Henry Wallace's presidential bid (although he broke with the Progressive Party before the election after he recognized that it had been taken over by Communists). One wonders what might have happened under more favorable political circumstances: with his intelligence, articulateness, and Brahmin manner, he might have risen to great heights.

Even as his scholarly career took off in the 1950s, Hughes remained deeply involved in left-wing causes. His most spectacular political adventure came in 1962, after he had taught at Harvard for four years: he ran on a disarmament platform for a U.S. Senate seat in Massachusetts. (His autobiography contains a photo of him giving a campaign speech on top of a truck, microphone in hand.) Among his advisers was Martin Peretz, who later bought the *New Republic* and became a political enemy. Peretz always said that the election was lost when a reporter asked Hughes about his religion, and he answered, with imprudent candor, that he was an agnostic. Hughes himself was inclined to blame the Cuban missile crisis. Nonetheless, he still managed to get fifty thousand votes. (The winner, of course, was Ted Kennedy.) After the defeat Hughes remained politically active, but in a more buttoned-down way: along with Benjamin Spock he became the head of SANE, the Committee for a Sane Nuclear Policy. As a sophisticated man, he knew that his political views were overly optimistic, even utopian, but he never made the move to the right so common among his intellectual contemporaries. At the University of California at San Diego after 1975, his longtime acquaintance with Herbert Marcuse, a fellow OSS alumnus, blossomed into one of the most important friendships of his later years. I myself recall Hughes's telling me, during a visit in the 1980s, that whenever Ronald Reagan came on the television he felt an irresistible urge to go to bed.

He was teaching at Stanford in 1956 when he received the call to Harvard. Apparently the History Department had agonized over whether to offer the position to Hughes or Carl Schorske. In *That Noble Dream*, Peter Novick implies that the decision between Hughes and Schorske ultimately came down to a question of which of the two was the less offensive politically: "David Owen [the department's modern British historian] thought that in the case of modern European historians Hughes's lack of 'political sagacity' was a relevant consideration; but, Owen said, 'Carl's record, if anything, has been worse than Stuart's.'" Others were of the opinion that Harvard naturally favored a Wasp over a Jew. Doubtless there was something of a rivalry between Schorske and Hughes. They resembled one another in several ways. Born within a year of each other, both received their Ph.D.'s at Harvard, both served in the OSS under their Harvard professor William Langer, and both were men of the left. They were also friends. In *Gentleman Rebel* Hughes recounts their intimacy during the war: "Closest to me was Carl Schorske, Langer's adjutant, bubbling over with a rich vein of humor, laced with German turns of phrase. On convivial evenings I would prompt him, 'Lieber Carl, jetzt sollen wir singen,' and he would lead off in his well-trained baritone, the rest of us one by one joining in." Perhaps most important, Hughes and Schorske became, along with Leonard Krieger and Peter Gay, the leading European intellectual historians of their time. But they chose very different scholarly paths. Schorske wrote intricate and profound studies of relatively limited historical phenomena: German Social Democracy before the First World War, Viennese culture in the fin-de-siècle. Hughes by contrast was drawn to the large panorama. In his most important books he produced broad-brushed accounts of European thought in the late nineteenth and early twentieth century and of French and German thought in the interwar years. The two men were also subject to opposite criticisms: Schorske was judged insufficiently productive, while the more prolific Hughes was sometimes found superficial. However intense their professional rivalry, in the end they came to view each other as comrades in arms. When in 1997 the French booted out the Conservatives and elected the Socialist Lionel Jospin, Hughes could think of no one with whom to share his jubilation other than Schorske, and he promptly dialed him up.

Unlike today's practitioners, Hughes did not think of himself exclusively as an intellectual historian. Half of his books, in fact, treat general topics in modern European history. He published a successful textbook, *Contemporary Europe,* as well as an admired study of Italian society and history, *The United States and Italy.* Later in his career came *Sophisticated Rebels,* an examination of political dissent in Europe during the two decades after the Prague and Paris uprisings of 1968. But doubtless Hughes will be best remembered for his books on modern European thought. He began in 1950 with *An Essay for Our Times,* part intellectual history, part political manifesto, which revealed his devotion to the great innovators of the early twentieth century, figures whom he would examine more thoroughly in *Consciousness and Society.* It was followed by *Oswald Spengler: A Critical Estimate,* in which he sought to rescue Spengler from his Nazi appropriators and to advance a qualified case for the academically disreputable genre of meta-history written not just by Spengler but by Arnold Toynbee, Petrim Sorokin, and Alfred Kroeber. The book, which Hughes later called "an 'estimate' and no more," betrayed his lingering ambivalence about the profession.

That ambivalence was mastered with *Consciousness and Society: The Reorientation of European Social Thought 1890–1930,* which was both a *succès d'estime* (to use Hughes's own phrase) and, by scholarly standards, a remarkable commercial success as well: it sold over 100,000 copies. He hadn't yet written a line of it when the invitation to Harvard arrived, and he convinced himself that he would not deserve the Harvard job unless the book was finished. So he drove himself relentlessly over seven months between 1956 and 1957, and by the time he arrived in Cambridge the manuscript had been sent to the publisher. The story, told in his autobiography, reveals the anxious contingencies behind a work that has become the standard account of Europe's intellectual transformation in the early twentieth century.

Consciousness and Society shows Hughes's powers of synthesis at their most impressive. The book treats the generation of intellectuals who invented what we now think of as the modern way of thinking. It contains deft analyses of the period's foremost innovators—Émile Durkheim, Georges Sorel, Benedetto Croce, and above all the two towering figures of the age (and the heroes of the book), Max Weber and Sigmund Freud. But the distinctive feature of Hughes's treatment is his skill in identifying the common denominators—the intellectual affinities—that united the thinkers of that time in a common conceptual enterprise. The book succeeds in defining the spirit of the age, that allusive body of shared assumptions and aspirations that lent unity and coherence to what at first blush seem entirely unrelated ideas. In effect Hughes did for the early twentieth century what Ernst Cassirer had done for the Enlightenment or what M. H. Abrams would do for romanticism: he defined an intellectual era. In recent years scholars have become increasingly unwilling to undertake broad syntheses of this sort. Indeed, synthetic studies have come under fire for doing violence to the complexity and nuance of individual thinkers and texts. But Hughes believed that the highest and most delicate task of the intellectual historian is precisely to attempt such integrative portraits.

He hoped to follow *Consciousness and Society* with a book that would tell the story of Europe's intellectual life in the interwar years. After wrestling with the project for a while, he concluded that there were in fact two stories, which would require separate books. One was that of the emigration of Central European (above all German) thinkers to England and the United States as a result of the rise of Nazism, an event that not only transformed British and American intellectual life but stimulated the Continental Europeans to a number of important innovations. Hughes's account, in *The Sea Change*, focused on such émigré figures as Hannah Arendt, Theodor Adorno, and two friends from his State Department days, Franz Neumann and Herbert Marcuse. The other story was the obverse of the first: the relative isolation of French intellectuals, who, of course, did not participate in the emigration. The French stayed home, he argued in *The Obstructed Path*, and the result was a certain intellectual provincialism. Hughes was disappointed that neither of his books about the interwar period (which he later reissued as a single book, *Between Commitment and Disillusion*) enjoyed the success of *Consciousness and Society*.

One of Hughes's great strengths was his prose: his writing was clear, efficient, and graceful. Here also, as in his devotion to the big picture, he parted company with those younger historians whose work is afflicted by postmodern opacity. He learned his literary craft from the great novelists, who always remained his favorite reading. He had a special partiality for Roger Martin du Gard, whom he once told me he preferred even to Proust. He was also an avid reader of European newspapers, above all *Le Monde* and the *Frankfurter Allgemein*. He prided himself on his knowledge of foreign languages and was apt to drop French, German, or Italian expressions into his conversation. That conversation, moreover, was of a piece with his prose: he spoke elegantly, even aristocratically, in a voice that was sinuous and tinged with irony.

When I was Stuart Hughes's Ph.D. student in the 1960s our relationship was cordial but distant. Harvard at the time was something of a factory, so it is hardly remarkable that I saw very little of him. He was in Europe the year I wrote my dissertation, and the entire enterprise was carried out by mail. But the accidents of history contrived to bring us together in the last decade and a half of his life, so that I had the rather odd—and wonderful—experience of becoming his friend some twenty years after I had been his student. The accidents in question were that he left Harvard for San Diego and San Diego was my home town—where I grew up and where my brother continues to live. Sometime in the mid-1980s I began visiting Stuart and his wife, Judy, regularly when I was in San Diego to see my family. We established a routine of going out for dinner at least once a year.

I last saw him less than two months before he died. He was confined to bed and a wheelchair by the ravages of diabetes and Parkinson's disease, but he bore his troubles with patience and good humor. Friends from UCSD visited daily, and Judy cared for him with obvious affection. During the hour I spent with him he was eager to enlist me to speak at a memorial service he was planning. But, as always, he also wanted to talk about books, politics, and people. Even as his body betrayed him his distinctive voice and way of speaking remained unchanged: the pitch a bit elevated, the words precisely chosen, the tone earnest but also ever so slightly amused. I went to Harvard in 1963 aware that he was an important scholar and intellectual, but at the end I found myself thinking of him more as a charming and admirable man whose company I would miss.

CHAPTER SIXTEEN

Three Essays on Writing

These short essays, published in the New Republic *in 1979 and 1980, contain my defense of a certain kind of writing. The first speculates on what inspires academic writers to carry on in spite of the discrepancy between the energy and anxiety expended in writing and the number of readers they are likely to attract. The second defends my adherence to correct usage, even while recognizing that the cause is undemocratic, often unkind, and finally doomed. The last extends my defense of tradition (with, I hope, sufficient irony) from words to punctuation marks.*

Why Write?

I won't address the paradox of writing an essay that raises doubts about writing. Suffice it to say that I think the question interesting—interesting, obviously, to those who write; interesting also, probably, to those who are considering writing, and perhaps even to those who don't themselves write but find writers compellingly mysterious. I should add that I am thinking of nonfiction writing, especially the academic variety, though much of what I have to say is relevant to fiction as well.

For most of us, writing takes a long time; normally we devote several years to a book. And although a writer does other things as well, he typically spends thousands of hours before delivering his work to the publisher, and even then his labors aren't over. Because it takes us so long, we are astonished, even angered, to learn that a book has been written in a matter of days. Marshall Kilduff's book on the Guyana massacre, *The*

Suicide Cult, apparently was finished in 96 hours and published in less than two weeks. The book was actually the joint effort of a newspaper staff (that of the *San Francisco Chronicle*), but even so it entirely contradicts our notion of how much time must be invested before one has a real book.

Indeed, the question, "Why write?" arises precisely because we sense a disparity between the amount of labor we put into a piece of writing and the knowledge, edification, and entertainment that readers extract from it. I have speculated that if one could calculate all the hours spent by all readers in reading a book, they often would add up to fewer than the hours spent by the author in writing it. I hardly need say that I'm thinking not of the Shakespeares and Arthur Haleys of this world but of the rest of us scribblers.

For purposes of analysis, "Why write?" can be divided into two subquestions: What are the motives for writings? And who is the audience? The most likely answers to these questions all seem inadequate.

One writes to make money. Some writers—largely of fiction and textbooks—do, of course, make money, and a larger number write, at least in part, in the hope of making money. But most authors know that there's no money in writing, and those who don't know find out soon enough. By "no money" I intend a comparative judgment: ridiculously little money against what one can earn as a doctor, dentist, lawyer, businessman, or even a schoolteacher. These are the relevant comparisons, because writers, on the whole, are intelligent and industrious people who, aside from a temperamental disinclination, doubtless would succeed well enough in the high-paying professions. I have sometimes imagined trying to calculate my hourly income as a writer. If I counted only royalties it would be embarrassingly low, probably less than 50 cents, and even if I counted half my salary as a professor (under the assumption that Stanford is paying me to write as well as teach) it might at best approach the government's minimum wage. If one considers the matter statistically, then, only fools write for money.

One writes to get tenure. This, in a sense, is an academic variation on the above. It's true, but much less so than most students are inclined to believe. One's motives may change as one grows older, but I've noticed that an inordinately large percentage of scholars keep writing after they've gotten tenure. Are they stupid? There is a marginal economic incentive in that one's salary tends to reflect one's productivity, but the differences are too small to justify the time and energy senior scholars put into their writing.

One writes to gain a reputation. There's more to this motive, but it's a deceptive matter, and highly selective. Reputation is closely tied to the question of readership. I do not doubt that most writers desire esteem, but I think that they often delude themselves about who's listening, as I will try to show in a moment.

One writes to tell the truth. This is the most attractive, because the most disinterested, motive, but it has suffered irremediable damage in the twentieth century. In nearly all fields of inquiry, from the natural sciences to the humanities, the notion of truth has been under assault, and along with it the old cumulative model of intellectual enterprise—the "march of scholarship." Max Weber, Thomas Kuhn, and Richard Rorty (among others) have persuaded us, in varying degrees, that intellectual life consists not in replacing false ideas with true ones but in replacing impracticable ideas with useful ones. Naturally we still have to tell the truth, but I don't sense that authors write primarily to dispel error. The search for truth is by no means a negligible concern, but it doesn't hold the power it once did.

THE QUESTION OF READERSHIP is exceedingly complex: scholars of the book, like Robert Darnton, have spilled a great deal of ink trying to figure out who reads and what they read. But in terms of one's commitment to writing, actual readership is less important than imagined readership. Moreover it's not enough just to know who reads. We also want to know how they read—in what spirit and with what degree of comprehension. If these qualitative considerations are borne in mind, one can argue that many writers labor under a false conception of their audience. Who is listening, then?

Friends and family are listening. It would be more accurate to say that they are trying to listen. I doubt that I am unusual in finding that most of what I write makes very little sense to my friends and family. I dedicated my second book to my mother, an intelligent and well-educated woman, and she made a heroic effort to get through it. I received weekly letters with lists of words that were unfamiliar to her. (How often, in the course of normal literate conversation, does one say "empirical"?) As I recall, she finally gave up somewhere around page 70.

Most authors already acknowledge this sad truth in the way they approach the question, posed by a nonscholar, "What are you writing about?" When I was working on my book about opera and intellectual history, my answer to the question invariably consisted of a series of dodges. "Opera" posed no difficulty, but "intellectual history" was a bottomless pit; the phrase, I found, meant virtually nothing to most people. (Nor is there any reason it should have.) Moreover, even if I conveyed what I meant by intellectual history, the task of explaining how it might relate to Mozart, Verdi, and Wagner still stretched before me like the labor of Sisyphus. In short, I was always relieved when my friends didn't ask, though not at all because I considered the enterprise trivial.

Reviewers are listening. Yes, but only in order to write reviews. Anyone who has reviewed a book knows the exploitative frame of mind in which one approaches the task: one's primary goal is not to learn but to figure out what one is going to say.

Students of the subject are listening. Yes, but only some, and, like reviewers, they tend to listen exploitatively. Too much is written for us to read more than a fraction of the publications relevant to our work, and we read largely in the spirit of "getting through." Books, even those of our friends, are hurdles. We dash over them, maybe picking up a few items that we can put to good use, and we are relieved to have them behind us. It strikes me as quite mad to think that one should spend so many years writing a book just to create the occasion for these little flurries of intellectual anxiety. Contemplating such an insane ritual, a rational person must conclude that most books are written to be written, not to be read.

There are exceptions, needless to say. Not just the writings of the great, the "immortals," but some "ordinary" books are so well conceived, so beautifully executed, that we read them in the spirit in which, presumably, they were written. In my own recent reading, Donald Howard's *The Idea of the Canterbury Tales* falls into this category. I mention it in particular because it contains a discussion of the beginning of reading and of books (what Howard calls "bookness") that throws striking light on our current predicament.

But the inescapable point is that such books are, as noted, exceptional. If one needs evidence, I recommend a casual tour through the stacks of a major library. Pick any book off the shelf, and the chances are you will hold in your hand a piece of scholarship that hasn't been consulted in years, though it may have won its author tenure at some university or—even more daunting—"crowned" a distinguished career. And there it sits, as dead as a medieval chronicle. Its only hope of survival is in the transformed guise of a primary source for some young scholar writing a history of the discipline. But even as the species cannibalizes itself, the prospects for any given tome are dim. At such moments one recognizes that writing is hedged about with insanity.

Yet we continue to write, and few of us are carted off to the loony bin. I have been able to think of only one explanation for this mystery, and that is that we write for ourselves. The proposition would sound more plausible if I had confined my remarks to fiction, because it is generally conceded that poets, novelists, and playwrights are engaged, at least partially, in acts of self-exploration and self-definition. But I believe the same is unconsciously true of writers of nonfiction, and that their writing would gain in clarity and force if the motive were raised to the conscious level. At the very least it might inhibit the attacks of purposelessness to which writers are peculiarly subject.

The best evidence that we write for ourselves is the fact that we are our own best audience. No one reads what we write with the attentiveness or affection that we ourselves bring to it. The author is the only reader who reads in a nonexploitative fashion. And the author is the only reader who recognizes the intellectual triumphs contained in certain perfectly unassuming phrases that took hours to bludgeon into shape. I suspect that if Shakespeare were to return to life and could find time to read all the criticism on just one of his plays, he would at first marvel at the many things literary critics have detected that he himself didn't know were there, but he would also have cause to complain that some particular felicity of expression, some ambiguity, or some inner rhyme has gone unappreciated.

Likewise, the author usually knows best where slippage has occurred in his argument, thus making him not only the most appreciative but in certain respects also the most critical reader of his own work. Viewed from this perspective, writing is an act of self-clarification, in which we bring order to those ideas and sentiments that otherwise would remain muddled and inarticulate.

Above all, the writer reads his own work with greater pleasure than any other reader. The late John Wasserman, who was among the most entertaining of writers I know, understood this home truth perfectly. He was famous for laughing out loud as he read his own columns and articles, and he loved to draw his colleagues' attention to particularly wicked turns of phrase he had hit upon. In effect, he had very sensibly embraced the narcissistic logic that protects writers from madness.

Only when the writer acknowledges that he writes for himself does he transcend the more petty forms of narcissism that plague writers: the desire for money, advancement, esteem. Ironically, the self stripped of its lesser vanities is also the most selfless point of reference for a writer: it becomes an instance of humanity. I recognize that I have entered murky waters here, but I believe it is psychologically correct to say that the writer who feels he is writing for himself also feels he is writing for mankind, and that the conviction is not tied to the question of whether or not he will be read. In exploring and clarifying one's own thinking, one has the sense that the mind of the species is also clarified. The proposition may sound implausible on first hearing, but its plausibility should be tested against that of the other motivations I've considered, which, it seems to me, are far less convincing.

I HAVE THOUGHT of a final reason why we write, one that relates to the universalizing implications of writing for oneself. Sometimes we write to say thank you, to render gratitude to a member or a portion of humanity that has given us pleasure, elevated us, and made us think better of ourselves. Such is the motivation we sense and find so moving in the opening sentence of Fernand Braudel's great study of the Mediterranean world in the sixteenth century: "I have loved the Mediterranean with a passion . . . . " I discovered a similar motive in myself as I wrote my study of opera and intellectual history. Part of the energy for the project, I found, came from wishing to reciprocate. I have spent thousands of hours listening to Mozart, Verdi, Wagner, and the other great opera composers. Indeed, measured in purely quantitative terms, nothing has given me more pleasure. A writer is in the fortunate position of being able to acknowledge such a gift in a more fully satisfying fashion than those who don't write.

This last motive, I believe, is also relatively independent of the possibility of finding an audience. Writing in this sense is a form of private correspondence, and its gratifications are exactly those derived from writing a friend. Only here the friend—or, more precisely, the benefactor—serves as a singular yardstick for the writer: because you and he are both members of the same species you are able to identify with him, but because he is one of its extraordinary examples, he reveals your limitations, the distance between yourself and what it is possible for a human being to achieve.

There are other reasons for writing, not least among them a sheer love of the language and its proper use, a motive stressed by George Orwell in his essay, "Why I Write." But at the heart of the enterprise, I'm persuaded, lies the enormously gratifying dialectic of self, other, and humanity.

Lost Causes

I. "Hopefully, Jimmy Carter won't be re-elected."
II. "Just between you and I, I hope he is."
III. "He ain't got a chance." An improbable exchange, both ideologically and linguistically, but one that suggests some useful distinctions. Party III is the most easily disposed of: he has made a mistake. Moreover everybody agrees that he has made a mistake. His sole linguistic defense is to insist that he is speaking the argot of a particular subculture. But if that were the case, he probably wouldn't be talking to Parties I and II.

Party II has also made a mistake, but it is less likely to be recognized as such. It might be called an upwardly mobile mistake. "Me" sounds plebeian (as in "Ralph and me went bowling"), so our cultural aspirant seizes every opportunity to substitute subject for object. His only linguistic defense is to appeal to our tolerance: since his meaning is clear and his intention innocent, to correct him would be small-minded.

But has Party I made a mistake? Here opinion among experts is divided. The floating "hopefully" (meaning "I hope" rather than its proper significance of "in a hopeful manner") is just the sort of issue that separates linguistic conservatives from linguistic liberals. It arouses enormous polemical passions. And rightly so: for the way one thinks about the propriety of this utterance reveals the essence of one's linguistic sensibilities. "Hopefully" is a classic example of a lost linguistic cause. Its incorrect use is now so common that only a fool would expect to recover its earlier meaning. And yet it does not follow that one acts foolishly in avoiding the new usage oneself or in correcting it in others. Lost causes, I would like to argue, still need to be championed.

These reflections were prompted by a conference I attended, The State of the Language, sponsored by the English Speaking Union of the United States and held in San Francisco's Mark Hopkins Hotel in the fall of 1979. The inspiration for the conference was not entirely pure: its guiding lights, Leonard Michaels and Christopher Ricks, had just edited a book, also entitled *The State of the Language*, containing essays and poems from 63 contributors, and the conference was intended, in part, to launch the volume on a successful commercial course. Twenty of the contributors attended the San Francisco meeting. Among them were two celebrities, John Simon and Alistair Cook (a noncontributor), who lent glamour to the proceedings. The floating "hopefully" was the object of recurrent attention.

Listening to the various participants, I became preoccupied with the psychological valence of the linguistic debate, the unconscious drama hidden beneath so much talk about the language. The speakers quickly divided into two camps, and both groups proved remarkably inventive in devising new labels for their fundamental disagreement. I heard it expressed in all the following ways: permissivists versus prescriptivists, linguists versus grammarians, democrats versus elitists, the descriptive versus the normative, the demotic versus the hieratic. In terms of my example, the former party defended the new use of "hopefully," while the latter excoriated it.

I was amused, but hardly surprised, to find the academics rushing to line up on the permissive side, while the media personalities argued for the maintenance of strict standards. Both camps were victims of considerable self-deception.

The conservatives, headed by John Simon, used linguistic propriety as a vehicle for their aggression. They were distinguished mainly by their mean-spiritedness. Simon even admitted to correcting complete strangers in Bloomingdale's, making me nervously aware of the ways our commitment to correct speech is tainted by self-assertion. One is easily deceived here because important values are at stake, above all the possibility of exact, witty, and profound expression. Yet much of our correcting is contaminated by an unconscious desire to affirm ourselves at the expense of others. If you don't think that's so, reflect for a moment on what you feel when someone corrects your own grammar or pronunciation. You know beyond all doubt that you have been aggressed against. The world of correct speech, it seems, is a loveless one.

I've put the matter psychologically. But several of the participants in the conference made the same point in social and political terms. Ishmael Reed made it with respect to black English, while Richard Rodriguez gave a rending account of what he had lost in the way of intimacy and a sense of community when the nuns in his school taught him to speak proper English. Both men made one vividly aware of language's function in the stratification of society. Indeed, you could almost visualize a two-tiered structure: the haves and the have-nots, those who speak correct English and those who don't. That structure was mirrored in the conference room where Reed and Rodriquez spoke. The audience was almost entirely white and over 40, and it sported identification tags with names like Whitaker, Dickey, and Crawford. They politely disapproved of Reed's linguistic separatism (as I must disapprove of it myself), and they applauded Rodriguez's conviction that in learning the master language he had gained more than he had lost. Under the circumstances one could hardly ignore that our language—which enables us to be intelligent, funny, and sometimes even passionate, and which moves and delights us—has a dark secret. It also oppresses. It is an instrument of violence. Like all great cultural achievements, it has come at a price.

The permissivists were playing an entirely different game. It might be called "with-it-ness," a form of intellectual slumming. Academics have fragile identities. They hate to be thought stuffy, out-of-it, or un-sexy. They want desperately to prove that they, too, are real people. At the conference the audience was treated to a lot of bold and embarrassing talk about the greatness of Bob Dylan, the virtues of bureaucratese, and the ways the language has been enriched from the linguistic netherworlds of television and consciousness-raising. Beating the drum for a cause like "hopefully" was not only pointless but, much worse, snobbish. Thus the permissivists avoided the spite of their conservative opponents only to fall into an even more self-indulgent modishness.

John Simon muddied the waters by providing the academics with the perfect excuse to slum. Only a few sentences into his opening remarks he forgot his appointed role and went in for a little slumming of his own: "I don't give a flying fuck whether people speak in the right tone or grada-tion, but I do care about grammar and syntax." Thereafter the professors rushed to prove that they, too, could say "flying fuck." A more ideal opportunity to establish one's authenticity could hardly have been imagined, and the room was quickly suffused with an aura of self-congratulation. Before it was over I found myself sympathizing, how-ever reluctantly, with the beleaguered Mr. Simon, who lamented, "As long as the language has linguists, it has no need of enemies." And for the first time I also understood Lionel Trilling's remark, "I find righteous de-nunciations of the present state of the language no less dismaying than the present state of the language."

Is there any way one can think and talk about the language without falling into the complementary traps of vindictiveness or mindless modernity? Perhaps not. But I have arrived at two working principles, one moral, the other intellectual, that at least help.

The first is to remain as conscious as possible of the social and psy-chological reality underlying the struggle for correctness. In the most immediate instance this means attending to the aggression implicit in one's own verbosity. We can't—and shouldn't—stop correcting, espe-cially those of us who happen to be teachers. But at least we can learn to distrust our motives. When the delicate balance between a love for accu-rate expression and the wish to assert oneself shifts dangerously in favor of the latter, it's time to call a halt.

My intellectual guideline is that conservatives should come to terms with history: words and phrases evolve over time, and thus propriety is always a relative matter. It does not follow, however, that whatever people say is right. The issue is vastly more interesting and complex. The best formulation I can give it is that language exists in a kind of tension, and if there are no forces to resist the inevitable process of evolution, the result will be linguistic incoherence. Therefore conservatives should think of themselves as performing an essential role in a historical drama. They know that certain causes are lost, but they must fight them nonetheless, because that is their part in the play. "Hopefully" is just such a cause, and linguistic conservatives realize their historical function by contesting it to the bitter end. If nothing else, they distract the forces of change from launching a premature assault on some other hapless word or phrase.

One would like to see the language defended with more intelligence and love. The participants in the San Francisco conference were short on both.

The Philosophy of Punctuation

Punctuation absorbs more of my thought than seems healthy for a man who pretends to be well adjusted. The subject is naturally attractive to all with character structures of the sort Freud dubbed anal, and I readily confess to belong to that sect. We anal folk keep neat houses, are always on time, and know all the do's and don't's, including those of punctuation. Good punctuation, we feel, makes for clean thought. A mania for punctuation is also an occupational hazard for almost any teacher, as hundreds of our hours are given over to correcting the vagrant punctuation of our students.

One approach to punctuation is by way of rules. In my very favorite book, *The Elements of Style,* by William Strunk and E. B. White, we may read, for example, Rule Number 2: "In a series of three or more terms with a single conjunction, use a comma after each term except the last." I couldn't agree more heartily, and I love the quaint formulation. Better than that, I have inserted the missing comma in countless sentences written by students and colleagues of mine. I have also suffered no little distress seeing that comma removed from my own prose after it has been sent to the *New York Times Book Review* or (yes, I'm sorry to say) the *New Republic,* both of which clearly have adopted policies of eliminating this serial comma so beloved by purists.

Rules are important, no question about it. But by themselves they are insufficient. Unless one has an emotional investment, rules are too easily forgotten. What we must instill, I'm convinced, is an attitude toward punctuation, a set of feelings about both the process in general and the individual marks of punctuation. That set of feelings might be called a philosophy of punctuation.

I say "a" philosophy, because I'm not yet so opinionated as to insist that everyone adopt my own. I recognize legitimate alternatives, and I'm quite aware that punctuation has a history. A single page of Thomas Carlyle, or any nineteenth-century writer, reminds us, for instance, that a comma between subject and verb—for me the most offensive of all punctuation errors—was once perfectly acceptable. A colleague of mine, whom I consider a fine writer, punctuates, as it were, by ear. That is, he seeks to reduplicate patterns of speech, to indicate through his punctuation how a sentence is supposed to sound. Consequently his punctuation lacks strict consistency. But I can respect it as guided at all times by what I consider philosophical principles.

Given my character, my own philosophy is more legalistic. My colleague, you might say, is a Platonist in punctuation, while I am an Aristotelian. My punctuation is informed by two ideals: clarity and simplicity. Punctuation has the primary responsibility of contributing to the plainness of one's meaning. It has the secondary responsibility of being as invisible as possible, of not calling attention to itself. With those principles in mind, and on the basis of reading what now passes for acceptable writing, I have developed a set of emotional responses to individual marks of punctuation. Precisely such emotional responses, I believe, are what most writers lack, and their indifference accounts for their errors.

Let me now introduce my dramatis personae. First come the period and the comma. These are the only lovely marks of punctuation, and of the two the period is the lovelier, because more compact and innocent of ambiguity. I have fantasies of writing an essay punctuated solely with periods and commas. I seldom see a piece of prose that shouldn't, I feel, have more periods and fewer of those obtrusive marks that seem to have usurped their natural place. The comma, as noted, was once overused, but it now suffers from relative neglect. The missing comma before the "and" introducing the last item in a series is merely the most obvious example.

Periods and commas are lovely because they are simple. They force the writer to express his ideas directly, to eliminate unnecessary hedges, to forgo smart-aleck asides. They also contribute to the logical solidity of a piece of writing, since they make us put all our thoughts into words. By way of contrast, a colon can be used to smooth over a rough logical connection. It has a verbal content ranging anywhere from "namely" to "thus," and it can function to let the writer off the hook. Periods and commas, because of their very neutrality, make one an honest logician.

Semicolons are pretentious and overactive. These days one seems to come across them in every other sentence. "These days" is alarmist, since half a century ago the German poet Christian Morgenstern wrote a brilliant parody, "Im Reich der Interpunktionen," in which imperialistic semicolons are put to rout by an "Antisemikolonbund" of periods and commas. Nonetheless, if the undergraduate essays I see are representative, we are in the midst of an epidemic of semicolons. I suspect that the semicolon is so popular because it is the first fancy punctuation mark students learn of, and they assume that its frequent appearance will lend their writing a properly scholarly cast. Alas, they are only too right. But I doubt that they use semicolons in their letters. At least I hope they don't.

More than half of the semicolons one sees, I would estimate, should be periods, and probably another quarter should be commas. Far too often, semicolons, like colons, are used to gloss over an imprecise thought. They place two clauses in some kind of relation to one another but relieve the writer of saying exactly what that relation is. Even the simple conjunction "and," for which they are often a substitute, has more content, because it suggests compatibility or logical continuity. ("And," incidentally, is among the most abused words in the language. It is forever being exploited as a kind of neutral vocalization connecting two things that have no connection whatever.)

In exasperation I have tried to confine my own use of the semicolon to demarking sequences that contain internal commas and therefore might otherwise be confusing. I recognize that my reaction is extreme.

But the semicolon has become so hateful to me that I feel almost morally compromised when I use it.

Before leaving the realm of epidemics, I want to mention two other practices that are out of hand: the use of italics for emphasis and of quotation marks for distancing. These are ugly habits because of the intellectual tone they set. Italics rarely fail to insult the reader's intelligence. More often than not they tell us to emphasize a word or phrase that we would emphasize automatically in any natural reading of the sentence. Quotation marks create the spurious impression of an aristocracy of sensibility. Three paragraphs back I originally put quotation marks around "fancy," to suggest quite falsely that I would never use such a word myself, being of too refined a temperament.

At the opposite pole are two marks of punctuation that have grown increasingly obsolescent, the question mark and the exclamation point. Appropriately, the disappearance of the question mark largely reflects the disappearance of questions, which sound unpleasantly rhetorical to us. But even real questions, if they are long enough, are now apt to end in periods. The exclamation point is obviously too emphatic, too childish, for our sophisticated ways. Psychologically speaking, the decline of these two marks is the inverse of the semicolon epidemic. Questions and exclamations betray a sense of inquisitiveness and wonder that is distinctly unmodern, whereas semicolons imply a capacity for complex, dialectical formulations appropriate to our complex times. As part of my campaign against the semicolon—no doubt irrationally—I am endeavoring to develop friendlier relations with these neglected gestures. But I'll admit that it's not easy.

Then there are parentheses and dashes. They are, of course, indispensable. I've used them five times already in this essay alone. But I think one must maintain a very strict attitude toward them. I start from the proposition that all parentheses and dashes are syntactical defeats. They signify an inability to express one's ideas sequentially, which, unless you're James Joyce, is the way the language was meant to be used. Reality may be simultaneous, but expository prose is linear. Parentheses and dashes represent efforts to elude the responsibilities of linearity. They generally betoken stylistic laziness, an unwillingness to spend the time figuring out how to put things in the most logical order. Needless to say, they also betoken a failure of discipline. Every random thought, every tenuous analogy gets dragged in. Good writing is as much a matter of subtraction as creation, and parentheses are the great enemy of subtraction. In all that I write I try to find ways to eliminate them.

A monstrous variation on the parenthesis is the content footnote. What, after all, is a content footnote but material that one is either too lazy to integrate into the text or too reverent to discard? Reading a piece of prose that constantly dissolves into extended footnotes is profoundly disheartening. Hence my rule of thumb for footnotes is exactly the same as that for parentheses. One should regard them as symbols of failure. I hardly need add that in this vale of tears failure is sometimes unavoidable.

Only one issue of punctuation generates no emotion in me, namely, the rules governing the placement of punctuation marks with respect to quotation marks. Those rules are simple enough, but perhaps because they differ between England and the United States they possess for me only the arbitrary authority of commandments and none of the well-nigh metaphysical significance that I associate with the period, the comma, the parenthesis, and the semicolon.

CHAPTER SEVENTEEN

Cats

Essentially a jeu d'esprit, this little essay reflects on what we can learn about our-selves and our "civilization" (in Freud's sense) from living with cats. When the essay appeared in the Stanford Alumni Magazine *(Spring/Summer 1979) it elicited a torrent of angry letters from cat-lovers. I suppose it might be regarded as a futile effort to curb the human impulse to anthropomorphize. I might add that I wrote the essay before I acquired the two cats—sisters—that have lived with me now for 19 years. They have only confirmed my prejudices.*

Cats can tell us important things about ourselves, more striking things, I believe, than can any other animal with which we have frequent contact. Cats occupy a unique space in our culture: they move back and forth be-tween a natural and a civilized realm, but without ever adopting the attri-butes of the latter. No other common pet has quite this quality. Fish and birds are isolated in an artificial environment, and in most cases they are rather too small to make much of an impression on human beings. Dogs, unlike cats, have been seriously compromised by civilization. They have been incorporated into the work of society—leading the blind, guarding the rich, herding sheep, and cutting down on marijuana consumption— and to a categorically greater extent than cats they have absorbed certain human attributes: loyalty, affection, and, most important of all, deference to authority. Because dogs have been so compromised, our relations with them are very different from those with cats. Apparently there is some evidence that cats can be trained to do many of the things that dogs do, but the relevant fact for their influence on human beings is that they don't. They exist among us as foreign creatures, and in their foreignness they illuminate what it means to be human.

One of the most important differences between cats and people is in perception. Cats dramatically lack the powers of visual abstraction that humans take for granted. They are unable, for example, to translate a two-dimensional symbol into a three-dimensional reality. Television is meaningless to them, as are reflections—even their own—in a mirror. A simple consideration of these facts should remind us of how complex human vision has become. Our visual life, seemingly the most passive and animalistic dimension of our existence, is shot through with effort and conceptualization. Immanuel Kant's assertion, in *The Critique of Pure Reason*, that the human mind imposes order on the external world always sounds somewhat fanciful—the kind of thing only a philosopher would dream up—but if you attend to how cats view reality the proposition begins to take on a certain plausibility.

Even in the three-dimensional world, cats don't see the same things we do. Or rather, they don't necessarily think of them as things. Among the "objects" of human perception that I'm convinced cats see at best intermittently are human beings themselves. David Hume said that personal identity was merely a convenient myth: nothing proves that the creature having eggs for breakfast today is the same as the one who had waffles yesterday. Hume's skeptical glance at identity, as the example suggests, was primarily historical: he raised doubts about continuity over time. The modern biologist who tells us our bodies contain not a single cell they contained seven years ago says virtually the same thing. We instinctively feel that both are wrong; we know that we endure, cells or not. Cats, however, are more radical skeptics than even Hume. Not only do they make their way through life without the benefit of the category "human being," they only irregularly regard us, their loving owner, as an entity. Their skepticism, unlike Hume's, is not temporal but spatial. Much of the time we are merely a set of parts, loosely and accidentally associated. We are a hand that feeds and strokes or, more astonishingly, a toe moving under a blanket, which our imaginative pet "pretends" is a mouse. The thought may be too devastating for most cat owners to bear, but not only do our cats not love us, they don't even know we exist.

Unlike people, cats also have no general understanding of how the world is put together. By that I don't mean they lack a unified theory of reality but rather that their practical knowledge of the world is curiously flawed. Naturally cats know all about jumping, climbing, and the like, but they have no general conception of the practical effects of gravity. One of the funniest cat scenes I have witnessed involved a quarrel between two cats on my back porch. The older—and ornerier—cat backed the younger one up until he slipped over the edge and hung by his paws. Any creature understanding gravity would have recognized that the moment for decisive action had arrived: the enemy was defenseless. But the bully stood frozen in the same glowering pose, as if the younger cat might at any moment miraculously lift himself back onto the porch. Both remained so stationed, making hideous noises, for as long as a minute, before the younger one ran out of steam and dropped to the ground below. The whole scene presumed a distorted conception of reality, which to us seems extraordinary.

Another important difference between cats and people is their way of relating to infancy. Modern men and women, at least, have become almost morbidly preoccupied with their lost childhood. From Wordsworth through Freud, Proust, and beyond, modern intellectuals have explored, usually nostalgically, an infantile past that can be recaptured only in memory, often only in art. Cats, by way of contrast, remain in what might be called physical contact with their earliest days. Their infancy remains within them, and it is regained the moment someone dangles a piece of string in front of them. They then behave in a fashion comparable to adults making mud pies. They remind us, in other words, of how profoundly developmental the human animal is—of our powerlessness before the processes of growth and decay, both physical and mental.

Cats also enable us to establish relationships that our received romantic ideology has pronounced impossible: nonreciprocal love affairs. Self-deluding cat owners may convince themselves that their pets feel affection for them, but the clear-eyed know that cats don't love. Love is a sentiment well beyond their psychological means. This fact has often been misinterpreted along moral lines. Cats are said to be devious, exploitative, disloyal, or whatever. But these vices, like affection, presume mental capacities they don't possess.

Still, we love our cats very much. We enjoy their company, we want to pet them, even (horrors) to kiss them. We find them charming, and we devote hours to their well-being. Yet they care not a whit for us. Or, if you find that too strong, whatever they feel for us doesn't begin to approximate what we feel for them. The relationship is profoundly unsymmetrical. Perhaps the emphasis here should be on the ways we seek to mystify this reality, so incompatible with out general notion of love. Thus we argue that our cats show affection when, for instance, they sit on our laps, repressing for the moment the consideration that they are drawn there simply by the heat (the same thing that makes them bed down on top of television sets). Nonetheless, I find it remarkable that in spite of our romantic totalitarianism we manage to enjoy an emotional attachment that is fundamentally one-way, and I don't believe that we take the gloss we have put on that attachment very seriously.

All this raises intriguing questions about strictly human relations. It suggests that we may have overlooked the pleasures of unrequited love among human beings—that we are perhaps guilty of a kind of visceral romanticism in considering the person who pursues an impossible object tragic or even pathological. In reality we love many things that can't return our affection, and that love is often a constructive element in our experience. We invest our libido in such things as books, historical figures, and unattainable contemporaries. The love we feel for cats is an archetype of this unilateral love that is both gratifying and enriching.

Ultimately, cats are compelling, I believe, because they recall our ambivalence about civilization. Their very manner of existence brings to mind the odd and exacting demands civilization makes on us. Consider just one thread in the complex fabric of civilization: planning. We are forever planning. We plan big things like lives or presidential campaigns, medium things like trips to Europe or courses of study, and minutia like what to have for dinner or what to wear to work. Cats never plan. They have not the slightest idea of where they will be in one hour, even in one minute. They don't organize "their day." Instead, the decision to lie in the sun or chase flies is inspired (if that's the right word) by the most fleeting mental images.

This magnificent aimlessness makes cats perfect inversions of ourselves. Part of our ambivalence toward civilization is expressed in the attempts we make to attribute human motives to cats. We compulsively deny their otherness—deny, in effect, what we have lost. We try to incorporate them into the human realm so as to repress a full awareness of the burdens of civilization. But our efforts along these lines are only too flimsy. The brute fact of the matter simply can't be ignored. Every morning after we climb out of bed, shower, dress, and arrange our briefcase, we take a moment to open a can of cat food. Then we exit purposively by the front door, contemplating the events of the coming day. At the same moment our cat wanders out the back door, thinking of virtually nothing, indeed without any notion that what he has just launched is his "day." Living with cats doesn't make us hostile to civilization, merely more conscious of its costs. It's a kind of practical version of Freud's argument in *Civilization and Its Discontents:* civilization, cats remind us, is a wonderful thing, but we don't get it for nothing.

EPILOGUE

My Afterlife

Nothing I have written has elicited greater response than this account of my liver transplant, which originally appeared in the Stanford Historian *in 1995. The experience and my recording of it are linked in my mind to a growing fascination with autobiography, particularly the autobiographies of gay men, which culminated in my publishing* Gay Lives: Homosexual Autobiography from John Addington Symonds to Paul Monette *in 1999. The reader will not have failed to notice autobiographical moments in earlier pieces in this collection, especially "The Opera Queen" and "Dear Paul." "My Afterlife" brings the story of my intellectual evolution—not to mention my physical survival—right down to the present.*

In July 1988, when I was forty-seven, I got a new liver. I was in fact the tenth recipient of a liver transplant at Pacific Presbyterian Hospital (now California Pacific Hospital) in San Francisco. No more than two weeks before the operation I hardly knew that liver transplantation existed, or, to the extent it had entered my consciousness, I assumed that, as a hepatitis sufferer, I would not qualify for it. After all, I reasoned, hepatitis is in the blood and would remain in my body to destroy the new organ.

Hepatitis is a curious disease, above all in its unpredictability. In my case the most striking thing about it was its episodic progress. I would enjoy long periods of seemingly good health and then, inexplicably, suffer an attack. I became infected, I believe, in the late 1970s, an inference I base on a routine blood test I took in 1980 or 1981 as part of a Kaiser multiphasic exam. The test showed that I had elevated liver counts. Nothing explicit was said about their significance, and no further testing was proposed. I can't recall whether I had any inkling of what was wrong, although I doubt it. Nonetheless, several years later, in the summer of 1985, when I was unable to shake a cold and felt generally exhausted, I sought out a doctor who specialized in liver problems and told him I suspected I had hepatitis. A biopsy confirmed my suspicion and also revealed the early signs of cirrhosis.

Perhaps because hepatitis is so unpredictable or because doctors have learned not to tell sufferers too much about what might lie ahead, I always assumed that I could contain the damage with a proper regimen of diet and medication. And, indeed, at each stage of the disease's evolution my doctors prescribed medicines or dietary changes that alleviated my symptoms and allowed me to carry on with my life. In other words, I did not think of myself spiraling inexorably downward to an early death but rather engaged in an indefinite regime of coping.

The period from my diagnosis in the summer of 1985 until late spring 1988 constitutes, in recollection, a more or less unified span in which the disease progressed through its familiar stages and I developed a particular set of psychological mechanisms to deal with it. Let me chart the progression and, as best I can, recreate my state of mind during that period, because it bears on how I responded to the trauma and deliverance of my transplant.

I recall three phases of my physical deterioration. I had given up drinking over a decade earlier, so I didn't need to make any immediate changes in how I lived. But I became convinced that the attack I suffered in the summer of 1985 was brought on by anxieties relating to publishing a book I had just finished. And because my doctor concurred that a person's mood could play a role in provoking the disease, I resolved to minimize my worries, including not obsessing about my mortality. I now recognize this ritual of avoidance as my first method of coping with the disease.

Sometime in 1986 or 1987 I entered the next phase: I experienced internal bleeding, caused by increased pressure on the veins of my esophagus and stomach as my liver grew more inefficient. I found blood in my stool and even vomited blood, which, combined with renewed attacks of the virus, left me weak enough to require brief hospitalizations and transfusions. The prescribed response was pharmaceutical: I began taking a widely used drug, Zantac, that reduces digestive acids and hence the chance of hemorrhaging.

Only a few months passed before I experience a new complication: the retention of fluid in the abdomen ("ascites" it is now called, although in Beethoven's day it bore the more colorful name of "dropsy"). It caused considerable bloating and discomfort but nothing so scary as the bleeding. It too was treated with drugs: in this case, diuretics, above all Lasix, which worked fairly well until my rapid decline just before the transplant. I also eliminated salt from my diet.

The final stage came in perhaps the last two months of my coping regime: mental disorientation, brought on, I was told, by excessive amounts of nitrogen (unprocessed by my failing liver) in the brain. As before, a specific medication was prescribed, a dreadful syrup that I found intensely unpleasant and whose effectiveness—in contrast to the antacid and the diuretics—seemed doubtful.

Throughout this roughly three-year period of trying to cope with the disease I grew increasingly anxious. I worried not that I would die but that my particular symptoms—exhaustion, bloating, above all the weakness brought on by bleeding—might interfere with my responsibilities at Stanford. I felt embarrassed by even the appearance of incapacitation. I was so compulsive about my duties that I don't believe I missed a single class. Somehow I managed to arrange even my hemorrhages to fit my schedule, and, although I doubtless looked thin and bedraggled, I didn't become jaundiced until the very end. Still, I can recall some panicky moments—days when I lectured on sheer will power, sometimes right after passing a bloody stool and just before carting myself off to the emergency room. The idiosyncratic character of university work—a lecture here, a meeting there—lent itself to my coping routine much more readily than would a normal nine-to-five job.

I must also set my response to the disease against the background of anxieties peculiar to the historical moment and to my situation at Stanford in those years. The broadest context—improbably as it might sound—was the Reagan Revolution. As a liberal Democrat and sometime radical, I, like many academics, experienced a persistent low-level depression that I traced to this ugly, triumphalist exercise in greed and self-congratulation. The 1980s, as Barbara Ehrenreich has written, were the worst decade in living memory, and their evil seemed to resonate with my sick body. Perhaps more to the point, as a gay man living in San Francisco, I experienced my illness in the shadow of AIDS. Indeed, I experienced it almost as my own version of AIDS—an equation grounded in the presumption that both diseases were sexually transmitted. There even came a moment when a spot on my wrist sent me to a dermatologist terrified that I might be infected. As part of my ritual of avoidance, I took no HIV test (a policy I defended on psychological grounds, uncertainty being preferable to despair). I got tested only after I was hospitalized for the liver transplant, which, of course, would have been denied me had I been HIV-positive. But as more friends died and the plague increasingly absorbed our collective imagination, my hepatitis united me to its victims. To be sure, unlike AIDS, my disease wasn't a death warrant (or so I thought), nor was it so transparently a gay man's disease. Yet inescapably I felt myself caught in the shameful miasma that was engulfing my community.

Finally, despite my belief that stress was to be avoided, I yielded to ambition and duty in order to assume two administrative posts at Stanford, both of which caused me much grief and contributed, I am persuaded, to my deterioration. In 1985–86 I served as chairman of the History Department, in which capacity I had to deal with two very unpleasant personnel cases, one a foreign scholar who sued the university when his appointment failed to materialize, and the other an assistant professor who was denied tenure. Inevitably I was the point man for both of these grievances, and my health suffered accordingly. Not having learned my lesson, I agreed in 1986 to become director of Stanford's Western Culture Program, devoting much of my (declining) energy in 1987 and 1988 to the highly contentious debate that resulted in that program's being redesigned to give it a more multicultural profile. The compromise I hammered out, through hundreds of hours of negotiation, ultimately proved a success, but the heat of the battle was intense and often unpleasant, not least when Jesse Jackson and William Bennett managed to turn Stanford's modest curriculum reform into a national political football. The anxieties induced by the Western Culture Debate fed into and fused with those stemming from my illness.

In June 1988, having barely made it through spring quarter—when the curriculum controversy came to a head and when I also endured the strain of moving to a new home on the Stanford campus after twenty-one years in San Francisco—I suffered my most severe attack of the virus. I became so exhausted and had so little appetite that I barely stirred from bed. But I still assumed I only had to wait it out. Thus I was taken by surprise when, in July, my doctor told me that I had reached a watershed. The disease was no longer responding to treatment and had become critical. For the first time a transplant was mentioned. I put up not the slightest resistance to being hospitalized at Presbyterian as a possible recipient. Getting told that you are on the verge of death makes all such decisions simple; as the man said, it concentrates the mind. Almost instantaneously my elaborate coping routine collapsed like the proverbial house of cards. If anything, I felt relieved.

I was in the hospital for nearly two months, substantially longer than most liver transplant patients, mainly because I was so very sick when I entered. But precisely because I was so sick I was spared the usual long and agonizing wait for a donor organ. Once my doctors determined that I had nothing wrong with me beyond hepatitis, I was moved to the top of the list and operated on after less than two weeks. The operation lasted the usual fourteen to sixteen hours. I associate the period right afterward with intense (but not unrelenting) pain, darkness, immobility, the strangest dreams of my life (which merged into daytime hallucinations), and a general sense of being out of it. And in fact my early recovery did not go well, mainly because, once again, the transplant took place when I was sicker than most recipients. I am not sure how close I came to dying, but I believe my life was very much in the balance. Sometime in the first week I was opened up again as the doctors tried to figure out what might be wrong. Thirteen days after the transplant they operated a third time in order to give me a new kidney, my own having failed. Thereafter I gradually improved, but because I had been bed-ridden so long I needed physical therapy to get back on my feet. I also suffered from the familiar jitters that are the main side effect of Cyclosporine, the immune-suppressant drug that transplant recipients must take (in decreasing doses) for the rest of their lives. Still, despite the pain and delirium, I found my long stay in the hospital strangely agreeable. At one level I relished being liberated from the struggle of work and life, not to mention the disease. Moreover, my mind was sufficiently muddled that the daily course of TV soap operas constituted a perfect intellectual fit. But underlying these banal comforts was the gently exhilarating sense that my "afterlife" had begun.

I don't want to belittle either the trauma of the operation or the difficulties I faced in my first year of recuperation. That year constituted a kind of interregnum, during which, although I was thrilled to be alive, my fate was still very much in doubt. I was given a quarter's leave from the university as I struggled to regain strength and weight. By January 1989 I felt well enough to return to teaching, but in the following months I took a turn for the worse: instead of getting stronger I got weaker. I feared that the hepatitis had revived and that I was on my way out again. My thoughts grew more morbid than ever before. A blood test confirmed that the virus was indeed still present (in a certain number of transplants, apparently, it is eradicated), but my doctors assured me it was active at such a low level that it couldn't be causing my weakness. Instead, the blood-pressure medicine I used to counter Cyclosporine-induced hypertension was pronounced the culprit. And in fact when I switched medicines I soon felt better.

Although I never had another scare of the same magnitude, my recovery was punctuated by two further setbacks that prevented me from embracing my new life with full confidence. A little less than a year after the operation I suddenly had an attack of fever and nausea that sent me back to the hospital. I was diagnosed as suffering from a not uncommon complication of liver transplantation: a clogged bile duct. It required yet another operation, reopening the original incision, so that the duct could be attached at a different spot on the digestive track. Compared with the original operation this was a brief and essentially mechanical affair. It had considerably less impact on my state of mind than did my relapse of the preceding winter, but it served to remind me that I was not yet out of the woods. My doctor took the occasion to tell me that I might at some point need a second transplant. Strange as it may seem, I embraced this intelligence gratefully, because I had feared that if my new liver failed I might not be given another chance.

The final complication occurred a year later, in the summer of 1990, when I again developed a sudden fever and nausea and was hospitalized just over a week with a liver infection ("cholangitis"). The infection was effectively treated with antibiotics, and I felt entirely well again after a few days. I was kept in the hospital mainly for observation. But a biopsy revealed that my new liver in fact showed signs of "early cirrhosis," so that I carried away a lingering awareness that I might yet need a second transplant.

I WANT TO SET this narrative of post-operative tribulations against my overwhelming sense of having indeed entered on an "afterlife." Since my final hospitalization in 1990 that sense has been unqualified. I'm intensely conscious of how lucky I am to have gotten sick at the right historical moment: liver transplantation has been available less than two decades; I would be dead had the disease attacked me anytime before 1980. I am thus a man who has been granted a reprieve, a pardon without parole. I have resumed all the activities of my previous existence with no diminution in efficiency or enjoyment. The completeness of my restoration is most evident to me in my work as a teacher and scholar. If anything, I have become even more intensely focused on my calling than before. Above all, I was able to muster the energy and discipline to write a new book. *Freud and His Critics* appeared in 1993 and was dedicated, appropriately, to my doctors ("who gave me a new liver but left me my old spleen"). I like to say that it is the best book ever written on a transplanted liver. I regard it, almost fetishistically, as concrete evidence of my restored powers and confidence.

I offer my experience, then, primarily to argue that liver transplantation can effect a full physical and emotional recovery. In virtually all particulars there is no difference between the way I live now and the way I lived before I got sick. Of course I still have hepatitis and may yet need another transplant. But I have no symptoms of the disease and almost never think about it. The most striking thing about my mental estate is that it, too, is indistinguishable from what it was before my illness. I sometimes wonder if I am hopelessly superficial: surely, having come so close to death only to enjoy a miraculous recovery, I ought to be a changed man. The story puts one in mind of the extreme experiences of Saint Paul or Saint Augustine. But, on a day-to-day basis, I think not about life and death but about the quotidian tasks and pleasures immediately before me. My tolerance for existential heavy-breathing and self-important philosophizing is as low as ever. Perhaps this relentless insouciance is the way my unconscious wards off anxiety. But I regard the very banality of my state of mind as the clearest evidence of just how fully I have been restored to what I was. I may be enjoying a sort of afterlife, but it is manifestly constructed of the same psychological and intellectual stuff as my old self.

I HAVE HAD ONLY one extraordinary experience in the years of my recuperation. In late 1989 a young woman named Sharon Thomas wrote to tell me that the two of us had received transplants from the same donor and she hoped I might join her in Phoenix to make a television commercial encouraging organ donations. The medical story she recounted was uncanny, with, I am convinced, decidedly philosophical implications. Sharon had been dying of lung disease, and to get new lungs she had to give up her perfectly good heart, because lungs can't yet be transplanted independently. Her heart, in turn, was transplanted into a man with terminal heart disease, whom she also invited to Phoenix. There, on February 6, 1990, gathered three human beings previously unknown to one another but linked by the most intimate physical bonds. Our bodies had become intricately entangled. The situation inspired thoughts about how transplantation had lent the old Hegelian ideal of the unity of mankind a heretofore unimaginable concreteness.

But the Phoenix meeting brought an even more remarkable revelation. Sharon Thomas had somehow managed to identify the young man from whom we received our new organs. Moreover, she had persuaded his parents to fly to Phoenix to participate in our television commercial. When I met Don and Barbara Montgomery my first thought was how astonishingly young they were: to be precise, still in their thirties. They came from a small town in Nevada, where he was a farmer and handyman and she worked in the school cafeteria. I learned that their fifteen-year-old boy, Edward Joseph (whom they called E.J.), had been killed in a freak accident when he fell out of the back of a pick-up truck. Apparently a nurse at the local hospital recognized that, except for the fatal damage to his brain, he was in perfect physical condition and thus an ideal candidate for organ donation. As it happened, his older sister had been preoccupied with transplantation for some time, and she persuaded her parents to make the sudden and difficult decision to have E.J. sent to an organ donation center in Phoenix, where a number of doctors—including my own—converged in the next few hours to "harvest" his various organs (why do I find the verb so distasteful?). Different people received not only his heart, lungs, kidneys, liver, pancreas, and corneas but also his bone marrow and even parts of his skin (for burn grafts).

I don't know how to characterize the few hours I spent with the Montgomerys that February afternoon and evening. We shared two meals and, between them, made our little television spot. We experienced the usual awkwardness of strangers from very different walks of life. Yet at the same time we enjoyed a curious familiarity. I was astonished by their composure under circumstances that had to bring back painful memories. They talked almost dispassionately about E.J., showing us pictures of him as well as an article, from the school newspaper, about his death and the memorial service held for him. He was an athlete, good looking, and interested mainly in cars. (Is my new liver vaguely erotic?) Barbara Montgomery obviously felt a comfortable affection for Sharon Thomas, to whom she had already spoken on the phone. With me both parents were more reticent. What did we in fact feel? Was this a new kind of family? Did they think of their son as alive in me? Had this quiet couple in their thirties somehow become my parents? In spite of my almost professional cynicism, I again indulged in thoughts about the new human connectedness that transplantation has ushered into existence. At some level my afterlife is also E.J.'s. The metaphor of human community seems to have become rooted in our bodies.

From time to time, Don and Barbara Montgomery send postcards filling me in on the details of their life and inquiring after my health. I reciprocate with copies of my books. We have no plans for a reunion, but the intrepid Sharon Thomas may yet engineer one. Perhaps I am not entirely my old self after all. Indeed, the very idea of the self may have suffered a ruder shock from transplantation than it ever has from David Hume or Michel Foucault, its severest philosophical critics. Our boundaries are no longer as sharply etched as they once were. We have become commingled.

INDEX